Do Morals Matter?
A Guide to Contemporary Religious Ethics

Ian S. Markham

© 2007 by Ian S. Markham

BLACKWELL PUBLISHING
350 Main Street, Malden, MA 02148-5020, USA
9600 Garsington Road, Oxford OX4 2DQ, UK
550 Swanston Street, Carlton, Victoria 3053, Australia

The right of Ian S. Markham to be identified as the Author of this Work has been asserted
in accordance with the UK Copyright, Designs, and Patents Act 1988.

First published 2007 by Blackwell Publishing Ltd

2 2008

Library of Congress Cataloging-in-Publication Data

Markham, Ian S.
Do ethics matter? / by Ian S. Markham
p. cm.
Includes bibliographical references and index.
ISBN 978-1-4051-5377-5 (hardback: alk. paper)
ISBN 978-1-4051-5378-2 (paperback: alk. paper)
1. Ethical problems. 2. Christian ethics. I. Title
BJ1275.M366 2007
170—dc22
2006004751

A catalogue record for this title is available from the British Library.

Set in 10.5 / 12.5 pt Dante
by The Running Head Limited, Cambridge, www.therunninghead.com
Printed and bound in Singapore
by Fabulous Printers Pte Ltd

The publisher's policy is to use permanent paper from mills that operate a sustainable forestry
policy, and which has been manufactured from pulp processed using acid-free and elementary
chlorine-free practices. Furthermore, the publisher ensures that the text paper and cover board
used have met acceptable environmental accreditation standards.

For further information on
Blackwell Publishing, visit our website:
www.blackwellpublishing.com

Do Morals Matter?

01/06

For Luke Stephen Austin Markham
Above all things, I pray, may you be virtuous

Contents

Acknowledgments

I have lived and worked in the world of ethics for almost 20 years now. This book is the result. As with all such labors, colleagues, friends, and students have helped me develop the arguments in this book. For the many lives that have intersected with mine and shaped my worldview, I am grateful.

In particular, I am extremely grateful to the following:

– for my teachers, John Keast, Keith Ward, Brian Hebblethwaite, and Gordon Dunstan;

– for the privilege of serving on the Advertising Standards Authority in the United Kingdom and especially the wisdom and insight of Matti Alderson, Lord William Rodgers, Elizabeth Filkin, Roger Wisbey, and Claire Serle;

– for the privilege of working on the Joint Working Party on Euthanasia of the Royal College of Physicians and the Royal College of Surgeons;

– for the focus in ethics at Liverpool Hope University College developed by Simon Lee and led by John R. Elford;

– for Richard Burridge and his insights on the use of the Bible in ethics;

– for Heidi Hadsell, Worth Loomis, and Kelton Cobb – members of the team of ethicists here at Hartford Seminary;

– for the advice on contentious questions from Stefan Weber and Eva Weber;

– for the many conversations on ethical questions with George Newlands, Leslie Houlden, Martyn Percy, Gareth Jones, and Lewis Ayers.

In the shaping of this manuscript, several people deserve special mention. My executive assistant Yvonne Bowen put the manuscript into final form for Blackwell Publishing. Worth Loomis brought his considerable expertise in business ethics to my chapter on this subject. The chapter is much improved because of his comments. My colleague Kelton Cobb read the manuscript and encouraged me to complete the project; it is undoubtedly true that but for his help this book might not have seen the light of day. Heidi Gehman was my co-teacher in "Theological Ethics and the Personal Life," where much of this material was tested with the class. For her help and insights, I am very grateful. My commissioning editor and good friend Rebecca Harkin has been very helpful. Her capacity to understand a project and advise how best that it might progress is remarkable. My brother Anthony Markham discussed the developing ideas in the book on a walk on the Ridge Way (near Newbury in the UK) on New Year's Day 2004. Ian Croft provided material that helped me shape chapter 15. And finally my wife Lesley. She joins the ranks of those partners who have helped academics to write: she read and edited each chapter. For all that we share, I am truly grateful.

The book is dedicated to my son. It was a promise I made as I wrote the book. He has asked that his network of friends should also be celebrated in the acknowledgments. A request I am more than happy to grant. So on his behalf, we express our gratitude to the following key friends: Ben Thumma, James Mullin, Max Weber, Randy Kayser, Kyle Raney, John Lawlor, Connor LaPointe, Tim Panella, Ethan Swain, and Kevin Shea. In addition, he wants to recognize his teachers: Mrs. Staffaroni, Mrs. Flores, Mrs. Wrubel, Mrs. Antoinetti, and Mrs. Hall.

Luke is truly an inspiration. Never a day passes without an expression of gratitude to God for the gift of Luke.

Permissions

The author and publisher gratefully acknowledge the permission granted to reproduce the copyright material in this book:

The thought exercises at the start of chapters 12 and 14 are reproduced from *101 Ethical Dilemmas*, Martin Cohen, © 2003, and Routledge. Reproduced by permission of Taylor & Francis Books, UK.

Chapter 7 is a slightly amended version of my article reprinted from *Encyclopedia of Applied Ethics*, vol. 3, 1998, 'Religion and Ethics', pp. 799–808, with permission from Elsevier.

The case study at the start of chapter 10 is adapted from Richard T. De George's description in Richard T. De George, *Business Ethics*, fourth edition, © 1995, pp. 221–2. Adapted by permission of Pearson Education, Inc., Upper Saddle River, NJ.

Every effort has been made to trace copyright holders and to obtain permission for the use of copyright material. The publisher apologizes for any errors or omissions in the above list and would be grateful if notified of any corrections that should be incorporated in future reprints or editions of this book.

1

Thinking about ethics

Thinking about ethics can be dangerous. So it is with some nervousness that I invite you to join me on a journey around the ethical world. The problem is this: rational reflection can expose certain tensions in a person that were hitherto hidden. As the old slogan goes: ethics are caught not taught. Parents are the primary vehicle for ethical education and the process for this is not argument but example. In a healthy family, children are provided with good role models. Kindness and love permeate the home. Constructive mutual affirming habits are formed – one learns that as one is kind to others so others are kind to you. Discipline does not need to resort to violence and uncontrolled violence is never seen. In this environment, the basis of morality is laid. Certain assumptions – do unto others, as you would have them do unto you – become part of the furniture of your mind.

Given all this, the trouble with ethical reflection as an adult is that you can inadvertently unpack all the good work that your parents did when bringing you up. Suddenly you start asking awkward questions: what is wrong with selfishness? How do I know what is right and good? Given sex is pleasurable, why not seek as many pleasurable sexual experiences as possible? As the questions are raised, so the unthinking assumptions are challenged. Suddenly alternative answers which have not occurred to you before emerge. These alternatives become temptations. In short, this book needs a health warning: thinking about ethics can damage your ethical health.

So why write it? And from your point of view, why read it? We live at a moment in history when interest in ethical questions is considerable. The collapse of Enron and the difficulties facing Parmalat has revitalized interest in business ethics; medical options, such as cloning or genetic screening, have forced us to think about the unthinkable; and for many the threat of suicide bombers needs us to revisit the conventional discourse about "just war." With this renewed interest in ethics, we do need a new map of the ethical territory. This map must include all the major landmarks from the past, and add comment, reflection, and analysis in the light of this changing world. In writing this book, my goal has been simple – it is to provide an up to date, accurate, interesting map of this changing ethical world.

Any map that opens up new ethical questions will have to face the possibility that some readers will become preoccupied with some of the old fundamental questions and perhaps arrive at answers that damage their current healthy ethical assumptions. This is an unavoidable risk.

However, to mitigate this a little, this map does have a suggested route – a message. It will introduce you to the concept of a *morally serious person* (MSP). This is a person who takes ethical discourse seriously and strives to live in a positive and constructive way. As you work through each chapter, you will see serious ethical exchanges about the nature of ethical discourse and the appropriate way to think about certain questions. At the end, I shall argue that regardless of the position you actually take on many questions, the responsible obligation on us all is to take part in the conversation and be motivated by the quest for a position that is life enhancing and committed to the care of others.

In the more descriptive chapters, I have attempted to be as fair as I can be to the main arguments and positions in the various debates. I have tried to be "objective." Naturally, in this postmodern age, we now know that strict objectivity is impossible. Value judgments are involved at every stage. I have made a selection of views that I consider important: at this point, I am clearly making a judgment. Perhaps more seriously, there are certain points in the narrative where I develop an argument. In chapter 4, I strongly suggest that consequentalist and deontological positions (terms that will be explained in that chapter) can be transcended with appropriate emphasis on the "responsible self." In chapter 9, I argue that Roman Catholics are the only major group who can consistently oppose homosexuality. And in chapter 10, I attempt to show that business ethics are in the interests of good business. However, beyond this, my goal has been to describe the options – not to decide between them.

Naturally I do hold opinions on such tricky issues as the significance of religion, abortion, and environmentalism. So in the very last chapter I do present my ethical worldview. In so doing, I trust it will help to demonstrate how one goes about making ethical judgments. The danger of just being presented with arguments on both sides is that it compounds the impression that there is no way of deciding between options. This last chapter should help overcome that impression.

Before we start the journey, there are certain preliminaries that need to be established. This we shall do now.

Ethics and morals

For many, these two words are synonyms. However, a distinction between "morals" and "ethics" can be helpful. Ethics is the realm of "rational reflection upon human behavior." As Peter Baelz puts it: "Ethics, then, is a reflective, or theoretical, business. It aims in the first instance at understanding rather than decision. It takes stock of the moral scene. It steps back from the immediately practical and attempts to discover some underlying pattern or order in the immense variety of moral decisions and practices both of individuals and societies."[1] Morals are the actual practical problem that we face in a particular situation or circumstance. Although most chapters start with a moral problem, this book is a primer about ethics – so it stands back and deals with the big picture.

Another distinction is commonplace in the literature. This is the distinction between *descriptive ethics* and *normative ethics*. Descriptive ethics simply – as the word implies – describes the major ethical traditions both historically and today. The task is understanding. Normative ethics, on the other hand, will try to adjudicate between positions. It will attempt to suggest what is right, rather than describing the ways that others believe are right. This book weaves these two types of ethics together: it will describe the main ethical traditions, yet also offer the arguments of those who take a position. The last chapter is where your author and guide offers an adjudication about the strength and weakness of the arguments that have been considered in this book.

Thought exercises and case studies

Each chapter (with the exception of the last two) will start with a thought exercise or a case study. A thought exercise is an abstract exercise that seeks to think through a principle. It constructs an imaginary scenario, which often serves as part of an argument. The famous article by Judith Jarvis Thomson called "In defense of abortion" started with a thought exercise that she hoped would invite the reader to concede a principle that she wants to use in her pro-abortion argument. You will find this thought exercise reproduced at the start of chapter 11. A case study is an actual moral problem that identifies a pivotal issue for decision-making. Case studies are realistic and often actual dilemmas.

The reason why each chapter begins with a thought exercise or case study is that ethical discourse needs to be grounded. In other words, they link our ethical reflection with moral problems. The ethical arguments in this book have implications for the way that we behave, the things we do and say, and the priorities for our future. The thought exercise or case study should make these connections.

Do please use the thought exercise or case study as dinner time conversation.

As one finds your guests exhausting the normal topics of children, schools, mortgages, and pensions, it is good to introduce a few moral problems into the conversation. It may liven the whole thing up!

Let the journey begin

With these preliminaries out of the way, you are now ready to embark on the journey. The book divides into three sections. Chapters 2 to 8 deal with meta-ethics (or philosophical ethics). We start with the basic question: "why not do wrong?" and move through the whole debate about the fundamental nature of moral discourse and its relationship with religions. You will be introduced to Immanuel Kant and John Stuart Mill; natural law and virtue ethics will be described; and by the end of this section, your vocabulary will include such terms as "deontological" and "consequentialist." Although the focus is on the western philosophical traditions, chapter 6 does look at the major areas of ethical agreement and disagreement across the major world religions and chapter 8 provides a sympathetic description and critique of the secular humanist tradition.

The second section is much more applied. Chapter 9 looks at the realm of human sexuality; chapter 10 examines business ethics; chapter 11 embarks on the complex area of medical ethics; chapter 12 explores the moral problems involved in war; chapter 13 takes up the problems of government and power; and chapter 14 looks at environmental ethics. It is perfectly possible to move straight to the second section or to read particular chapters. Each chapter is a separate entity that can be read on its own.

As already mentioned, it is in the third section that I become a conversation partner. In chapter 15, I make explicit the implicit argument of the book that we all need to take ethical discourse seriously. You can be almost anything and an MSP (gay, Catholic, or rich); it is an approach or disposition to life that is characterized by the sense that moral discourse matters. In the last chapter, I discard my apparent neutrality and explain precisely how I see the issues that we have explored together. If you don't want to be subjected to my ethical prejudices, then feel free to skip this section.

Finally, I do hope this book is enjoyable. Although my goal is to cultivate an MSP, the seriousness is not meant in terms of sober or miserable. Indeed the opposite is true: our seriousness should run parallel with the capacity to appreciate the ironies of life that cannot help but produce a smile. The moral life can and should be fun; and reading about it should also be fun.

Notes

1   Peter Baelz, *Ethics and Belief* (London: Sheldon Press 1977) p. 2.

Part One

Philosophical Ethics

2

Why not do wrong?

Thought exercise

Imagine if you can a large lever located in an extremely secure computer room within a prestigious university. Imagine further that this lever triggers a complex cyber-reaction which courtesy of numerous satellites, results in the death, ostensibly of natural causes, of a middle-aged man in Bangladesh. The obscenely rich independent backer of the project invites you to pull the lever. He offers you $5 million to do so. Would you accept the offer?

The place to begin our exploration of ethics is with a simple fundamental question. What is wrong with being selfish? The word "ethics" implies that we need to reflect upon our behavior. However, reflection is simplified considerably if we start with the assumption that the "right" action (and the inverted commas captures the potential ambiguity of that word) is simply the one that furthers most effectively our self-interest. This thought exercise challenges us to decide whether an ostensibly "immoral act" can be justified by the enormous potential personal gain. The dilemma is simple: would you murder another human being for a large financial gain? And if not, why not?

There are a whole set of obvious questions that need to confronted. How could I be sure that the backer would indeed pay me? How would I cope with the guilt? Surely I should not pull the lever because I wouldn't want someone to pull the lever on me?

For the purpose of this case study, let me respond to these objections as follows. The financial backer has the cash there in front of you; he can clearly afford to pay you and anyway you know from others in different situations he has indeed paid up. He also offers you a course of Prozac and a team of personal and confidential counselors to help you talk through any post-lever guilt. And given the technology underpinning the lever is unique, one need not worry about the lever being pulled on you.

At this point you might object that the whole exercise is a nonsense: the lever doesn't exist. Murdering for money is difficult and messy. Yet the thought exercise does confront us with the basic issue about the character of morality. For a person with considerable power, for example Stalin, there are moments when human life can be sacrificed for a personal gain. And the thought exercise is intended to eliminate all the other factors that often cause us to be moral, for example, detection, guilt, and fear of reprisal. Detection is eliminated because it is not in the interests of anyone to expose the deed; guilt is eliminated by the promise of medication and therapy; and reprisal is eliminated because this is a unique machine underpinned by unique technology. It zooms in, then, on our fundamental attitude to human life. "Thou shalt not kill" proclaims the Decalogue and the question is: are we committed to that truth even when the potential gain would be enormous?

Standing back from the thought exercise

At the heart of this thought exercise is the question about the nature of "ethics." On one level a definition of "ethics" is easy: it is an attempt to analyze the reasons for certain actions. But on another level the definition of ethics is extremely difficult. This is because the ethical vocabulary is a little strange.

Consider the words "ought," "right," and "wrong." This is the language of ethics. Yet what precisely do they mean. When I explain that "I really *ought* to go to my son's soccer match," I am not, normally, saying "I really *want* to go to my son's soccer match." One constructs that sentence when a friend has turned to me and said, perhaps, "would you like to come to the baseball game tonight?" The implied explanation is that my personal preference would indeed be to see the Yankees beat the Red Sox; however, I am feeling this obligation that makes me think that to do that particular action would be wrong. Instead my sense of obligation makes me think that the right thing to do is to watch my son's soccer match. So we seem to have a clash between our personal preferences and our ethical obligation. It almost sounds as if something external to myself is pushing down on me and telling me that the right thing to do is something that I don't want to do (or at least, left to myself, it would come in as a second preference to the baseball option).

Or let us think about the language of right and wrong. Imagine a conversation where you are discussing an old man wanting a sexual relationship with a 10-year-old child. Now I think that is wrong: I have a variety of reasons for thinking it is "wrong," even if the 10-year-old is showing exceptional maturity or expresses a desire for the relationship. If others disagree with me, then the word "wrong" extends to them. I would say that they are "wrong"; they are "mistaken." In invoking the word "wrong," I seem to be making a universal claim that applies to everyone. It isn't simply my opinion but it is a universal claim that I expect everyone to agree with.

So the word "ought" seems to imply an external agency pushing down on me that requires me to take a course of action that conflicts with my preferences; the word "wrong" (and conversely when I use the word "right") seems to imply a universal claim that applies to all people, even if (perhaps especially if) they disagree with me.

Ethics and religion

Once this point is grasped about ethical language, one can immediately see why one doesn't go very far in the ethical discussion before one encounters religion. It might come as a surprise to a "secular" westerner that religion still matters, but when it comes to ethics, it matters a great deal. It is clear, as Alasdair MacIntyre has shown, that ethical categories emerged in a culture that assumed the truth of a religious universe.[1] The "ought" made sense because God had built into the universe certain moral truths that are then binding upon us. We will look later in the book at precisely how this works – it is called the idea of "natural law." But for now let us note how the external nature of moral discourse coupled with its all-embracing universal claims make perfect sense if you believe in a God who created the world and cares for it.

Now the project of providing a secular account of moral discourse has been a major preoccupation of many post-Enlightenment secular thinkers, and we will look at some of the major secular accounts, especially Utilitarianism, in later chapters. However, before we all go along with the assumption that any convincing account of morality needs to do without God, because many people today are irreligious, it is worth pausing and challenging that assumption.

There is a widespread view, most recently defended by Steve Bruce, that with the European growth in science and technology there comes, inevitably, an increasing lack of commitment to religion.[2] This lack of commitment to religion, or to put it more accurately, the decline in the authority of religious institutions, is often called the secularization process. However, it is worth noting that this view has come under increasing attack. The obvious exception, which was always recognized, is "America." Religious participation in the United States remains steady and strong at approximately 40 percent, and, moreover, the true "exception" is not the United States but Europe! It is clear that as other parts of the world embrace technology and science (e.g. Asia, the Middle East), they are not embracing secularism. As Grace Davie has shown, European secularism is marked by both a growing failure of memory and an inability of people to engage in common activities.[3] It is often claimed that football is the new religion of Britain, but this is clearly false. Gathering at football matches has itself declined since the 1950s in even faster numbers than gathering at churches. Many more watch football on television than attend games, and it is equally true that many millions watch religious activities on television. The funeral of Princess Diana might be seen as the religious equivalent of the World Cup Final – and the religious ceremony won by a large margin. In addition, not only churches and football matches but also, trade unions, political parties, and women's organizations are all in trouble. In fact, church attendance decline is less dramatic than many of these "secular" activities. People in Europe are simply ceasing to "gather." It is clearly a separate point whether Europe's exceptionalism is desirable or not.

Religion will be a significant theme in this book about ethics, but it will not assume that to be ethical one need be religious. Empirically, it is clear that is not the case: there are plenty of remarkable people who are deeply virtuous (to lapse into moral language without any explanation of what precisely I mean); and there are plenty of religious people who are deeply unpleasant, intolerant, and cruel. However, at the level of justification and common usage, it does look at first sight as if the religious people have an advantage. The words "ought" and "wrong" often seem to make more sense or to be more at home within a religious worldview.

With these preliminaries out of the way, we are now at the point that we can return to the question underpinning our thought exercise. What is wrong with selfishness? Why not do wrong? One possible answer to this question is "nothing." This was the answer given by the nineteenth-century genius, Friedrich Nietzsche.

Introducing Friedrich Nietzsche[4]

Friedrich Nietzsche (1844–1900) was the son of a Lutheran pastor. He had a strict classical education. At age 8 there were signs of a philosopher emerging. At 12 his slightly obsessive streak was beginning to show: he would wake up extremely early and then work all day long into the evening. Perhaps because of this punishing schedule, he was to be haunted by illness throughout his life. At the age of 24, when he was made Professor of Philosophy at Basel, his mind would play tricks on him: he worried about unseen forces "behind the chair." More generally, he suffered from stomach pains, vomiting, headaches, and pains in and around his eyes. All things considered, perhaps, it is not surprising that his life was to relatively short. He died when he was 56. And for the last 10 years of his life, he was unable to construct any coherent arguments. It is as if this genius worked himself to death.

His intellectual journey had several significant resting places. When he was a young man, in his twenties, he was sympathetic to the philosophy of Schopenhauer (1788–1860). However, Schopenhauer proved insufficiently radical for Nietzsche, so he moved on. He devoured the work of Charles Darwin; he sensed the growing skepticism about God in his culture. He anticipated both naturalism (i.e. the view that asserts there is nothing beyond the natural world) and certain forms of "postmodernism" (i.e. the challenge to the belief of modernity and premodernity that there is a explanation for reality that we can identify as true). He left a considerable corpus of writing, and he covered a range of themes: the need to regenerate European culture; the nature of education; the implications of science for our view of ourselves; a "yes to life"; the nature of morality; the death of God – and many more. Anyone wanting to appreciate our modern period needs to grapple with the thought of Friedrich Nietzsche.

Interpreting Nietzsche

Nietzsche is probably one of the most controversial of all philosophers. The range of interpretations of Nietzsche's work is considerable. It has, for example, been viewed with considerable suspicion because of the use made of it by Hitler and the Nazis. He was apparently Hitler's favorite philosopher. It was thanks to Walter Kaufmann that this suspicion was overcome and Nietzsche was liberated from such associations. Kaufmann turned Nietzsche into a relatively straightforward humanist existentialist (i.e. one who places considerable stress on experience) and pragmatist (one who uses the criterion of "usefulness" to evaluate assertions), who denies all metaphysics – and then confronts the ethical implications of such a denial.[5] The problem with this interpretation is that there are just too many parts of Nietzsche which are much more radical than it implies. Repeatedly he denies the possibility of all knowledge, describing science as "an interpretation and arrangement of the world . . . and not an explanation of the world."[6] This led to the quest for the "new Nietzsche," with which I am in sympathy. On this view, Nietzsche's views are a radical challenge to truth and morality as traditionally understood.

His initial work operated within the accepted conventions of academic writing. For example, he delivered five very clear lectures called "On the Future of Educational Institutions" at the University of Basle. However, fairly rapidly he moved beyond such conventions. He uses wit, irony, and hyperbole to make his point. Stylistically, he is confusing. He does not provide a neat, clear, exposition of an argument for a position. Indeed his style is part of the problem of interpreting Nietzsche. Because of this, along with the Hitler association already mentioned, many philosophers do not read him. What they miss, however, is that Nietzsche's style is clearly part of his message. In *Ecce Homo*, he comments explicitly on his style:

I shall at the same time also say a general word on my art of style. To communicate a state, an inner tension of pathos through signs, including the tempo of these signs – that is the meaning of every style; and considering that the multiplicity of inner states is in my case extraordinary, there exists in my case the possibility of many styles – altogether the most manifold art of style any man has ever had at his disposal. Every style is good which actually communicates an inner state, which makes no mistake as to the signs, the tempo of the signs, the gestures – all rules of phrasing are art of gesture. My instinct is here infallible. – Good style in itself – a piece of pure folly, mere "idealism," on a par with the "beautiful in itself," the "good in itself," the "thing in itself" . . .[7]

Nietzsche here contrasts his style with "good style" (i.e. good and clear arguments). The problem with good argument is that it is pure folly: it is comparable with other equally foolish ideas like reality or goodness. The style is internalized. He talks elsewhere in *Ecce Homo* of the pain involved in writing and his capacity to intuit, even "to smell."[8] So the picture emerging here is of a man who has internalized the cultural moment forced on Europe by the Enlightenment. And as he writes his opaque prose is itself part of the message: knowledge is difficult; truth is fiction; and, for our purposes, morality now must be invented.

In *The Joyful Wisdom*, Nietzsche tells the story of the "madman." The scene starts in a marketplace, where people are completing the normal chores of life. The "insane man" is trying to disrupt this normality and point out what exactly has happened culturally, namely the achievement of the western world to make God redundant:

The Madman – Have you ever heard of the madman who on a bright morning lighted a lantern and ran to the market-place calling out unceasingly: "I seek God! I seek God!" – As there were many people standing about who did not believe in God, he caused a great deal of amusement. Why! is he lost? said one. Has he strayed away like a child? said another. Or does he keep himself hidden? Is he afraid of us? Has he taken a sea voyage? Has he emigrated? the people cried out laughingly, all in a hubbub. The insane man jumped into their midst and transfixed them with his glances. "Where is God gone?" he called out. "I mean to tell you! We have killed him, – you and I! We are all his murderers! But how have we done it? How were we able to drink up the sea? Who gave us the sponge to wipe away the whole horizon? What did we do when we loosened this earth from its sun? Whither does it now move? Whither do we move? Away from all suns? Do we not dash on unceasingly? Backwards, sideways, forwards, in all directions? Is there still an above and below? Do we not stray, as through infinite nothingness? Does not empty space breathe upon us? Has it not become colder? does not night come on continually, darker and darker? Shall we not have to light lanterns in the morning? Do we not hear the noise of the grave diggers who are burying God? . . . God is dead! God remains dead! And we have killed him! How shall we console ourselves, the most murderous of all murderers? . . . Is not the magnitude of this deed too great for us? Shall we not ourselves have to become Gods, merely to seem worthy of it? There never was a greater event, – and on account of it, all who are born after us belong to a higher history than any history hitherto!" Here the madman was silent and looked again at his hearers; they also were silent and looked at him in surprise. At last he threw his lantern on the ground, so that it broke in pieces and was extinguished. "I came too early," he then said, "I am not yet at the right time . . ."[9]

Nietzsche's argument can be understood in this way: with the rise of science and the social sciences, God has ceased to be a cultural option. We no longer need to appeal to the mysterious transcendent to explain the weather: a virgin does not need to be sacrificed to ensure the sun will rise again. In addition, the social sciences (sociology and anthropology) explain why we have different cultures with contrasting moral and scientific beliefs. Given that they are all different, then how can a particular culture have the metaphysical truth about the universe? In *Human, All Too Human*, Nietzsche points out that since Darwin we are now all committed to the proposition that the human mind is simply a result of nature. In this respect, Nietzsche is anticipating the work of the founding father of psychology, Sigmund Freud. The point, explains Nietzsche, is this: if the human mind is simply a result of nature, then all the thoughts in the human mind must be a result of nature, which implies that all morality, art, religion, and even the quest for truth are chance inventions of nature. We have eliminated God, yet not faced up to the implications. Everything, explains Nietzsche, has changed. Nothing can be the same. The concept of truth must change; and of course, the character of moral discourse can never be the same.

Nietzsche understood the transcendent nature of traditional moral language. Embedded in the word "ought" is the sense of a moral fact transcending our life and world. However, if science and the social sciences have explained the world without reference to God, then it is no longer intelligible to believe in a transcendent life that determines our moral code of behavior. Morality as traditionally understood must go: we need to reinvent the meanings of the language, even the language itself, that makes up moral discourse.

Our task now, argues Nietzsche, is to create our own meaning. He wants to offer this as a challenge but also as an opportunity. He shares with other post-Enlightenment thinkers a strong antagonism to religion: he thought it pathetic that humans should spend their time groveling around worshipping this invisible ego, who threatens to send all those who refuse to affirm "how wonderful God is" to hell. So our cultural "moment" brings the opportunity to break the shackles of religion.

He invites us to consider the Superman. He recognized that only a minority would have the strength to face up to our historical moment. The herd will still need to be led. However, this minority will recognize our obligation: this is the will to power. Power is located in our decision-making processes. The Superman is the one who can accept the truth of our situation, accept the very absurdity, welcomes the ultimate emancipation and irresponsibility. This is, explains Nietzsche, joyful wisdom.

Is this rational egoism? This is a difficult question to answer. Nietzsche does invite us to formulate a morality of a certain type. He wants us to become "efficiently human": he thinks it important to impose our will on nature. He thinks our invented morality should include strength, power, and the control of the herd. If you want to invent a morality made up of hedonism and the indulgent satisfaction of the senses, then Nietzsche would disapprove.

The value of Nietzsche

This chapter is called "why not do wrong?" The question underpinning that one is that of the meaning of moral terminology. Nietzsche has a clear position: moral terminology, as things stand, is dependent on religion. Religion is no longer a cultural option in the West because of the rise of the physical and social sciences. Therefore traditional morality must go and moral words need new meanings.

When we encounter a great philosopher, our task is to start a conversation. For the person of faith reading this, Nietzsche assumes too much. He overstates the significance of the Enlightenment and the implausibility of the language of faith. However, the religious person might agree that Nietzsche does pose a challenge to the secular humanist (a person who believes in love and justice but is not religious): how can one use moral language given morality depends so much on religion?

For the humanist, Nietzsche perhaps sees the historical moment and then commends a morality that seems needlessly harsh and demanding. Why can't one invent a morality that retains certain "traditional" commitments? We will look at this humanist tradition later on in the book.

As we converse, perhaps we also need to think a little harder. What is the underlying character of the moral discourse? Are there moral facts? Or is it all an invention? It is to this question that we turn in the next chapter.

Notes

1 See Alasdair MacIntyre, *After Virtue* (London: Duckworth 1985).
2 See Steve Bruce, *God is Dead: Secularization in the Modern World* (Oxford: Blackwell Publishing 2002).
3 See Grace Davie, *Religion in Modern Europe: A Memory Mutates* (Oxford: Oxford University Press 2000).
4 Parts of what follow are taken from my *Truth and Reality of God* (Edinburgh: T & T Clark 1999) chapter six.
5 See Walter Kaufmann, *Nietzsche: Philosopher, Psychologist, Antichrist*, fourth edition (Princeton, NJ: Princeton University Press 1974).
6 F. Nietzsche, *Beyond Good and Evil*, translated by R. J. Hollingdale with an introduction by Michael Tanner (Harmondsworth: Penguin 1990) section 14, p. 44.
7 F. Nietzsche, *Ecce Homo*, translated by R. J. Hollingdale, introduction by M. Tanner (Harmondsworth: Penguin 1992) p. 44.
8 Ibid. p. 18. Nietzsche writes, "I perceive physiologically – smell – the proximity or . . . the innermost parts, the 'entrails,' of every soul."
9 Nietzsche, *Nietzsche Selections*, edited by Richard Schnacht, (New York: Macmillan 1993) p. 114.

3

Is the ethical a human construct or a factual realm?

Thought exercise

The setting is an apartment in New York. A young couple are sitting having breakfast in their kitchen; Mary is reading the *New York Times*; John is trying to balance his fork on top of the egg cup.

Mary looks up: "Female circumcision is disgusting. It says here that female genital circumcision is performed on young girls in much of Africa, the Middle East, and the Far East. They use a razor blade or knife to remove part or all of the clitoris, without anesthesia. It leaves these poor girls with reduced or sometimes no sexual feeling. And, as they grow older, orgasms are sometimes impossible to experience. It is completely wrong. It makes me mad."

John had been listening intently. He thinks for a while before responding: "On what basis are you saying it is completely wrong? Who are you to impose your cultural values on a different culture? There are plenty of things that we do that those involved in female circumcision want us to stop. They might disapprove of the fact that we drink or that our best friend is gay. What gives you the right to announce that their rituals are wrong?"

Mary retorts. "Understand this: no culture is permitted to impose this surgery on a young girl. You will be saying that cannibals are allowed to eat people in their culture next. That is crazy."

"But how do you know your ethical values are right and their ethical values are wrong?" John replies. "I don't see how you can just sit there and be so sure," he went on, "After all, those performing this operation – come to that, the cannibals eating the people – believe that their values are right as well. You are completely wrong to want to change them."

Who is right? Mary or John?

In chapter 2 we have already touched on this question. As we saw, Nietzsche's great contribution to the history of ideas was that the ethical was a human construct, which therefore provokes the question: what is wrong with selfishness? In this chapter we shall locate this question and explore the fundamental nature of ethical discourse.

This is, probably, the most important question to reflect upon as we start our journey into the world of ethics. We need to decide on the nature of ethical assertions. And there are two main options. The first sees the ethical as an aspect of the "factual realm" (i.e. something that has been built into the nature of the universe in some way). This means that ethics is a matter of discovery and truth, not invention or opinion. This is the position of Mary. The second sees the ethical as relative to culture and therefore a human construct that frees individuals to pick and choose their own ethical system. This is the argument offered by John.

This chapter will look at these two options. We shall start with John's position and his arguments for and against the *subjective* or *non-cognitive* nature of ethics. Ethical subjectivists deny objective moral truths with the implication that morality is *entirely* a human construct. Then we shall move to Mary and look at the arguments for and against the *objective* or *realist* nature of ethics.

Argument for a human construct view of morality: subjective or non-cognitive accounts of ethics

For his book, *Ethics: Inventing Right and Wrong*, J. L. Mackie chose a telling sub-title, one that expresses exactly the subjectivist claim.[1] Morality is no longer a question of truth and discovery, but of feeling and invention.

Mackie offers two reasons for this position. First, the argument from relativity, which

> has as its premise the well-known variation in moral codes from one society to another and from one period to another, and also the differences in moral beliefs between different groups and classes within a complex community . . . Disagreement about moral codes seems to reflect people's adherence to and participation in different ways of life.'[2]

So there are certain cultures that permit polygamy; there are others that insist on monogamy. Whether you believe polygamy is permissible will be determined by the culture to which you belong. Different cultures developed different moral systems according to their particular historical experience. You cannot resolve a disagreement over polygamy or any other substantial moral issue, Mackie argues, since morality is more a matter of cultural invention than discovery.

Embedded in this argument is a further one: there are anthropological explanations for the diverse moral codes in the world. Anthropologists study different cultures and very contrasting accounts of the ethical emerge. In India, the caste system developed. Order in India is considered a social priority and one way of sustaining order is this highly stratified society. Everyone has a place; all relationships between people are determined by their place in society. Meanwhile in North America the western doctrine of individualism took hold. Here the ethic is the opposite: anyone can be someone and it is wrong to let "social" expectations hold you back. The explanations offered by anthropologists are local (i.e. the ethic developed pertains to the social factors in that part of the world); it does look as if each culture develops the ethic that makes sense for that region.

Mackie concedes that the fact of disagreement in morality is not decisive evidence for subjectivity. Scientists disagree constantly over the best way to describe the universe, but clearly the subject matter is objective. He thinks that no parity can be found between a moral disagreement and a scientific disagreement. Scientists look at the "objective" world they are studying through a microscope or telescope and can construct arguments that make sense of the evidence; ethicists have nothing equivalent to this process.

J. L. Mackie offers a second argument against objectivity. This is the argument from queerness. Mackie thinks that it is odd (he uses the word queer) to talk about moral facts. Put simply, Mackie points out that the objectivist needs to explain exactly where these moral values are located and how we discover them. With the scientific facts that divide our scientists, their "facts" are much more obvious than the supposed "moral facts." Different cultures have recourse to different sources for their ethical rules. Many cultures cite a religious book – the Bible, Torah, the Qur'an, or Upanishads. But these books are all different; they contain different rules; and there is no way we can be sure which one is the "real" authoritative guide to human behavior.

Mackie is very unsympathetic to religion. One of his other books is called *The Miracle of Theism*,[3] which he explains in the introduction is so called because he thinks it is a miracle that there are any theists. Religion runs parallel with morality; it is a construct of society. Both religion and morality arose at a point in human evolution when the mystery of the universe needed a God or gods to make sense of it all. A divine lawgiver – to keep order in society – was a perfect tool. But given the transformation of our understanding of the world by science, it seems rather odd to continue to affirm that religion and the divine lawgiver are true. Let us now turn to the arguments for the ethical objectivity.

Arguments for ethical objectivity

The first task for the defender of ethical objectivity is to explain why J. L. Mackie is mistaken. One way to do this is to revisit his first argument, which was the "ethics are culturally relative." Mackie asserts that scientific arguments are completely different from moral ones. However, is this true? Consider the following thought exercise: we manage to arrange a meeting that includes Aristotle, Newton, and Einstein. We further manage to gather considerable biographical, sociological, and psychological information on each participant. We then settle down to witness the exchange. The argument is heated, with each scientist arguing for his cultural position. Aristotle argues for a universe with set purposes for every plant and animal; Newton is arguing that the universe is best understood as a large machine; and Einstein is arguing that the universe involves a radical relativity especially at great distances and speeds. And as we watch we suddenly notice that a correspondence can be seen between the mechanistic views of Newton and his psychological and sociological background. Let us imagine that as a child he was obsessed with marbles and machines. We appear to have an explanation for the mechanistic views of Newton. Now along comes our "human constructivist advocate" who argues that all we have here are different projections, and the physicists are not making objective truth-claims.

Even though, some in our postmodern world would be quite comfortable with the possibility that there is no truth in science, most of us would feel some unease. In science, there is obviously a world that scientists are seeking to explain. And the point of this exercise is simple. The fact of disagreement and the possibility of psychological explanation does not reduce all truth-claims to merely subjective preferences. Every viewpoint and discovery will have a psychological motivation or aspect, but this fact cannot determine whether the matter involves issues of truth. One can still believe in the objectivity of value and concede that cultural factors do affect our judgment about what we believe that objective moral code consists in. Related to this is another consideration: if morality was simply a matter of personal preference, then argument would be pointless. I like carrots and my wife dislikes carrots. This is a difference in taste; nothing can be gained by a furious argument over carrots. The usual explanation for disagreement is that an issue involves complicated matters of fact. Our three scientists disagree over the ultimate nature of the universe precisely because it is complicated. Likewise a moral objectivist would want to say that disagreement over morality arises because discovering the moral truth is difficult.

What about Mackie's second argument? Where is the source for the objective ethical values? Which holy book gives the truth? Mackie is requiring that the objectivist offer a framework in which objective moral values would be intelligible. This is perfectly reasonable. And a variety of possible frameworks can be offered. For the Marxist (the traditional ones that use to exist before 1989), these objective moral values are located in the dialectic of history. For the theist, these values are located in the character of God. Interestingly, Mackie concedes that,

> To meet these difficulties, the objectivist may have recourse to the purpose of God: the true purpose of human life is fixed by what God intended (or intends) men to do and to be . . . I concede that if the requisite theological doctrine could be defended, a kind of objective ethical prescriptivity could be thus introduced. Since I think that theism cannot be defended, I do not regard this as any threat to my argument.[4]

Arguments for and against the existence of God are beyond the scope of this book. Suffice it to say, this is also a matter of lively debate and Mackie's confidence that there are no good arguments for the existence of God is not shared by everyone.

There are three main reasons for affirming objective moral values. The first is the character of moral discourse. We alluded to this in chapter 2. The point is that close examination of the nature of moral language seems to imply an obligation from beyond us that often conflicts with our self-interest. When for example I say "I really ought to visit my grandmother this evening," I seem to be implying that there is a conflict between morality and self-interest. We can imagine this person going on to say, "I would rather go out for a drink, but I really ought . . ." Moral action seems to be in conflict with my personal inclination. Consider, further, that this "ought" is describing an obligation, a compelling feeling which needs to be satisfied. The language seems to imply an external obligation to act in a certain way. We cannot avoid this obligation anymore than we can wish away the earth's roundness. Or, to take another example, consider a disagreement over abortion. The pro-life advocate argues that abortion is murder, the pro-choice advocate argues that it is wrong for anyone else to make decisions for a woman over her body. This disagreement is a disagreement over the truth. Each participant is not saying, "Well, for me, it is wrong to have an abortion, but for you . . ." Both use the language of morality to imply that this assertion is wrong or right for the other person. Or as C. S. Lewis puts it:

> Everyone has heard people quarrelling . . . They say things like this: "How'd you like it if anyone did the same to you?" – "Give me a bit of your orange, I gave you a bit of mine" – "Come on, you promised." . . . Now what interests me about all these remarks is that man who makes them is not merely saying that the other man's behavior does not happen to please him. He is appealing to some kind of standard of behavior which he expects the other man to know about. And the other man very seldom replies: "To hell with your standard."[5]

The point is that both parties in an argument are appealing to an external standard that is binding on the other person. Clearly, the language of moral assertions is intended to be "objective." Moral assertions appear to refer to an external set of moral truths that are universally true. Terms like "good," "right," "wrong," "ought," and "should," sound as if they are external to our mind. Morality is a matter of truth and discovery, not invention. In moral philosophy, there was a period when philosophers were sympathetic to the "expressivist theory." This states that moral assertions are just a strange way of articulating one's likes and dislikes. So, for example, "I think stealing is wrong" really means "I don't like stealing." For defenders of objectivity in ethics, this cannot be misguided. For most people the only time one thinks about stealing being wrong is when one is tempted to steal. Even though they would like to steal, they think it is wrong. With the statement, "I really ought to visit my grandmother," there is a clear implication that I do not really want to visit my grandmother. On this account, the expressivist theory is wrong because moral assertions are normally in conflict with our individual preferences. For defenders of moral objectivity, the nature and use of moral assertion provides clear evidence that moral values are objective.

The second reason is the nature of justice. Two cultures disagree over the validity of slavery or female circumcision. Now the subjectivist is stuck. She might be able to express her personal (and cultural) dislike of slavery, but she cannot provide any reason why slavery is wrong for a different culture. The objectivist then goes on to point out that if one reduces this to individual crimes, all the assumptions of our legal system start to disintegrate. One defense that is never permitted in our courts is the argument that, given moral relativity, my morality is different from yours and you have no basis on which to judge my action. But of course law-courts must judge and punish a person who commits assaults from racist or anti-Semitic motivations, even if (or perhaps especially if) that person regards her anti-Semitism as morally justifiable. Justice presupposes the objectivity of value.

The third reason is that there are areas of agreement in the ethical code advocated by many cultures. C. S. Lewis made this central to his moral argument. He writes:

> If anyone will take the trouble to compare the moral teaching of, say, the ancient Egyptians, Babylonians, Hindus, Chinese, Greeks, and Romans, what will really strike him will be how very like they are to each other and to our own.[6]

Just imagine, Lewis goes on to argue, what a culture with a "totally different morality" would look like. He explains:

Think of a country where people were admired for running away in battle, or where a man felt proud of double crossing all the people who had been kindest to him. You might just as well try to imagine a country where two and two made five. Men have differed as regards what people you ought to be unselfish to – whether it was only your own family, or your fellow countrymen, or everyone. But they have always agreed that you ought not to put yourself first. Selfishness has never been admired. Men have differed as to whether you should have one wife or four. But they have always agreed that you must not simply have any woman you liked.[7]

The last argument has already been developed in the last chapter. We concluded that chapter with the "rational egoist." A rational egoist is a person who opts to use the criterion of "self-interest" as the basis of all ethical decisions. If morality is just "subjective," then there is no argument against "rational egoism." Indeed it makes perfect sense.

Now how would the defender of moral subjectivism respond to these arguments? To the first, Mackie, for example, would concede that moral language has its roots in religion and that it therefore does sound as if it were "objective." The source of law for a premodern society was divine lawgiver. Therefore the transcendent (that it seems to be above human communities) and universal (it applies to everyone everywhere) character of moral language did develop. However, to think of the ethical in these ways today is impossible for our modern culture. We need to find a fresh way of interpreting it.

To the issue of justice, Mackie is sympathetic. He wants to argue that it is possible to see that most basic ethical injunctions are in one's self-interest. One does not steal because one does not want to be stolen from; one does not kill because one does not want to be killed; and one does not lie because one does not want to be lied to. If society commits to these values, then it is appropriate for society to punish those who choose not to live in these ways.

To the third argument, Mackie would concede that some agreement across cultures is inevitable; it is difficult to see a culture that valued the person who wanted to murder other people. It would disintegrate very quickly. However, Mackie would also say that it is easy to overstate the agreement. As we shall see in chapter 7, when we look at the different ethical insights in different religious traditions, there are plenty of substantial areas of disagreement. To the last difficulty, Mackie argues that being ethical is in the interests of a rational person who wants to pursue self- interest.

At this point there is a danger that the reader might be getting frustrated. J. L. Mackie provided two strong arguments for subjectivism in ethics, i.e. the argument from cultural relativism and the queerness argument. The defenders of objectivity countered these two arguments, and then offered four arguments for the opposite position, i.e. the arguments from the nature of moral discourse, the assumptions of justice, the widespread agreement across cultures, and the problem of the rational egoist. J. L. Mackie came back with his response to those arguments. The defenders of objectivity might then push back again: they might, for example, point out that Mackie's ethical system, which is built on egoism, runs into a self-confessed difficulty. He explains:

> It leaves unanswered the question "Why should I not at the same time profit from the moral system but evade it? Why should I not encourage others to be moral and take advantage of the fact that they are, but myself avoid fulfilling moral requirements if I can in so far as they go beyond rational egoism and conflict with it?" It is not an adequate answer to this question to point out that one is not likely to be able to get away with such evasions for long. There will be at least some occasions when one can do with impunity and even without detection. Then why not? To this no complete answer of the kind that is wanted can be given. In the choice of actions moral reasons and prudential ones will not always coincide.[8]

So for the objectivist, this is a significant difficulty. Egoism will not always justify moral behavior. And Mackie can give no reason why the character at the end of chapter 2 cannot, for example, pull the lever and kill an innocent person if the gain is great enough and detection is very unlikely.

This back and forth can seem frustrating. And at this stage it is important that one just gets use to it. We are dealing with a complex subject matter, where many of the arguments and issues are finely balanced. Thus far J. L. Mackie has been placed in conversation with C. S. Lewis. However, there are many other positions, which before we conclude this chapter we need to mention.

Positions in between

In this section I shall describe briefly *dispositionalist* (Michael Smith), *contractualist* (Peter Carruthers), and *ideal observer* (Michael Martin). And we start with the dispositionalist view.

Considerable interest has been shown in the last 10 years or so in "response-dependent" accounts of moral discourse. Along with the subjectivist, there is a recognition that ethical values are determined by human responses to the world. However, along with the objectivist, there is also a recognition that ethical values are not simply arbitrary; the fact that an individual murderer thinks that murder is "moral" does not make it so. A popular and often cited parallel is colors.

Tony Pitson offers an account of color which he calls "dispositionalist." Pitson starts by pointing out that colors are a result of light waves which are reflected or emitted from an object's surface – so on one level colors don't exist. Yet that sounds very odd – a great painting and a remarkable sunset are made great and remarkable by colors. So surely something must exist. Pitson then argues that:

> Red is, roughly speaking, a property of things in virtue of which they are disposed to look red to perceivers under such-and-such conditions, where their looking this way is a matter of perceivers having certain sorts of experience or beliefs.[9]

This is a response-dependent account of color: the idea is that given a certain set of conditions one should experience red.

It was David Lewis who developed a dispositionalist account of moral value.[10] And it is Michael Smith who has defended it in a variety of different places. Smith explains that "according to the dispositional theory of moral value . . . facts about moral values are facts about idealized desires."[11] Smith is a moral realist for "moral facts reduce to idealized psychological facts, facts which in turn constitute reasons for actions."[12] Now there are many complex issues embedded in these assertions. However, to simplify (rather crudely) the idea is this: all people, given a certain vantage point (i.e. fully rational), should value the moral quality of love. Smith explains that the version of dispositional theory of value he supports involves the following:

> When a subject judges it desirable for *p* to be the case in certain circumstances *C*, this is a matter of her believing that she would want *p* to be the case in *C* if she were in a state that elude all forms of criticism from the point of view of reason – or, for short, and perhaps somewhat misleadingly, if she were fully rational. More precisely, if still somewhat misleadingly, let's suppose that when a subject judges it desirable that *p* in *C* this is a matter of her believing that, in those nearby possible worlds in which she is fully rational – let's call these the "evaluating possible worlds" – she wants that, in those possible worlds in which C obtains – let's call these the "evaluated possible worlds" – *p* obtains.[13]

Smith is attempting to explain with some precision why exactly we affirm certain values. Primarily it is an exercise in rational recognition.

Now the analogy with colors is attractive for several reasons. First, it is a naturalist account. It does not depend on the concept of God to make the account intelligible. Second, it is a powerful analogy. It allows for argument (there are plenty of disagreements with my wife whether this particular color

of tie goes with my shirt and suit) yet it also recognizes that this is a real argument over a matter of fact. There is, underpinning this account, an intuition
that one should be just able to see why certain actions are right and others are
wrong.

There are difficulties with this account. Articulating exactly what is meant
by, for example, a fully rational person is difficult. In addition, the subjectivist
might want to suggest the sheer diversity of moral perspectives is not taken sufficiently seriously (there are people out there calling "white black" and "black
white"). The objectivist might argue that any adequate theory of moral value
must have a response to the rational egoist – and it is not sufficient to suggest
that "they are just not determining their values in a sufficiently rational and
all-embracing way." Yet the analogy between morality and colors continues to
fascinate. This is an account of morality which will continue to provoke considerable interest.

The second alternative is the contractualist account. Peter Carruthers, in a
delightfully well-written book called *The Animal Issue: Moral Theory in Practice*,
argues for a "weak objectivist" account of morality called contractualism. By
weak objectivism, Carruthers means "that ethics employs concepts (ideas in our
minds) with determinate conditions of application."[14] He uses the analogy of
scientific classifications to describe the world. It is clear that there really is an
external world that language seeks to understand and classify. And although the
distinctions between "animals" and "fish" are human constructs, they are not
arbitrary or capricious. Rational people cannot simply disregard the terminology. Carruthers explains:

> While it is true that I am sitting at a table, and hence true that individ-
> ual tables really exist, the difference between tables and other types of
> thing is not itself a part of the real world. It is rather something we
> impose on the world, in selecting the concepts we do.[15]

Carruthers goes on to argue that contractualism is the most plausible account of
moral language. He defines a contractualist moral theory as

> an attempt to justify a system of moral principles by showing that they
> would be agreed upon by rational agents in certain ideal circumstances.
> It is an attempt to exhibit the rationality of moral rules, not an attempt
> to legitimate those rules by appeal to past agreement or present self-
> interest.[16]

He acknowledges an enormous debt to John Rawls and Thomas Scanlon. John
Rawls was the author of *A Theory of Justice*.[17] He invited his readers to imagine

that we are creating the rules for society behind a "veil of ignorance" (i.e. so we are in a position where we do not know what our status will be in this society). Rawls argued that from this exercise certain fundamental principles of justice would be derived and agreed upon. From Thomas Scanlon, Carruthers takes the insight, that while Rawls might have idealized individuals reaching agreement, Scanlon faces up to the necessity that the participants in the contract are real people who want to reach some sort of moral agreement.[18]

So the basic idea is this: imagine a group of rational agents who are willing to set the rules for their society without knowing where in that society they would be (i.e. the veil of ignorance). What sort of rules would result? Carruthers argues that agreement would be reached on the following principles. First, there would be a respect for one another's autonomy. In addition to the rule that the act of injury to another is forbidden, we would also want a general recognition that "agents should be granted as much freedom to act and pursue projects as is compatible with a similar degree of freedom being granted to all others."[19] The second principle is the ideal of publicity; it would be essential that everyone must know the rules of the society. And the third is some sort of principle of beneficence (i.e. an agreement "to develop in themselves an attachment to the welfare of others, of sufficient strength to ensure that they do their fair share in alleviating suffering."[20]) The result, as he admits, is the basic ethical values of a liberal democracy.

For Carruthers, then, this account of moral language is a human construct in the same way that language is a human construct that organizes the world. He believes that contractualism captures an innate human justification for moral discourses that then form different moralities because of different metaphysical and cultural frameworks. It is weak objectivism because it captures an innate human need that enables us to live together in community.

A C. S. Lewis type objectivist could concede that Carruthers has captured one of the ways in which God has so organized the universe so that humanity can discover ethical truth. As we shall see later in this book, Roman Catholics could suggest that the innate human need is a modern version of the "natural law" approach. On this view, it is not surprising that our human reason can discern the basic rational values of certain ethical fundamentals. Meanwhile the strong subjectivist might respond that Carruthers is not facing up to the extent of moral diversity. And the suggestion that liberal democratic values are really universal moral values is deeply misguided. Once again, the conversation continues.

The third account – the ideal observer – has been recently vigorously defended by Michael Martin in *Atheism, Morality, and Meaning*. Martin's project in this book is to provide an objective account of morality which is intelligible and plausible for an atheist. Martin argues that the ideal observer theory provides both a theory of meaning and theory of justification that makes sense of moral discourse. According to Martin, the theory has its roots in the work of Adam Smith and David Hume. The basic idea involves the following:

> The meaning of ethical expressions such as "It was morally wrong of Jones to steal the book," "There is a prima facie moral duty to keep promises," and "Gratuitous torture is morally wrong" is analyzed in terms of the ethically significant reactions of an observer who has certain ideal properties such as being fully informed and completely impartial . . . Note also that the theory does not suppose that Ideal Observers actually exist. Rather, the analysis is stated in terms of a con-trary-to-fact conditional: if there *were* an Ideal Observer, it *would* react in certain way . . . [I]n order to be rationally justified in one's ethical judgments about some action or event one must base these judgments on one's estimate of the reaction of an ideal observer. One way of doing this would be to approximate to the characteristics of ideal observer and see what one's own reactions would be. For example, to be ethically justified in holding that it is morally wrong for John to lie to Mary, one could become well informed with respect to the rele-vant facts, be impartial, and so on and determine if one had a feeling of disapproval. The more one approximates to these and other ideal char-acteristics the more one's reaction would be morally trustworthy.[21]

So for Martin, moral judgments involve the following exercise. We are facing a moral dilemma. What we should do is to imagine an "ideal observer" – some-one who knows all the relevant facts and seeks to be impartial – and then see which course of action is favored as a result of this imaginative exercise.

Martin is building on the work of Roderick Firth.[22] Much like the disposi-tional theory, Firth draws an analogy with colors: although dependent upon people, moral values do have a quality that transcends people. For Firth, the ideal observer has the following qualities: omniscience (in respect to non-ethi-cal facts), omnipercipience (i.e. knowing all possible consequences of all possible acts), disinterestedness (i.e. impartial), dispassionateness (doesn't have a par-ticular animosity to an individual or party), consistency, and normalcy (i.e. is human rather than a God). Martin works through each of these criteria in turn. He modifies some and affirms others. Given he doesn't think that omniscience is coherent, he argues that the ideal observer is "as knowledgeable as coherence allows."[23] Martin also wants to add empathy and compassion.

There are two difficulties facing this account. The first is why anybody should

27

enter into this imaginative exercise. Martin believes that this is the fundamental intrinsic invitation at the heart of moral discourse. However, once it is exposed as simply an imaginative exercise, why should the Nietzschian skeptic participate? The second is that the ideal observer does sound like God. Martin is very hostile to this criticism.[24] And it is true that the Ideal Observer is not the Creator of the Universe. However, it is a "fiction" that deliberately tries to create the transcendental perspective for morality that theism provides. Whether this is significant or not is for you (the reader) to decide.

So is morality objective or subjective or somewhere in between?

At this stage, perhaps it is important to note the following. This is a very fundamental decision about the character of morality, however, it cannot be considered in isolation. Your judgment on this question will partly depend on your view of religion and the success or otherwise of anthropological explanations for morality. Moral issues connect with many things; at the end of this chapter, we find ourselves again linking ethics and religion. This is an issue that will be revisited again in later chapters in the book.

Notes

1 J. L. Mackie, *Ethics: Inventing Right and Wrong* (Harmondsworth: Penguin 1977).
2 Ibid. p. 36.
3 J. L. Mackie, *The Miracle of Theism* (Oxford: Clarendon Press 1982).
4 J. L. Mackie, *Ethics: Inventing Right and Wrong*.
5 C. S. Lewis, *Mere Christianity* (New York: Macmillan Company 1960) p. 3.
6 Ibid. p. 5.
7 Ibid.
8 Ibid. p. 190.
9 Tony Pitson, "The Dispositional Account of Colour," *Philosophia* 25:1–4 (April 1997) and available on the web at http://www.philosophy.stir.ac.uk/old/cnw/webpapers/pitson1.htm
10 See D. Lewis, "Dispositional Theories of Value," *Proceedings of the Aristotelian Society*, Supplementary Volume (1989) pp. 113–37.
11 Michael Smith, *Ethics and the A Priori* (Cambridge: Cambridge University Press 2004) p. 9.
12 Ibid. p. 9.
13 Michael Smith, "Exploring the Implications of the Dispositional Theory of Value," *Philosophical Issues* 12, *Realism and Relativism* (2002) p. 329.
14 Peter Carruthers, *The Animal Issue: Moral Theory in Practice* (Cambridge: Cambridge University Press 1992) p. 15.
15 Ibid. p. 16.

16 Ibid. pp. 35–6.
17 For John Rawls see *A Theory of Justice*, revised edition (Cambridge, MA: Belknap Press 1999).
18 For Thomas Scanlon, Carruthers acknowledges his debt to him: Thomas Scanlon, "Contractualism and Utilitarianism" in A. Sen and B. Williams (eds.) *Utilitarianism and Beyond* (Cambridge: Cambridge University Press 1982).
19 Peter Carruthers, *The Animal Issue*, p. 40.
20 Ibid. p. 43.
21 Michael Martin, *Atheism, Morality, and Meaning* (Amherst, NY: Prometheus Books 2002) pp. 50–1.
22 For Roderick Firth see "Ethical Absolutism and the Ideal Observer," in Wilfrid Sellars and John Hospers (eds.) *Readings in Ethical Theory*, second edition (Englewood Cliffs, NJ: Prentice Hall 1970) pp. 200–21.
23 Michael Martin, *Atheism, Morality, and Meaning*.
24 See ibid. p. 86.

4

Do you just do what is right or do you try to predict the outcomes?

Thought exercise

You are part of a group of people who are spelunking (what the British call potholing). After a morning of exploring various caves, the group settles down to a lavish lunch in a cave. As you are finishing the lunch, you notice some water gushing into the cave. You then make the mistake of sending the person who has consumed the most at lunch to leave the cave first. That person – much like Winnie the Pooh – gets firmly wedged in the exit. Meanwhile the water is rising rapidly. It looks like five people might drown unless the sixth is removed from the exit. In amongst your kit, you find a stick of dynamite and a match. Would you use the dynamite?[1]

This is a widely discussed thought exercise, which captures the theme of this chapter precisely. It is an obvious ethical axiom that the "killing of innocent people" is wrong. Indeed it is so basic, that one might presume that it should never be violated. However, this is a classic challenge to that assumption. What if the killing of one innocent person might save five other people?

The answer to this question will depend on whether you are a deontologist or a consequentialist (sometimes in the literature called a "teleologist"). Let us look at the difference around this thought exercise before exploring the history of these two positions in more detail. *A deontologist can be defined as a person who recognizes that there are absolute moral prohibitions that must be applied consistently to all situations.* One must do one's ethical duty regardless of the outcome or, to put it more technically, the right action always coincides with the good thing. John Rawls, probably one of the most distinguished political theorists of the twentieth century, explains that a deontological theory is "one that either does not specify the good independently from the right, or does not interpret the right as maximizing the good."[2] In other words one does not have to speculate about

30

what the appropriate outcome is: a certain course of action is both the right action and leads to the appropriate outcome. For a deontologist, there is a whole host of ethical absolutes – rape, torture, and treachery are simply forbidden. Taking an innocent life is also an absolute: therefore it would be wrong to blow up your friend, even if the intent is to save the lives of others.

A consequentialist is a person who insists that the goal of ethical action is to bring about the most desirable outcome: so the ethical task involves calculating the possible outcomes and acting accordingly. If to realize a certain end, it is necessary to take an "ostensibly" evil action, then it may be right to do so. If to save five innocent lives, it is necessary to kill one innocent life, then one should kill the innocent life. In terms of outcome, it is, explains the consequentialist, surely better that five people should live and only one die, rather than just one person living and five people dying. In short, the consequentialist believes that the "end can justify the means."

The deontologist would respond by explaining that it is unhealthy to turn the ethical domain into endless calculations about possible outcomes. Predicting the outcome is extremely difficult. The act of blowing up the friend might entirely shatter the cave and kill everyone. The act of murder has then led to everyone dying. Or perhaps moments after the murder, the remaining five potholers might meet the rescue party; then the murder would have been unnecessary. Furthermore human self-interest and ingenuity can find various neat ways of justifying all sorts of manifestly immoral behavior. Adultery will be justified as "simply an act of love" beyond the marriage, when really it is the total erosion of all trust and a denial of love. You could imagine torture being justified as a necessary means to fulfill the needs of a sadomasochist.

This is a key difference in ethics. It will shape one's attitude to a whole host of ethical dilemmas. Many opponents of abortion are deontologists; they argue that the taking of an innocent life is always wrong. While many advocates stress the consequences of an unwanted child in the world and the problems it would pose to the mother and existing children. We shall look at many of these dilemmas later in the book; for now, let us explore this distinction in more depth. We start with the deontological approach.

Deontological approaches

Elizabeth Anscombe (the Cambridge philosopher) in a famous article called "Modern Moral Philosophy" argued that modern English moral philosophy has taken a consequentialist turn, which has completely betrayed the Hebrew-Christian moral tradition. She describes the main characteristic of that tradition thus:

> For it has been characteristic of that ethic to teach that there are certain things forbidden whatever *consequences* threaten, such as: choosing

to kill the innocent, for any purpose, however good; vicarious punishment; treachery (by which I mean obtaining a man's confidence in a grave matter by promises of trustworthy friendship and then betraying him to his enemies); idolatry; sodomy; adultery; making a false profession of faith. The prohibition of certain things simply in virtue of their description as such-and-such identifiable kinds of action, regardless of any further consequences, is certainly not the whole of the Hebrew-Christian ethic; but it is a noteworthy feature of it.[3]

So the first deontological approach, Anscombe is suggesting, is the entire Hebrew-Christian moral tradition. Now there are many theologians who are less sure than Anscombe about the character and the uniformity of the Hebrew-Christian moral tradition. And perhaps what shapes Anscombe's view of the Christian tradition is her Roman Catholicism.

It is true that Roman Catholic moral theology has been heavily influenced by deontological assumptions, although the whole tradition of casuistry allowed some, at times a great deal of, flexibility. We shall look at the Roman Catholic approach in a later chapter. However, it is worth noting that Pope John Paul II has been a key opponent of consequentialism. He writes in *Veritatis Splendor*:

> Such theories however are not faithful to the Church's teaching, when they believe they can justify, as morally good, deliberate choices of kinds of behavior contrary to the commandments of the divine and natural law. These theories cannot claim to be grounded in the Catholic moral tradition.[4]

And later in the same encyclical, the Pope explains:

> If acts are intrinsically evil, a good intention or particular circumstances can diminish their evil, but they cannot remove it. They remain "irremediably" evil acts; per se and in themselves they are not capable of being ordered to God and to the good of the person.[5]

However, the main modern representative of a deontologist approach is that genius of the Enlightenment, the German philosopher Immanuel Kant (1724–1804). Immanuel Kant is a giant in philosophy. Although the vast majority of people in the West haven't heard of him (or only have a remote sense of his significance), he has shaped their assumptions and worldview. Although Königsberg, which was then part of East Prussia (today in Russia), was relatively calm, he was living at a time of dramatic change. Kant was the philosopher who brought out the significance of Sir Isaac Newton's work in England. He could see that the rise of modern science was going to have a dramatic impact on the way we think in the West. He also saw how science was a potential threat to morality. The picture of humanity emerging in science was "impersonal" and "almost machine-like." It was difficult to see how science could be reconciled with human free will; and if human free will were a problem, then morality would be a problem as well.

To understand Kant, one must locate his reflection on morality in the broad context of his philosophy. In *The Critique of Pure Reason*, Kant set out the limits of reason. Kant argued that knowledge is a result of sense-experience (what we see, touch, taste, hear, or smell) being interpreted by the categories in our mind. Kant saw with exceptional clarity that we do not have knowledge of the "way things are in themselves" – what he called the "noumenal world." All we know is the way the world appears to the mind (i.e. the phenomenal world): we cannot access any other world but that.

On morality, Kant argues as follows. First, he distinguishes between theoretical reason and practical reason. Theoretical reason is thought about our worldview (our theoretical understanding of the world). Practical reason is thought about actions. We should think differently and in different ways about these two aspects of life.

Second, the character of morality is grounded in what he called the "categorical imperative." Kant argues that the question we need to ask is this: "What could I legislate as a universal principle of action for all human persons, whatever situation they are in?" (Note, incidentally, how similar this is to the traditional "Golden rule" – "do unto others as you would have them do unto you.") So we are searching for universal principles that would attract the assent of all rational people. The central categorical imperative is this: "act only on a principle all rational agents could act on." From this, all moral obligations then emerge. Kant argued that these obligations would divide into two: first, to seek the happiness of others; and second, to fulfill the capacities of one's own intellect. It is called a categorical imperative because we arrive at an imperative (something we must do) and it is categorical (one does it simply because it is right – because it is an action that all rational persons would assent to). In the last chapter we reflected on the puzzling nature of moral discourse. The "ought" that calls for obedience and often conflicts with our desires is very puzzling. This sense of "morality" pushing down on us and requiring us to behave in certain ways is at the heart of Kant's understanding of the moral life. The language of morality, argues Kant, is deontological. When we are under a certain obligation, that obligation calls for obedience, not negotiation or discussion.

Now Kant has arrived at an account of morality that does not depend on "revelation" (i.e. accepting the authority of a particular religion); it is one that all rational persons should just recognize as true. There are, said Kant, innate in the human mind, necessary and universal moral truths. His next step was to reflect on the assumptions we need to make (what he called postulates of practical reason). When we make sense of our moral obligations, we are required to assume three truths about the universe. The first is human free will. Even if theoretical reason has problems with reconciling human free will with science (because in a world where everything is caused, how can you have an uncaused action), practical reason makes human free will a necessity. We cannot act morally unless we have genuine freedom. The second is eternal life; and the third is God. It isn't necessary at this point to look in detail at these two postulates. But in brief, Kant worries about the relationship between justice and morality and postulates God as the being necessary to bring about what he calls the *summum bonum* (the highest good – where justice and morality are reconciled) and eternity as the necessary venue to do this work. It is important to stress that God is not needed as the source of these moral principles; the moral principles are already built into humanity and his categorical imperative is his method of discovering those moral principles.

For our purposes, however, it is the character of the moral discourse that we need to appreciate. Kant sees embedded in the very language of morality an overwhelming obligation that must shape our behavior. When we have an "obligation" to behave in a certain way, then that is non-negotiable.

Nancy (Ann) Davis is right when she explains that contemporary sympathizers to a deontological approach tend to construct an approach to ethics that operates with three features. First the "deontological constraints" (as she calls them – the ethical obligations as I have called them) must be "negatively formulated."[6] "Thou shalt not lie" is a great deal clearer than "thou shalt tell the truth." It also opens up the option that you can keep silent (that, after all, is not lying), while always "telling the truth" would exclude that option. Second, the deontological constraint should be "narrowly framed and bounded."[7] "Do not harm the innocent" makes it clear exactly which class of action is excluded; "do not harm" could become much trickier to implement. Third, the deontological constraint needs to be "narrowly directed."[8] It must concentrate on the agent's intention in respect to the immediate action. So the moral question in the cave is: do I kill this innocent life? It is not: given the whole situation, what should I do?

One strength of the deontological approach to ethics is that it works very effectively in moral education. When one is training a child, one does not invite the child to consider a range of options for behavior and then evaluate which one is appropriate: a parent simply tells a child it is wrong to lie or to bully another child. We set out rules that are absolute.

The problem with deontological approaches, however, is that in the murky world of living we find it all too difficult. Sometimes our obligations conflict: the

obligation not to lie and the obligation to save innocent lives become very difficult to reconcile when the Nazi is asking you whether you are hiding a Jewish
family in the attic. And sometimes the obligation seems to conflict with a desired
outcome, like the dilemma in our thought exercise. It was these two rival tugs
that generated an alternative. Perhaps instead of seeing the moral life as simply
something given, we should attempt to work out the right and good by reflecting on where we want to end up. This is called consequentialism.

Consequentialism and utilitarianism

Any ethic that thinks that consequences need to be a major factor in determining what is right is a consequentialist ethic. The best known consquentialist ethic
is the English eighteenth-century "invention," albeit anticipated in the work of
David Hume (1711–76) and Thomas Hobbes (1588–1679), called utilitarianism.

Utilitarianism was developed in its most sophisticated form by Jeremy
Bentham (1748–1832) whose stuffed body is stored at University College,
London. Bentham was exceptionally bright; he went to Oxford University to
study law at the age of 12. He framed his ethical theory in the light of his commitment to social policy and legislation. This is important to recognize: he
wanted to find a way so that the political world could think "ethically." He developed his account of the ethical life in his best known work – *Introduction to the
Principles of Morals and Legislation*, which he published in 1789.

Bentham wanted to create a scientific approach to ethics. He proposed that
the goal of a moral action is the greatest happiness for the greatest number.
Bentham argued the key issue in moral decision-making is "utility" – the benefits (or usefulness) of a particular course of action. This means that you should
take the course of action that would benefit most people. His criterion was happiness, which he defined in terms of pleasure (hence this position is sometimes
called "hedonistic utilitarianism). He suggested a mathematical calculation of
pleasures and pains, which will then determine which course of action is right.
Peter Baelz provides a good summary:

> What all men want is pleasure, or happiness. That is the common
> thread running through all human aims and objectives. The value of
> men's actions, therefore, is to be assessed in terms of the happiness that
> they produce. Just as the individual, when he has only himself to think
> about, makes up his mind what to do in terms of what will give him the
> greatest pleasure, or happiness, so the member of society, concerned
> with the interests of others as well as with his own, must make up his
> mind what to do in terms of what will produce the greatest happiness.
> My single and overriding concern in any conflict of interests will be so

to act as to ensure that the greatest number of people enjoy the greatest amount of happiness."⁹

On this account of morality, one does not preclude at the outset certain courses of action for if a certain action will benefit many people then it must remain an option. So, for example, divorce might be wrong in general, but if in a particular situation a woman would be able to escape from a violent husband, thereby protecting her children, then the greatest number would benefit from the action of getting a divorce.

Jeremy Bentham started a movement. And it was a son of one of his closest friends that became the leading light of the movement in the nineteenth century. John Stuart Mill (1806–73) was equally precocious as a child: he started learning Greek at the age of three. He spent much of his life in France, returning to England to be elected to Parliament in 1865, only to lose his seat in 1868. His major book was called *Utilitarianism*, which was published in 1863 and served as the basis for his radical commitments to women's rights and prison reform.

Mill modified one key aspect of Bentham's scheme. First, he insisted that one must recognize distinctions in forms of happiness and not just its intensity. Bentham had maintained that the "quality of pleasure being equal, push-pin [a child's game] is as good as poetry."¹⁰ Mill argued that most people would prefer to be "Socrates dissatisfied rather than a pig satisfied." One cannot just equate "happiness" with "pleasure and the absence of pain." We need to work with a more elevated calculation of pleasure.

Many were attracted by the evident simplicity of the principle. Those in politics saw its immediate legitimacy: it provided a criterion for moral judgment and one that had manifest legitimacy in any democracy. It was influential amongst those who wanted prison reform. Rather than "lock up" the villain and throw away the key, one should recognize that reform of the criminal rather than simple social revenge is the way of bringing about the "greatest good for the greatest number."

Difficulties with utilitarianism

There are four major difficulties with utilitarianism. The first is who or what exactly do we include in the "greatest number"? If the criterion is pleasure and pain, then it would seem necessary to extend the greatest number to include all sentient beings (every person and all animals). J. L. Mackie develops the difficulty when he writes:

> A theory that equates good with pleasure and evil with pain would appear to have no non-arbitrary reason for excluding from considera-

tion any creatures that are capable of feeling either pleasure or pain. Does it include only those who are now alive, or also future generations; and if so, only those who will exist or also those who might exist?[11]

In much of the literature this is seen as a problem: surely it is impractical to consider every single human being, as well as animals and plants, both now and in the future? Yet as we shall see in the chapter on environmental ethics, there is a need for our ethical reflection to widen its concerns from the preoccupation with humans to the non-human realm. Critics might be right when they stress the difficulty of such a wide moral scope, but just because it is difficult doesn't mean it isn't necessary.

The second difficulty is that the democratic and egalitarian sympathies of utilitarianism do not recognize that some people should be given more regard in the individual's ethical decision-making. It is a recipe for child neglect if I give the same ethical weight to my child as to every other child in the world. I do not have the same responsibility to the child around the corner or in Latin America, as I do to my own child. My son Luke is entitled to expect me to turn up and watch him play soccer; I am not obligated to do that for every child in the world. As a parent, I have particular responsibilities to my child. J. L. Mackie calls the utilitarian expectation the "ethics of fantasy" and makes the criticism with some force:

> We cannot require that the actions of people generally should ever pass the test of being such as to maximize the happiness of all, whether or not this is their motive. Even within a small village or commune it is too much to expect that the efforts of all members should be wholly directed towards the promoting of the well-being of all. And such total cooperation is out of the question on the scale of a nation state, let alone where the "all" are to be the whole human race, including its future or possible future members, and perhaps all other sentient beings as well.[12]

On one level Mackie is entirely right. It is a physical necessity that a human occupies a body in a particular place. Given our finitude, at any one moment there are certain people we know better than others. It is right to say that our moral obligations extend out in concentric circles: our immediate family is entitled to be given a moral priority; our extended family are next; our physical neighbors who make up our community are next; then our town or city; then our country; and finally, then we should have a moral concern for the whole world.

However, on another level, Mackie is not right. Although humans are almost bound to organize their ethical priorities in this way, the utilitarian attempt to extend the moral discourse is good. It is especially good for those in power. For those in power, it is a temptation to promote family and friends to positions of power and wealth. This is nepotism. Although Tony Blair is not obliged to go to a football game with every child in Britain and, in that respect, is permitted to make that activity one that his children enjoy over other children, he is expected to ensure that his policies as prime minister do not focus on his children and do consider all children especially those furthest from his natural social circle.

The third difficulty is the problem of justice. This is perhaps the most significant difficulty. The utilitarian ethic requires us to opt for the course of action that brings the greatest happiness to the greatest number. Imagine, then, a situation where there are 20 sadomasochists and one non-sadomasochist. The sadomasochists love torturing non-sadomasochists. What is the right thing to do in this situation? Or less dramatically, should taxes go to fund a new opera house which only a (well-off) minority will use? Along with this conceptual difficulty, there are many more pragmatic illustrations of the conflict. Peter Baelz writes:

> It is debatable whether principles of justice are compatible with the principle of utility . . . What, for example, are we to say about Caiaphas' celebrated remark when, according to the Fourth Gospel, the chief priests and Pharisees were debating what to do about Jesus: "It is expedient for you that one man should die for the people, and that the whole nation perish not"? Do considerations of public interest justify judicial murder? Or what are we to say about the decision of the British Government at the end of the Second World War to hand over to the Russian allies the nationals who had been fighting on the side of the Germans, even though they were sending them to their deaths?'[13]

Churchill's decision is a good illustration of the problem. It was a utilitarian calculation by Churchill to return to the Russians the Austrians who had collaborated with the Nazi regime. These people were almost certainly slaughtered; however, he calculated that the potential advantage in terms of a better relationship with Soviet Russia was worth any potential injustice to the minority of people who were returned. This illustrates rather well why utilitarianism (and all forms of consequentialism) can be so difficult. Churchill predicted inaccurately the outcome: the Cold War still occurred and the Russians remained awkward players on the international scene. It is very unclear whether the sacrifice of these people for the putative greatest good really did achieve its desired end. Predicting consequences is extremely difficult.

Now thus far we have looked at what is called "act utilitarianism." One response to these difficulties with act utilitarianism was "rule utilitarianism."

Rule utilitarianism

In 1832 John Austin wrote a book called *The Province of Jurisprudence Determined*. His famous dictum stated that "our rules would be fashioned on utility; our conduct on our rules." The idea has two steps. Step one: we would start by considering the tendency of any act. If it tends towards making people unhappy, then it would be wrong; if it tends towards happiness, then it would be right. Step two: once we have classified the act, then it becomes binding on us.

Now all utilitarians accept that the "conventional rules" (e.g. do not lie) are helpful. They are the result of years of wisdom about actions that make people happy. However, rule utilitarianism wants to go further. These rules once formulated, using the principle of utility, are binding on us. The question is: what exactly does this mean?

On the one hand, it might mean that we should be formulating new rules for changing situations. So, for example, it is a rule that one should not lie. One can think of many situations where the greatest happiness is enhanced by observing that rule. However, if your friend is having an affair and the partner of your friend asks you whether this is the case, then we might need a modified rule. The rule might be "do not lie unless you judge that the consequences of the truth might damage a friendship," which then becomes binding in all situations. The problem is clear: endlessly revised rules mean a situation that is just like "act utilitarianism." On the other hand, these rules (such as "do not lie") once formulated using the principle of utility can end up losing the advantage of consequentialism. If the only utilitarian aspect to the ethic resides in its utilitarian justification, but from then on the rule must be applied to every situation, then it resembles a deontological ethic. The problem arises that one must not lie even to the Nazi soldier who wants to know about your Jewish friends hiding in the attic. It is a consequentialist ethic that has lost the advantage of consequentialism.

Before finishing this section on utilitarianism, it is worth mentioning a Christian version of Utilitarianism. It was formulated by Joseph Fletcher (1905–91) and was called 'Situation Ethics."

Situation ethics

Fletcher's book *Situation Ethics: The New Morality* appeared in 1966. In it, he distinguishes three approaches to ethics. First, the legalistic (i.e. the applications of laws to all situations); second, the antinomian (i.e. the lawless approach); and third, the situational. The argument of the book was that "situation ethics" was the Christian ethic that Jesus taught.

A key passage for this position is found in Mark's gospel:

One sabbath he was going through the cornfields; and as they made their way his disciples began pluck heads of grain. The Pharisees said to him, "Look, why are they doing what is not lawful on the sabbath?" And he said to them, "Have you never read what David did when he and his companions were hungry and in need of food? He entered the house of God, when Abiathar was high priest, and ate the bread of the Presence, which it is not lawful for any but the priests to eat, and he gave some to his companions." Then he said to them, "The sabbath was made for humankind, and not humankind for the sabbath; so the Son of Man is lord even of the sabbath." (Mark 2:23–8)

Fletcher's interpretation of this story is that Jesus is teaching that people matter more than principles. The rule that you should not labor on the Sabbath (and the act of "plucking heads of grain" was interpreted as labor) should not be applied to every situation. And in certain situations, argues Fletcher, Jesus is insisting that the needs of people should take priority.

Instead of "happiness" the criterion was now "love." Fletcher uses the leading New Testament word for love which is "agape." This is a love that overflows and is the word used to describe the love that God has for humanity. He refers to his fundamentals as follows:

1 The First Proposition: "Only one 'thing' is intrinsically good; namely, love: nothing else at all."[14]
2 The Second Proposition: "The ruling norm of Christian decision is love: nothing else."[15]
3 The Third Proposition: "Love and Justice are the same, for justice is love distributed, nothing else."[16]
4 The Fourth Proposition: "Love wills the neighbor's good whether we like him or not."[17]
5 The Fifth Proposition: "Only the end justifies the means; nothing else."[18]
6 The Sixth Proposition: "Love's decisions are made situationally, not prescriptively."[19]

One should, argued Fletcher, treat each situation differently and do that which is "the most loving action." The Ten Commandments become a guide for ethical behavior, not absolutes. If a situation calls for killing as the most loving action, then so be it. As with utilitarianism one attempts to predict the outcome and act accordingly. Also, as with utilitarianism, it is open to the problems of predicting consequences and the dangers of sacrificing a minority for the majority.

Transcending the deontological and consequentialist options

The quest for an account of the moral life that transcends these two options is ongoing. Some Roman Catholics, for example, Richard McCormick, have been arguing for "proportionalism." This takes the view that the deontological moral prohibition can only be broken in extreme circumstances. So a directly willed evil is normally wrong, but it is admissible for a very grave or proportionalist reason.

Pope John Paul II in *Veritatis Splendor* condemned proportionalism. Nevertheless, it does contain an important moral insight. It is capturing the idea that the ends can justify the means under two conditions: (1) the end must be extremely serious, and (2) the means must be the only way of obtaining that end. So, for example, the woman who is hiding a Jewish family in her home from the Nazis will need to lie to protect that family. The end is absolutely serious: the life of a family is at stake. And the lie is the only possible means: to "evade" the question or keep silence is an invitation to search the house. It is a very great end that needs deception as the means to that end.

In addition to this insight, we need to relocate this debate. It was H. Richard Niebuhr in his classic *The Responsible Self* who argued that the language of responsibility entails the idea of the human life as a moral work in process. He writes:

> In this situation the rise of the new symbolism of responsibility is important. It represents an alternative or an additional way of conceiving and defining this existence of ours that is the material of our own actions. What is implicit in the idea of responsibility is the image of man-the-answerer, man engaged in dialogue, man acting in response to action upon us . . . To be engaged in dialogue, to answer questions addressed to us, to defend ourselves against attacks, to reply to injunctions, to meet challenges – this is common experience.[20]

The concept of the "responsible self" is a way of locating the debates about rules and consequences (the term that H. Richard Niebuhr uses is "teleology"). He explains the relationship of responsibility to rules and consequences, when he writes:

> [W]e may say that purposiveness seeks to answer the question: "What shall I do?" by raising as prior the question: "What is my goal, ideal, or telos?" Deontology tries to answer the moral query by asking, first of all: "what is the law and what is first law of my life?" Responsibility, however, proceeds in every moment of decision and choice to inquire:

"What is going on?" If we use value terms then the differences among the three approaches may be indicated by the terms, the *good*, the *right*, and the *fitting*; for teleology is concerned always with the highest good to which it subordinates the right; consistent deontology is concerned with the right, no matter what may happen to our goods; but for the ethics of responsibility the *fitting* action, the one that fits into a total interaction as response and as anticipation of further response, is alone conducive to the good and alone is right.[21]

H. Richard Niebuhr is stressing the need for the total ethical context to be considered. The moral decision is not exclusively about an end – an outcome – nor is it simply a matter of determining what is right and doing that; instead it is the quest for the moral action that fits the situation – uniquely and appropriately.

H. Richard Niebuhr defines "responsibility" as follows:

> The idea of pattern of responsibility, then, may summarily and abstractly be defined as the idea of an agent's action as response to an action upon him in accordance with his interpretation of the latter action and with his expectation of response to his response; and all of this is in a continuing community of agents.[22]

So again the moral decision is located. Responsibility assumes the reality that our dilemma comes within a context. We are always making a moral decision because of some "action" towards us. If you find a wallet on the ground, then this event will force a response. We will then interpret that action: in this case, someone has lost this wallet and the wallet belongs to someone else. We do so in the context of "social solidarity,"[23] which, at a minimum, means that we need to do what will uphold civil society. Given all this, the responsible response is to make every effort to return the wallet to its owner.

We can now see a rich account of the moral life emerging. One problem with the consequentialist against the deontological debate is that it need not make the moral life very demanding. It can be very easy to observe negative prohibitions and lead a life of privilege. One might not lie or commit adultery, but one still enjoys an obscene lifestyle of affluence and decadence. Conversely, consequentialism can be an excuse for all sorts of dubious decisions. Two 14-year-olds are in a hayloft drinking cider on a warm sunny day. It is very easy to imagine that the "most loving thing to do" in this situation is to make love; it is much harder to cope with the consequences nine months later. The language of "responsibility" is a safeguard: it makes positive demands on the morally lazy deontologist; and it warns against the temptations of consequentialism.

Our task is to become morally serious, which we will discuss in depth later on in the book. However, for now it is worth noting that this is the quest for a level of consciousness that transcends the mundane (mortgages, soap operas, reality TV) and takes seriously one's moral obligation to the moments that we find ourselves living. Thinking and being responsible is the secret.

Notes

1 Versions of this thought exercise have been circulating for many years. I have been attempting to track down the person who originally constructed it without success however. For a similar version but put to a different use see Helga Kuhse, "Euthanasia" in Peter Singer (ed.) *A Companion to Ethics* (Oxford: Blackwell Publishing 1991) p. 300.
2 John Rawls, *A Theory of Justice* (Oxford: Oxford University Press 1972) p. 30.
3 Elizabeth (G. E. M.) Anscombe, "Modern Moral Philosophy," *Philosophy* 33 (1958).
4 Pope John Paul II, *Veritatis Splendor*, Encyclical Letter, August 6 ,1993, paragraph 76. 2.
5 Ibid. paragraph 81. 2.
6 Nancy (Ann) Davis, "Contemporary Deontology" in Peter Singer (ed.) *A Companion to Ethics* (Oxford: Blackwell Publishing 1991) p. 208.
7 Ibid. p. 208.
8 Ibid. p. 208.
9 Peter Baelz, *Ethics and Belief* (London: Sheldon Press 1977) p. 31. Baelz was writing at a time when inclusive language had not become the norm.
10 Jeremy Bentham, *Introduction to the Principles of Morals and Legislation* (Oxford: Clarendon Press 1996).
11 J. L. Mackie, *Ethics: Inventing Right and Wrong* (Harmondsworth: Penguin 1977) pp. 126–7.
12 Ibid. p. 130.
13 Peter Baelz, *Ethics and Belief*, p. 33.
14 Joseph Fletcher, *Situation Ethics* (Philadelphia, PN: Westminster Press 1966) p. 57.
15 Ibid. p. 69.
16 Ibid. p. 87.
17 Ibid. p. 103.
18 Ibid. p. 120.
19 Ibid. p. 134.
20 H. Richard Niebuhr, *The Responsible Self* (Evanston, IL, and London: Harper and Row 1963) p. 56.
21 Ibid. pp. 60–1.
22 Ibid. p. 65.
23 This is H. Richard Niebuhr's phrase, see ibid. p. 65.

5

Natural law and virtue ethics

Thought exercise

This is part of the opening statement in the Trial of 23 Nazi doctors, who were charged with committing inhuman experiments on German citizens and nationals of other countries.[1] The opening statement is made by Brig. General Telford Taylor (December 9, 1946):

> The defendants in this case are charged with murders, tortures, and other atrocities committed in the name of medical science. The victims of these crimes are numbered in the hundreds of thousands. A handful only are still alive; a few of the survivors will appear in this courtroom. But most of these miserable victims were slaughtered outright or died in the course of the tortures to which they were subjected.
>
> For the most part they are nameless dead. To their murderers, these wretched people were not individuals at all. They came in wholesale lots and were treated worse than animals. They were 200 Jews in good physical condition, 50 gypsies, 500 tubercular Poles, or 1,000 Russians. The victims of these crimes are numbered amongst the anonymous millions who met death at the hands of the Nazis and whose fate is a hideous blot on the page of modern history.
>
> The charges against these defendants are brought in the name of the United States of America. They are being tried by a court of American judges. The responsibilities thus imposed upon the representatives of the United States, prosecutors and judges alike, are grave and unusual. It is owed, not only to the victims and to the parents and children of the victims, that just punishment be imposed on the guilty, but also to the defendants that they be accorded a fair hearing and decision. Such responsibilities are the ordinary burden of any tribunal. Far wider are the duties which we must fulfill here.

'These larger obligations run to the peoples and races on whom the scourge of these crimes was laid. The mere punishment of the defendants, or even of thousands of others equally guilty, can never redress the terrible injuries which the Nazis visited on these unfortunate peoples. For them it is far more important that these incredible events be established by clear and public proof, so that no one can ever doubt that they were fact and not fable; and that this Court, as the agent of the United States and as the voice of humanity, stamp these acts, and the ideas which engendered them, as barbarous and criminal.'

An observation by Herman Goering, who was Reichsmarschall and Luftwaffe (Air Force) Chief; President of Reichstag; Director of "Four Year Plan" at the Nuremberg Trials: "This is a political trial by the victors and it will be a good thing when Germany realizes that . . ."

Is it true that the nations of the world are answerable to a "higher law"? Is it true that all people everywhere should recognize certain ethical fundamentals?

Thus far in our exploration of ethics we have looked at several different ethical schemes: we gave, for example, particular attention to Kant's categorical imperative and to Bentham's utilitarianism. In this chapter, we shall look at two traditions; the first is natural law; and the second is virtue ethics. These two traditions shared a similar history and often were linked together. The title of the chapter is stressing the "objective" nature of the natural law ethic: natural law assumes that built into the fabric of the world are certain moral facts. Using our reason, we should be able to work out these moral facts and recognize their binding power upon us.

Roots of natural law in antiquity

The tradition of natural law was most fully developed in the Roman Catholic tradition, supremely in the thought of that famous Dominican friar of the thirteenth century – St Thomas Aquinas. However, the idea was developed initially in the thought of Aristotle (384–322 BCE) and the Roman Stoics.

Aristotle distinguished between the laws of the city-state and the laws of nature. Both were "laws" and both argued Aristotle were binding. Aristotle went on to argue that human reason had the capacity to work what was right. In addition the entire concept of a "telos" (an end) to which nature was directed has its roots in Aristotle. For Aristotle, this was a "biological" claim. To understand the processes at work in nature, one must recognize the goals to which the various parts of nature are seeking. So the little acorn is not understood unless one recognizes that the ultimate end of that acorn is a vast oak tree; in addition, there is a sense in which the "potential" of the oak tree exists in the acorn. The concepts then of "human reason as the tool for discovering moral truths" and the doctrine of the "telos" in nature are vital in the natural law tradition.

The Roman Stoics contributed the sense that there was a natural law for absolutely everybody. This emerged from their distinctive religious disposition. They were pantheists (i.e. they believed that God and the world should be identified together). As a result both human nature and human reason were linked in a very real way with the divine, which in turn was the basis of our moral life. Given this was true for all people, then all people had the capacity to work out – provided they recognize the order in the universe – the universal moral laws. Naturally, amongst philosophers in Rome, different emphases emerged in their interpretation of natural law. Cicero (106–43 CE), for example, stressed the distinctive human capacity to reason as the main source of ethical knowledge, while Epictetus and Ulpian stressed physical nature, which of course is shared with the animals, as the primary guide for correct behavior.

These three characteristics (namely, a universal ethic, which uses reason, to detect the telos of nature) became the basis of the natural law tradition. Its influence has been vast: international law is based on the natural law tradition; as we saw in our opening thought exercise, it was cited at the Nuremberg trials as the Allies sought to find an ethical basis for holding the Nazis answerable to a higher law; and it continues to shape much of our language and discussion about morality. But this is to move on too rapidly, we need to pause and look at the development of the tradition in the thought of St Thomas Aquinas (1225–74 CE).

Aquinas and natural law

No one can deny the genius of Aquinas. His *Summa Theologica* remains compelling reading. Aquinas attempts to answer every conceivable question (given the limitations of his time – he doesn't, for example, answer questions about genetically-modified crops!) in a systematic way. The structure of the *Summa* reveals a remarkably organized mind at work. He poses a question: he then formulates all the possible objections to the position he holds; he then identifies the key argument for the position he will then go on and defend; and then he expounds the arguments concluding with a response to the objections he initially formulated.

Aquinas believes that the moral dimension of life applies to all human actions. This might sound rather odd: my decision to eat a MacDonald's burger or work on my golf swing does not seem to involve many moral considerations. But Aquinas would insist that we ask the question: why are we eating a MacDonald's burger? Is it appropriate? Even mundane human actions, insists Aquinas, need to be relocated into the moral realm.

We have already noted how the "end" of an action is important for Aquinas: it was a discovery he learnt from Aristotle. The "why" you are doing something is normally the "desired end" of an action. "I am chopping wood" because "I need wood for my fire to keep us warm during the long Connecticut winter"; the desired outcome determines the legitimacy of the action.

Aquinas distinguished between four different types of law. The first is the "eternal law"; this is the law that governs the universe. The second is the "positive divine law," which is revealed in Scripture (in the New and Old Testaments); these are the particular commands of God, which will include many insights that can be learned from natural law (which is the third category) but also go beyond natural law. The third is, as we have already said, natural law; and the last is "positive human law"; these are the commands of rulers in a particular state, which of course should be grounded in natural law.

Now turning to natural law: the ultimate end of all human action (or as Aquinas puts it "the first principle of practical reason") is that good should be done and pursued and evil avoided. Aquinas puts it like this:

> Therefore, the first principle of practical reason is grounded in the notion of the good: the good is that which all things desire. This, then, is the first precept of the law: good should be done and pursued and evil avoided. All other precepts of the law of nature are grounded in this one, such that all those things that are to be done or avoided pertain to precepts of natural law which practical reason naturally grasps as human goods.[2]

For Aquinas, this is self-evident. Much like the law of non-contradiction (something either is or is not; it can't be both), "good should be done and pursued and evil avoided" is the moral equivalent. All rational people, insists Aquinas, should just be able to see this general moral principle.

From this general moral principle, Aquinas identifies certain "inclinations," which are illustrations of the implications of these axioms. "For there is in man a first inclination to a good of the nature he shares with all substances,"[3] explains Aquinas. So we should seek to ensure our bodily survival (food and shelter are therefore good); and we should seek to avoid all that which might destroy us (so large quantities of heroin are bad). The second inclination in humanity is

> an inclination to more special things, according to the nature he shares with other animals. Following on this, what nature teaches all animals are said to be of natural law, such as joining of male and female, and the raising of young, and the like.[4]

47

So Aquinas is arriving at family and its related obligations as fundamental moral obligations. The third inclination to good in humanity is the result of our reason. Aquinas explains:

> Man has a natural inclination to know the truth about God and live in society. Accordingly those things which look to this inclination pertain to natural law, for example, that a man should avoid ignorance, that he should not offend others with whom he must live, and other such things which are relevant to this.[5]

Natural law, then, works as a system. Or as Ralph McInerny puts it: "The way in which natural law precepts are described may lead us to think of moral discourse as an axiomatic system: first set down the most general principles, the articulate less general ones, then proceed systematically toward the concrete and particular . . . Natural law is a theory about moral reasoning."[6] The point is this: "do good and avoid evil" sounds pretty banal; yet at moments of significant moral pressure or temptation, it is important to remind ourselves of this underlying principle, which actually is assumed a million times a day as we make moral observations and decisions.

The development of the natural law tradition

It was in the sixteenth century that the natural law tradition developed the tools that were going to be so significant for modernity. Francisco de Vitoria (1492–1546) is perhaps the key player. Vitoria has been acclaimed as the founder of "international law." He wanted the "law of nations" (i.e. the laws governing the behavior of the nations) to be formulated in such a way that it is binding on the nations of the world. The provisions of the law of nations would be a result of international agreement and "positive law" (i.e. human decision). However, Vitoria argued that it needs to be grounded in the natural law that governs all human conduct. Or as Stephen Pope puts it, "Natural law precedes and governs positive law."[7]

Hugo Grotius (1583–1645) developed this tradition using the natural law tradition to justify the language of "natural rights." Although he was a very sincere Dutch Protestant, he also, crucially, insisted that natural law does not need God, thereby creating a secular version of natural law. There are, argued Grotius, still these norms in nature that can be established through reason, which create moral obligations for humans. In addition, Grotius introduces to the world the idea that individuals can claim "a right." So an employee has a right to a "just wage." Natural law was giving birth to human rights.

We can now see how significant this tradition is for our modern world. Both the French and the American Revolutions invoked the language of human rights. The language was a key assumption in our thought exercise – at the 1946 Nuremburg trials of the Nazi war criminals. When the United Nations Declaration of Human Rights was written in 1948, the rights are grounded in natural law language. It is a remarkable legacy to the modern world. However, running parallel with this talk of natural law and natural rights is an equally important tradition, namely the whole tradition of the virtues.

The virtues

For Aquinas, this stress on natural law went together with a comparable stress on the virtues, which has a similar history to natural law – Greek antiquity and Roman society. However, the recent interest in virtue ethics amongst moral philosophers has, unlike Aquinas, seen virtue ethics as a contrasting ethical approach to natural law.

The major reason for this is that natural law (or come to that utilitarianism or Kant's categorical imperative or any major ethical theory) stresses the content of ethics; however, ethics is not simply a matter of making a decision about what is right. Rather it is a training. Good ethics are not taught, they are caught. In fact thinking about ethics can be a disaster. If you see someone drop their wallet, then you should not be standing around trying to weigh up whether it is in your interests to return that wallet to its owner. Instead, the ethical person is the person who, unthinkingly, gets up and returns the wallet to the owner. This is a person who has been trained in the virtues (i.e. the habits and dispositions that express themselves in ethical actions).

As we have already noted, the tradition of the virtues has its roots in classical antiquity. Plato (c.428–348 BCE) gives Socrates (469–399 BCE) the credit for thinking of the virtues as a form of knowledge, which Plato insisted needed to be grounded in the experience of the Forms, such as Goodness, Beauty, and Justice. (The Forms are the universals underpinning this world of matter.) Aristotle (Plato's famous pupil) took issue with Plato's understanding of the virtues and developed a contrasting account. Although the virtues are still a form of knowledge of practical wisdom (albeit one that involves both appropriate emotional responses as well as sound judgment), his strategy of determining the nature of the virtues did not need Plato's transcendent experience of the forms. Instead he talked of the virtues as the mean between two alternative forms of action: so courage, for example, is a virtue that is the mean between cowardice and recklessness. It is responsible (not moderate) action to bring about a state of affairs where there is more good.

Cicero – the Roman statesman and philosopher, who was briefly mentioned in the history of natural law – is the next important character in the story. He was responsible for the four-fold division of the virtues into prudence (or practical wisdom), justice, courage, and temperance – this division was influential on medieval discussions of the virtues. Cicero also took issue with Aristotle's view that the primary virtue was practical wisdom and insisted that justice was more important. As the contemporary moral philosopher Jean Porter observes, "It is not hard to see that this reflects yet another shift in socially sanctioned ideals of virtue, away from the intellectual qualities prized by Athenian society and towards the ideals of justice and equitable administration cherished by the Romans."[8] Naturally with the movement of time and as the Christian Scriptures became more significant, different "virtues" were identified as central: the New Testament talks about "faith," "hope," and "love" as the greatest qualities (1 Corinthians 13). Humility, as opposed to pride, was seen to be supremely exhibited in the life of Jesus. So these virtues became more central in the various schemes.

By the time we get to Aquinas a distinction had emerged in the tradition. There were now "infused virtues" (those made possible by redemption and the grace of God) and "acquired virtues" (those obtainable by all people making right use of their reason). Aquinas liked Peter Lombard's (c.1100–60) definition of virtue: "a good quality of mind whereby one lives rightly and uses no one badly and which God without our help works in us."[9] In one sense this captures the key to this tradition: good people are trained in certain habits. They are trained to respond, almost instinctively, in the right way. Virtuous people then are people who don't even think of passing on a juicy confidence in confidence; it does not occur to them to gossip maliciously about those around them; they wear their goodness with disarming humility; and they just see and act appropriately.

It was the philosopher Alasdair MacIntyre who created a fresh interest in the tradition of the virtues. In a masterful book called *After Virtue*, he complained that we (i.e. those of us living in the modern period) had lost the connection between moral words because we had lost the community practices and the tradition of the virtues that connected these words together. He starts the book with a thought exercise: imagine that there was a reaction against science and the entire discourse of modern science was destroyed. Further imagine that 300 years later people start using certain scientific words and ideas to describe their attitudes to life, to what extent would this development of the scientific discourse be true to the original intent of those words? The answer, of course, is that it would not be legitimate: scientific theories and discourse are attempts to describe what actually happens in the universe, not our attitudes to the universe. So, in the same way, argues MacIntyre, our use of moral terminology is equally fragmented: we have lost the traditions that hold this discourse together. This is the reason why it looks as if there is no solution or answer to moral arguments.

MacIntyre wants us to create communities that take moral talk seriously and knows how to coherently hold such talk together. For many Christians, it has led to renewed interest in the importance of the Church. Where moral talk in the public realm seems muddled and confused, the different Christian traditions have ways (albeit different ones in different traditions) to hold moral talk together, while at the same time providing a training in the virtues. What is true of Christian traditions is of course equally true for those in Islamic, Jewish, or other faith traditions.

This stress on the significance of the community, which for Christians is the Church, is a major theme of the work of Stanley Hauerwas. In *A Community of Character* Hauerwas argues for a vision shaped by the drama of the Biblical witness and transformed into a people of virtue.[10] Part of this would involve allowing the narrative of the Bible to transform us so we face up to the challenge of our "conflicting loyalties."[11] The challenge here involves living an appropriately integrated life. For Hauerwas, the challenge facing Christian ethics is not to make the world ethical, but to make the Church ethical. Crucially, this should involve recognizing the centrality of the Christian obligation to take up the cross of Jesus and therefore become the pacifist witness.

Difficulties with this tradition

Although there is much that is impressive about the traditions of natural law and the Virtues, it does have its critics. Stephen J. Pope helpfully identifies the three main ones. First, it is difficult to see how any factual description should give rise to a particular ethical obligation. It was David Hume (1711–76) who made this point originally in passing: you cannot dervive an "ought" from an "is." And it was G. E. Moore who named this the "naturalistic fallacy." It is true that one must be careful in deducing moral obligations from a description of the way things are, but defenders of natural law simply stress that description can suggest certain obligations, which is the link natural law needs. "My body needs food" (description), need not necessarily, but could be taken to imply that perhaps "I ought to get some food" (obligation).

The second difficulty many have is from those who are more pessimistic about people. Thomas Hobbes (1588–1679) had a very pessimistic view of humanity: we are, argued Hobbes, preoccupied with seeking our own selfish happiness and without the benefit of government we would behave in very cruel and antagonistic ways to each other. Some of the Reformers shared this pessimism: the problem with natural law, argued Luther, is that it assumes that human reason has not been damaged by the Fall into sin. However, given reason is depraved, along with every other human faculty, then it cannot do the work that natural law wants it to do.

The third difficulty is that some postmodern philosophers complain about the propensity of natural law to assume that human nature is the same everywhere and in every place. This is called "essentialism." Instead descriptions of human nature, this position holds, are social constructs (i.e. invented by society). Although there are insights in this view (especially when it comes to an analysis of gender and sexuality), it is easy to overstate. There are certain fundamental and shared human needs that need to be satisfied for survival; the natural law tradition helpfully recognizes this.

The achievements of the natural law tradition include the impact on international law, and the recognition of a universal ethic accessible to all people capable of rational thought. The achievement of the tradition of the virtues is the stress on ethical training. We will look at one major difficulty in chapter 9. Natural law is the basis of the Roman Catholic opposition to contraception and homosexuality. Many people think this is an example of Roman Catholic intransigence to the inevitable progress of modernity. In chapter 9 we will look at why the Roman Catholic Church continues to construct a natural law argument against certain sexual practices.

Notes

1 All the material for this thought exercise is taken from the excellent website, which is provided by Doug Linder. http://www.law.umkc.edu/faculty/projects/ftrials/nuremberg/nuremberg.htm

2 Thomas Aquinas, *Summa Theologica* IaIIae.94.2. This translation is taken from Thomas Aquinas, *Selected Writings*, edited by Ralph McInerny (Harmondsworth: Penguin 1998) p. 645.

3 Ibid.

4 Ibid.

5 Ibid.

6 Ralph McInerny, "Ethics" in Norman Kretzmann and Eleonore Stump (eds.) *The Cambridge Companion to Aquinas* (Cambridge: Cambridge University Press 1993) p. 212.

7 Stephen J. Pope, "Natural Law and Christian Ethics" in Robin Gill (ed.) *A Cambridge Companion to Christian Ethics*, p. 83.

8 Jean Porter, "Virtue Ethics" in Robin Gill (ed.) *The Cambridge Companion to Christian Ethics* (Cambridge: Cambridge University Press 2001) p. 99.

9 Thomas Aquinas, *Summa Theologica*. This translation is taken from Thomas Aquinas, *Selected Writings*, edited by Ralph McInerny (Harmondsworth: Penguin 1998) p. 658.

10 Stanley Hauerwas, *A Community of Character: Towards a Constructive Christian Social Ethic* (Notre Dame, IN : University of Notre Dame Press, 1981).

11 Stanley Hauerwas, "Casuistry as Narrative Art," *Interpretation* 37 (1993) pp. 377–88.

6

Ethics and the Bible

Case study

In 1788 Raymond Harris wrote a pamphlet entitled *Scriptural Researches on the Licitness of the Slave-Trade Shewing its Conformity with the Principles of Natural and Revealed Religion Delineated in the Sacred Writings of the Word of God.*[1] Consider the substantial extract below: do you think Harris is right that the Bible does support the licitness (lawfulness) of slavery?

DATA

I

That the Volume of the Sacred Writings, commonly called the Holy Bible, comprehending both the Old and the New Testaments, contains the unerring Decisions of the Word of God.

II

That the Decisions are of equal authority in both the Testaments, and that that authority is the essential veracity of God, who is Truth itself . . .

IV

That, as the Supreme Legislator of the World is infinitely just and wise in all his decisions respecting Right and Wrong, and there is no ways accountable to his creatures for the reasons of his conduct in the government of the World; so it must be a degree of presumption highly criminal in any creature to refute assent to those Decisions, only because he cannot comprehend the hidden principles of that impartial justice, which characterizes every decision of God . . .

VII

That, if one or more Decisions of the Written Word of God give a positive sanction to the intrinsic licitness of any human pursuit (for instance, the

SLAVE-TRADE), whoever professes to believe the incontrovertible veracity of the Written Word of God, essentially incompatible with the least degree of injustice, must consequently believe the pursuit itself to be intrinsically just and lawful in the strictest sense of the word.[2]

Section I

That period of years, which elapsed from the day on which God created Man in his own image (a), to the day, on which He gave his Laws to the Children of Israel on Mount Sinai (b), is generally called the period of the Law of Nature. The exact duration of the period is a matter of controversy among the Learned. Archbishop Ussher, whose chronological accuracy in the computation of Scriptural years is much admired, reckons 2513 years between the Creation of the World and the promulgation of the Mosaic Law. But be this as it may (for no difference in computation can affect the subject of my present Researches), it is evidence from the tenor of the Sacred Records, that, between the creation of Adam and the promulgation of the Mosaic Law, the Dispensation of the Law of Nature, commonly called Natural Religion, or the Religion of Nature, was the only true Religion in the World.

Simple as the principles of this Religion may appear, directed chiefly to worship One, Supreme, Eternal, Being, the Creator and Governor of all things, and to choose and act, in exact conformity to the inward dictates of found and unbiased reason in every transaction of life, where *Right* and *Wrong* were left to choice of Man; it would be exceedingly difficult, as well as perfectly extraneous to my present subject, to digest those principles into a regular Code of those particular laws and duties, which constituted the whole system of that Religion. I have not engaged to display the whole frame and structure of Natural Religion: aim to show no further, than that the principles and laws of that Religion, as far as we find them delineated in the Sacred Writings, not only never forbade the SLAVE-TRADE, or hinted the most distant opposition to the prosecution of it; but that, the fame being frequently exemplified in the constant and uninterrupted practice of some of the most faithful observers of the laws and principles of that Religion, under the visible protection of God, whose favorites they were the laws and principles themselves were in perfect harmony with the practice of the SLAVE-TRADE. Two very singular instances of this kind, verified in the conduct of two of the most distinguished Characters within the above period of the Law of Nature, ABRAHAM and JOSEPH, will, I flatter myself, be sufficient, without mentioning others, to justify my assertion, and set the present Controversy in the clearest light of Scriptural conviction.[3]

[There then follows an extended discussion of the many virtues of Abraham and Joseph, both of whom had slaves. Harris then considers passages from Exodus before coming to Leviticus.]

V

The further I proceed in my Scriptural Researches, the stronger the evidences appear to me in favor of the SLAVE-TRADE. Indeed, I have every encouragement given me in this Sacred Book of LEVITICUS to advance a step further, and maintain, that the SLAVE-TRADE, has not only the sanction of Divine Authority in its support, but also positively encouraged (I had almost said, *commanded*) by that Authority, under the Dispensation of the Mosaic Law. The following plain and explicit words of one of the laws respecting that Trade, and registered in this Book, can admit of no other construction.

"Both they bond-men and bond-maids, says the Supreme Law-giver, which thou shalt have, shall be of the heathen that are round about you; of them shall ye buy bond-men and bond-maids. Moreover, of the Children of the Strangers that do sojourn among you; of them shall ye buy; and of their families that are with you, which they begat in your land: and they shall be your possession. And yes shall take them as an inheritance for your children after you to inherit them for a possession; they shall be your bond-men forever." (Leviticus 25:44–6)

. . . AGAIN: the words of this Law, and they are the words of God, do expressly declare, that Slaves thus purchased from the Heathen and Sojourners among them, shall be the Possession, that is, the real and lawful property, of the purchasers: a property so strictly their own, that they shall bequeath it to their Children at their death, as a part of their just and lawful inheritance, a part of their paternal estate, an estate forever, *"for they shall be your bondmen forever,* says the Law: that is, an hereditary estate with all the emoluments arising from it; and, consequently, with all the children born from them, agreeably to the tenor of that Law of EXODUS, which has been explained in the IVth Number of this SECTION; for otherwise the children of a Heathen Slave or a Stranger would have enjoyed a privilege, which an Hebrew Slave was denied, though a Slave only for a limited time . . .

VII

From the most decisive, most explicit, and irrefragable authority of the Written Word of God, visibly encouraging the prosecution of the SLAVE-TRADE, and declaring in the most categorical language that words can devise, that a Slave is the real, indisputable, and lawful property of the purchaser and his heirs forever, it necessarily follows by force of consequence the either the SLAVE-TRADE must be in its own intrinsic nature a just and an honest Trade, and by no means deserving those harsh epithets and names with which it is so frequently branded and degraded; or, that, if it does still deserve those odious names and epithets in consequence of its intrinsic turpitude and immorality, the Almighty did so far forget himself, when he made the above Law, as to patronize a manifest injustice, encourage a most criminal violation of his other laws, and give his sacred sanction to what humanity itself must forever abhor and detest. As there can be medium between these two unavoidable inferences, and the latter is one of the most daring blasphemies that the human heart can conceive, I leave the religious Reader to judge for himself, which side of the Question is the safest to embrace.[4]

[After further discussion of other passages in the Old Testament, Harris moves to the New Testament. He gives extended attention to I Timothy 6:1–5]

. . .

XI

The Apostle in these words describes two classes of Christian Slaves, or Servants under the yoke of bondage: Slaves subject to unbelievers, and Slaves subject to true believers or Christians; and, according to their respect situation, he specifies the general duties belonging to each class.

1. The former are exhorted to *count their own Masters*, though Infidels, *worthy of all honor*: that is, they are exhorted to show their Masters, both in words and actions, such unfeigned marks of honor, submission, and respect, as they have a right to claim, for *they are worthy of all honor*, from the superiority of their rank and station in life, and the authority they have acquired over them by the possession of their persons . . .
2. The latter class of Christian Slaves, subject to Christian Masters, are earnestly exhorted, not only not to be less respectful and obsequious to the latter for being their brethren in Christ, and joint-members with them of the same Communion and Church, as if they were their equals in every respect, but to show, on this very account in their readiness and obedience to their lawful authority; not considering themselves upon a footing of natural equality with those whose Slaves they are, though entitled at the same time to all the promises and spiritual franchises of true Believers . . .

XIV

So far then from being true, that there is nothing in the Sacred Writings of the New Testament, that can be produced in vindication of the SLAVE-TRADE, the palpable evidence just produced in justification of the Trade from the authentic words of One of the very principal inspired Authors of those Sacred Writings, must convince every candid inquirer into the merits of the present Controversy, that, if the SLAVE-TRADE, as demonstrated in the two preceding Parts, appears so visibly warranted by the Writings of the Old Testament, the same is not less evidently authorized, but rather more explicitly vindicated from every suspicion of guilt and immorality by the Writings of the New: for, they do not only declare in formal words, that the teaching of the licitness of the SLAVE-TRADE, exemplified in the practice of the Primitive Christians, is a *Doctrine according to Godliness*, and according to *wholesome words, even the words of our* LORD JESUS CHRIST, but they even stigmatize the Teachers of the contract doctrine with epithets and appellations not of the most pleasing sounds.[5]

For Roman Catholics, the natural law approach to ethics dominates. However, for those shaped by the Reformation (the Protestants), the Bible is central. The Reformation was the moment when the western church divided. In Germany, it was Martin Luther (1483–1546) who took issue with Rome; in Geneva, John Calvin (1509–64) was the inspiration; and in England, it was King Henry VIII who challenged the authority of the Pope. Each of these 'founders" created different traditions. However, in all, the Bible as a text, which can be interpreted by the individual Christian, became much more important. Martin Luther, for example, argued that because the Catholic Church is comprised of sinful humanity, the resulting interpretation of the Bible is flawed. Therefore the Church's enthusiasm for the selling of indulgences (a device that released individuals from time in purgatory) was not only exploitative, but more important *uniblical*. Luther advocated *sola scriptura* (by scripture alone). Christians should read and trust the Bible as the sole authority in all matters relating to faith, doctrine, and morality. The Bible stands above all tradition, councils, and Popes. It is the Bible alone we should trust.

Today it is the "evangelicals" who make Biblical authority central. The term "evangelical" comes from the Greek word *euangelion*. Literally it means "good news." For evangelicals, the good news that Christ has made it possible for humanity to be saved from sin is central. Evangelical Christianity emerges in the eighteenth century; it is the result of three distinct strands – Anglican Reformed Protestantism, Puritan Calvinism, and European pietism. Evangelicals are found in all the major Protestant denominations.

For evangelicals, the Bible is a reliable authority. For some evangelicals, the Bible is inerrant (without error) in every respect – history, science, as well as theology and morals. Other evangelicals would limit the inerrancy of the text to the areas of theology and morals. A key text for the evangelical view of the Bible is 2 Timothy 3:16: "All scripture is inspired by God and profitable for teaching, for reproof, for correction, and for training in righteousness."

So in this chapter, we shall look at how the Bible can be used in ethics. We shall start by looking at those who are sympathetic to the evangelical tradition.

And then we shall explore some of the key difficulties surrounding the Bible as an authority in ethics.

Biblical authority and evangelicals

Evangelicals are very christocentric (i.e. Christ centered). They recognize entirely that Jesus is the "word" (the logos) of God (see John 1:1). But of course reliable knowledge of Jesus is found in the New Testament. And to understand the remarkable life of the Incarnation of God, it is necessary to appreciate both the way that the Hebrew Bible anticipates the life of Jesus and then the New Testament describes the impact of Jesus. Therefore the entire Bible is important for the challenge of understanding the life of Jesus.

All evangelical scholars are sensitive to the difficulties of interpreting the Bible. It is commonplace to find a warning against the "proof text" (a text that proves a doctrinal point) in evangelical literature. There is a widespread recognition of the problem of interpreting the Bible. The Bible is a rich world of images, stories, complex argument, and different responses to contrasting situations. One cannot simply wrestle a text out of context and insist that this proves that, for example, all Christians must "oppose abortion" or "advocate capital punishment."[6]

I. Howard Marshall starts his article "Using the Bible in Ethics" by outlining some of the key problems. He groups the problems under three main areas. The first is that *"the ethical problems which confront us today may not be directly presented in the Bible."*[7] So this area includes everything from scientific advances to the emergence of the nation state. The second is the *"character of the Biblical revelation."*[8] Marshall concedes that the Bible does not look or read like an "ethical textbook."[9] The third is the hermeneutical challenge. Determining the meaning and the application of the text to our present day is very difficult. There is no complacency here about the challenges faced in using the Bible as an authority in Christian ethics.

Marshall's own proposal builds on the work of Anthony Thiselton.[10] Marshall explains: "The essence of this approach is to suggest that when we come to a Biblical exhortation *we must inquire into the underlying theological and ethical principles* which are expressed in it, and then proceed to work out how to translate those principles into appropriate exhortations for today."[11] So then, to use Marshall's own illustration, the story of the footwashing in John 13 isn't simply a command to "wash each other's feet." Given most of us are not walking with bare feet in a dusty, sandy environment, there is no need to wash each other's feet. However, Marshall explains:

> It is, however, abundantly plain from the context that what Jesus was commanding his disciples to do was to display humility and mutual love and one appropriate way of doing this in the first century in Palestine

was by performing this service. So the principle in the action is apparent, and we are to fulfil that principle by showing humility and love in service for one another.[12]

Marshall believes then that one should wrestle with the text (and it is the entire text of the Bible that Marshall wants to take seriously) and seek the underlying principle. It is that principle that then needs to be converted into a present injunction, which then requires obedience.

Marshall concludes his essay recognizing that questions and problems remain. However, one can see how such an approach might work. So, for example, the problem with homosexuality is less the proof text in Leviticus 18:22 ("You shall not lie with a male as with a woman; it is an abomination") and rather more the teaching of Jesus in Mark 10. Here in the context of divorce, Jesus explains how in creation God always intended one man to commit to one woman for as long as they both live. Therefore the underlying principle is that heterosexual monogamy is God's intended norm. On this view gay marriage becomes a problem because it is undermining this intended norm.

There are plenty of other equally thoughtful approaches to the Bible amongst conservative Christians. And I shall now look briefly at two such: Esther D. Reed from the University of St Andrews and Richard B. Hayes of Duke Divinity School. Starting then with Esther D. Reed, who is clearly orthodox and deeply committed to the Bible, but has a highly distinctive approach to Scripture. Reed argues that there is a strong Biblical witness to polyphony. Polyphony is a concept developed by Mikhail Bakhtin to describe a distinctive way to author a novel. Reed explains, "The polyphonic authorial point of view is not single, fixed or monologic, but multiple and dynamic, almost creating chaos and lack of direction because many different voices coexist and interact."[13] As Reed turns to the Bible, she finds the theme of polyphony embedded both in the Hebrew Bible and the New Testament. As she reflects upon Deutro-Isaiah's prophetic critique of captivity in Babylon, she writes: "The lives of the people are expressed in their many voices, Israel's many voices – which have many times contested the ordering of community life – risk everything in confessing God in the face of the powers of Babylon."[14]

And in the New Testament, there is the coming of the Spirit of God in Acts. The day when the disciples speak in many languages, leading to powerful preaching and widespread recognition by others that God was present. Reed writes, "The New Testament witness is that many voices proclaim the glory of God. The polyphony of faith follows from the distributive and personal work of the Holy Spirit."[15] Her overall point is that the Biblical witness endorses a liberty in the Spirit. Reed explains that she wants to develop the concept [of polyphony] in relationship to personal freedom in the Spirit and the many-voicedness that characterizes Christian testimony to the truth revealed in Christ. The intention is to link Christian ethics clearly to the work of the Holy Spirit in enabling believers "to have the mind of Christ" (1 Corinthians 2:16).[16]

Richard B. Hays' landmark text *The Moral Vision of the New Testament* offered both a description of New Testament ethics and, at the same time, a strategy for appropriate and consistent use of the New Testament as an ethical authority.[17] While admitting the value of recognizing four sources of ethical teaching (scripture, tradition, reason, and experience), he wants to make Scripture central.[18] Therefore as he outlines the different visions of moral life in the New Testament, he argues that three images can provide a tool for appropriate interpretation. The first image is community. Hays writes: "The church is a countercultural community of discipleship, and this community is the primary addressee of God's imperatives."[19] The second image is the cross. Hays explains, "Jesus' death on a cross is the paradigm for faithfulness to God in this world."[20] Hays introduces the third image in the following way: "The church embodies the power of the resurrection in the midst of a not-yet-redeemed world."[21] This is the image of new creation. So while recognizing the diversity of voices in the New Testament, he argues that these three major themes and images can help illuminate an appropriately Biblical position. He applies his methodology to five ethical issues: violence, divorce and remarriage, homosexuality, anti-Judaism, and ethnic conflict and abortion.

With Marshall, one searches for underlying principles and appropriately translates those principles into the modern period. For Reed, one recognizes that the Spirit of God is at work in the many diverse voices that characterize the Church's witness to the Gospel. For Hays, one takes certain dominant New Testament themes, which become the prism through which the New Testament is interpreted, and then arrive at certain ethical obligations.

In all three cases, there is a deep desire to demonstrate how the Bible can be used appropriately as an ethical authority.

However, there are problems with Biblical authority. And it is to those problems that we turn next.

Difficulties with Biblical authority

Even for those sympathetic to Biblical authority, we have already seen that it is not easy. For some Christians, the difficulties are simply overwhelming. In this section, there are five major difficulties I shall examine.

The first is the *canon*. Christians disagree about what precisely makes up the

Bible. Christians agree about the Hebrew Bible (the Old Testament) and the New Testament, but disagree about the status of the Apocrypha. Although there are many books that are considered part of the Apocrypha (which simply means "hidden"), there are 15 or so which some Christians claim should be considered part of the canon. These include: the first and second book of Esdras, Tobit, Judith, the rest of the chapters of the book of Esther, the Wisdom of Solomon, Ecclesiasticus, Baruch, A letter of Jeremiah, the Song of the Three, Daniel and Susanna, Daniel, Bel and the Snake, the Prayer of Manasseh, the first and second book of Maccabees.[22] The problem arises because the Greek translation of the Hebrew Bible, the Septuagint, which was produced in Alexandria, Egypt in 300–200 BCE, included these books. Given it was this version of the Hebrew Bible that the early church used, it was not surprising that these books were considered "inspired" (indeed they would have been included in the "all" of 2 Timothy 3:16). However, Jerome (340–420 CE) in 382–390 CE when translating the Hebrew Bible into Latin decided that these books were problematic because he could not find Hebrew versions of these texts. Protestants have largely agreed with Jerome, while the Roman Catholics and the Orthodox churches have continued to recognize the authority of the Septuagint.

The problem here is obvious. If one is going to consider the Bible an authority in ethics, then it obviously helps to know which books are in this authority. And there are texts which carry significant ethical teaching. For example, the injunction in Ecclesiasticus 8:9, "Never sit at table with another man's wife or join her in a drinking party, for fear of succumbing to her charms and slipping into fatal disaster" could have all sorts of implications for Christian dinner parties!

More important, however, than the additional ethical material is the problem of "who decides." Who decides exactly which books are in the canon? There was considerable disagreement over which books should be in the New Testament canon. The Gnostic gospels, for example, were all rejected. Given this, it looks like the authority of the Bible is dependent on the authority of the Church. If this is the case, the Roman Catholic points out, then it does not make sense to talk about "Scripture alone."

The second difficulty is the *relationship between the two Testaments.* This problem torments the Church right from the start. We can see the issue emerge in one of the earliest disagreements between the Apostle Paul and the Apostle Peter. Paul's missionary work amongst Gentiles posed a real challenge to the Jewish Christians, especially Peter and James. Jesus was a Jew; Jesus had been circumcised. Surely, the Jewish Christians argued, the followers of Jesus should be circumcised. It is commanded in the Hebrew Bible. However, Paul felt very strongly that Jesus had so transformed our relationship with God that circumcision was not necessary. Indeed he was deeply critical of Peter in Antioch (see Galatians 2:11ff).

For Luke the historian, it was inappropriate to describe in too much detail the depth of antagonism between the apostles. In his abridged history, Luke described how Paul and Barnabas agreed to go from Antioch up to Jerusalem[23] to the first Church council. And Luke summarized the problem thus:

> When they reached Jerusalem they were welcomed by the church and the apostles and elders, and reported all that God had done through them. Then some of the Pharisaic party who had become believers came forward and said, "They must be circumcised and told to keep the Law of Moses." (Acts 15:4–5, *New English Bible*)

Luke goes on to describe the classic compromise. Peter takes the lead and conceded that it was clear that these Gentile Christians have the Holy Spirit and were saved. James then followed it up with the following ruling:

> My judgment therefore is that we should impose no irksome restrictions on those of the Gentiles who are turning to God, but instruct them by letter to abstain from things polluted by contact with idols, from fornication, from anything that has been strangled, and from blood. (Acts 15:19–20)

The Gentile Christians did not have to get circumcised, but they must recognize certain fundamental food laws (the basic rules of kosher) and abstain from fornication and food offered to idols. This looks like a classic trade: Peter conceded on circumcision, while Paul conceded that the food laws were still binding.

This illustrates nicely the problem of affirming the authority of the Hebrew Bible and, at the same time, recognizing the changed circumstance brought about by Christ. However, the modern day Christian has two additional difficulties. The first is that other parts of the New Testament do not agree with the Acts 15 solution. It was Paul who undermined it. Given the heathen deities do not exist, Paul didn't really feel that the Christian should worry too much about food consecrated to these deities (see 1 Corinthians 8). Perhaps out of consideration for the weaker brother, one might restrain one's freedom to eat any type of food, but there was no theological reason why you should do so (Romans 14:1–4). Paul might have signed on to the Acts 15 compromise, but in his letters he took a more liberal approach. So the question for the Christian today is this: do we accept Acts 15 or the more liberal Paul? And on what basis do we decide? The second difficulty is that the work of thinking through the status of injunctions in the Hebrew Bible in the light of Christ performed by the Church in Acts 15 is work that we need to do on a thousand different topics. What about slavery? Is capital punishment still appropriate? Should the Church be pacifist? And so on. These are difficult questions. And it is not clear how we start to answer them.

The third difficulty is that *there are parts of the Bible that many modern Christians would consider unethical*. With the lectionary (the preaching cycle of readings used in some churches) often being very selective, many Christians never read the more horrific aspects of the Bible. Sitting down and reading the first 11 chapters of Joshua is a harrowing experience. This is a summary:

> So Joshua defeated the whole land, the hill country and the Negeb and the lowland and the slopes, and all their kings; he left no one remaining, but utterly destroyed all that breathed, as the LORD God of Israel commanded. (Joshua 10:40 New Revised Standard Version)

Everything living was slaughtered. There is in this passage no sensitivity to the non-combatants. Later we find King Saul's downfall was due to his disobedience to this command:

> Samuel said to Saul, "The LORD sent me to anoint you king over his people Israel; now therefore listen to the words of the LORD. Thus says the LORD of hosts, 'I will punish the Amalekites for what they did in opposing the Israelites when they came up out of Egypt. Now go and attack Amalek, and utterly destroy all that they have; do not spare them, but kill both man and woman, child and infant, ox and sheep, camel and donkey." (I Samuel 15:1–3)

Saul's mistake was that he spared King Agag and the best of the cattle. And for this the Lord God (and Samuel – the messenger) become very angry.

These are deeply awkward passages. Although there are explanations for the ruthless behavior in the text and in our knowledge of the period (e.g. the practice of child sacrifice, the need for tribal purity, the antagonism of these nations towards Israel, and the fact that all warfare in this period took this form), it is still disturbing to discover these values extolled in the Holy Scriptures.

The fact is the Bible is a text that captures human life as it was. When the Psalmist cries out in his (and it is almost certainly a "his" rather than a "her") pain and anger against his Babylonian captors, it is a classic example of the human capacity for revenge and anger.

> O daughter Babylon, you devastator!
>   Happy shall they be who pay you back
>   what you have done to us!
> Happy shall they be who take your little ones
>   and dash them against the rock! (Psalm 137:8–9)

But to plead that Babylonian children should be smashed against the rocks is not a very good example of Christian love and forgiveness.

Perhaps the most problematic example is the use of the Bible to support slavery. Slavery was instituted in the Hebrew Bible (Exodus 21), condoned by St Paul in the New Testament (Philemon), and supported by many Christians for centuries. If one compares the Biblical case for slavery with the Biblical case against homosexuality, then the slavery case is overwhelming while the homosexuality one is rather opaque. (See chapter 9 for further discussion on homosexuality and the Bible.) Given almost all Christians today do not support slavery, this does demonstrate that there is no such thing as a straightforward Biblical Christian.

The fourth difficulty builds on the problem of slavery. *As a text, the Bible has not always been used to support the case for liberation and justice.* The thought exercise at the start of the chapter illustrates this well. However, there are many other cases where the Bible has served the interests of the oppressor rather than the oppressed. Perhaps the best illustration is the whole issue of patriarchy and women's rights. When the United Nations collected certain statistics for the 1995 conference on women, which was held in Beijing, it showed that women account for 70 percent of the world's poor, do two-thirds of the world's work, yet earn between 5 and 10 percent of the world's wages and own 1 percent of the world's property. This is in 1995! Historically the problem of patriarchy and abuse of women has been worse.

Although St Paul's declaration in Galatians is remarkable ("There is no longer Jew or Greek, there is no longer slave or free, there is no longer male and female; for all of you are one in Christ Jesus" Galatians 3:28), it has been overshadowed by other passages relating to women. The claim that a woman was responsible for sin led to the implication that the woman must be kept under control. The author of 1 Timothy 2 (almost certainly not Paul) writes:

> Let a woman learn in silence with full submission. I permit no woman to teach or to have authority over a man; she is to keep silent. For Adam was formed first, then Eve; and Adam was not deceived, but the woman was deceived and became a transgressor. (1 Timothy 2:11–15)

It is because Eve misbehaved that a woman cannot teach or have authority over a man. This along with the injunction that wives must obey their husbands (Ephesians 5:22) has provided more than enough Biblical justification for patriarchy. Granted these texts (and others) can be read in a different way, but the historical fact is that this didn't happen. Men enjoyed the divinely sanctioned power over women.

The final difficulty is at the level of *justification*. Why exactly do we treat the Bible as the revealed word of God and not the Qur'an or some other holy book? At this level the Bible tends to come out of the argument badly. Unlike the Qur'an, which starts each sura with a declaration that this is written by Allah, the Bible reads more like a narrative *about* God rather than *by* God. It is also a text written over centuries, which leads to the internal inconsistencies and differences. It was at this level that the Muslim apologist Ahmed Deedat constructed his arguments against the Bible and in favor of the Qur'an.[24] And if the exercise is simply at the level of internal consistency and coherence, then it is true that Qur'an seems to come out the stronger.

For the fundamentalist Christian (the Christian who believes that the Bible is the inerrant word of God), this is a problem. For the majority of Christians, this is less of a problem. Ultimately, the Word of God is Jesus (the life, death, and resurrection). And the Bible is the book that explains the significance of Jesus. Richard Burridge has shown that the key theme of the New Testament is the "imitation of Christ."[25] The Gospels are modeled on ancient Graeco-Roman biographies, where the purpose of the genre is to demonstrate the importance of Jesus as a model of life, which we are called to imitate. In this way, it is the life described and contained in the Bible, which is the Word of God.

But all this is to move beyond the remit of this chapter. The overall point of this chapter is to demonstrate how difficult it is to use the Bible as an ethical authority. It also shows the care with which Biblical texts should be used. As we shall see when we discuss sexual ethics, it is difficult to use the Bible consistently.

Notes

1 Rev. Raymond Harris, *Scriptural Researches on the Licitness of the Slave-Trade Shewing its Conformity with the Principles of Natural and Revealed Religion Delineated in the Sacred Writings of the Word of God* (Liverpool: printed by H. Hodgson, Pool-Lane 1788). In reproducing extracts, I have updated the spelling, but retained all the other stylistic features (e.g. the italics and capitalization are all from Harris).

2 Ibid. pp. 9–10.

3 Ibid. pp. 12–13.

4 Ibid. pp. 41–3.

5 Ibid. pp. 62–5.

6 I am indebted to many conversations with Richard Burridge on this theme.

7 I. Howard Marshall, "Using the Bible in Ethics" in David F. Wright (ed.) *Essays in Evangelical Social Ethics* (Exeter: Paternoster Press 1981) p. 40. His italics.

8 Ibid. p. 41.

9 Ibid.

10 See Anthony Thiselton, *The Two Horizons: New Testament Hermeneutics and Philosophical Description* (Grand Rapids, MI: Eerdmans 1996).

11 I. Howard Marshall, "Using the Bible in Ethics" in D. Wright, *Essays in Evangelical Social Ethics*, p. 50. (His italics.)

12 Ibid. p. 50.

13 Esther D. Reed, *The Genesis of Ethics: On the Authority of God as the Origin of Christian Ethics* (London: Darton Longman and Todd 2000) p. 123.

14 Ibid. p. 126. Reed is here commenting on Isaiah 43:11–13.

15 Ibid. p. 127.

16 Ibid. p. 122.

17 Richard B. Hays, *The Moral Vision of the New Testament* (San Francisco, CA: Harper-Collins 1996).

18 Ibid. pp. 209–11.

19 Ibid. p. 196.

20 Ibid. p. 197.

21 Ibid. p. 198.

22 Lists of the books which should be included in the Apocrypha do vary. This list has been taken from *The New English Bible*. Roman Catholics include in their canon seven books, namely, Tobias, Judith, Baruch, Ecclesiasticus, Wisdom, first and second Maccabees; and the additions to Esther and Daniel.

23 A comparison with Paul's letter to Galatians shows significant differences with Luke's account. In Galatians, Paul had been converting the Gentiles for 14 years before this meeting in Jerusalem; in Acts Paul had a short pilot project (it does not specify the time, but it is clearly brief).

24 For Ahmed Deedat's work see his website http://www.ahmed-deedat.co.za

25 I am grateful for numerous discussions with Richard Burridge. This is the theme of his next major book. For his work on the genre of the Gospels see *What Are the Gospels? A Comparison with Graeco-Roman Biography* (Cambridge: Cambridge University Press 1994).

7

Learning from the wisdom of the world

Thought exercise

The witness of the major, orthodox, religious traditions of the world is that homosexuality is wrong. In Christianity, homosexuality is condemned because of Scripture and natural law; Orthodox Judaism cites the prohibition in Leviticus; the Qur'an builds on the story of Lot to condemn homosexuality and the Hadith advocates the death penalty for such behavior; in Buddhism the third of the five precepts states that one should abstain from sexual misconduct, which is normally (but not always) taken to include homosexuality; Hinduism disapproves of homosexuality because it is non-married sex, which cannot lead to children.

On what basis do we agree or disagree with this world wide ethical judgment? Does the fact that the vast majority of people take a certain position make a difference to our own view?

Thus far the focus of the discussion has been on the western secular conversation with western religion. Our ethical map would be incomplete if we didn't consider the wisdom and insights of the other main religious traditions in the world. To make this manageable, we shall confine our brief discussion to Hinduism, Buddhism, Judaism, Christianity, and Islam. We shall first look at the ethical methodology, which is found across these traditions, and then examine certain shared ethical insights before concluding with the identification of the main differences across these traditions.[1]

Ethical methodology

We have already noted how religious traditions agree on the objective character of moral discourse. Morality for almost all religions is a matter of discovery and truth. So there are "moral facts" that are analogous to scientific ones, which transcend individuals and human communities and are, in some sense, built into the structure of the universe. So in the same way that the existence of the moon is true for all people everywhere (regardless of their own perception), so Roman Catholics – to take one significant religious community – believe the moral command that "you should not take innocent life" is true for all people everywhere. Morality in a religious account is conceived as objective (transcending human communities) and absolute (when the moral truth is discovered it is true for everyone).

So although there is disagreement between the religions about the content of morality, there is agreement about the character of morality. Ronald Green, probably the most able contemporary writer on interfaith ethics, has argued that this extends far beyond the simple assertion that ethical discourse is objective. He believes that most religions have a deep ethical structure composed of three components. First, "a method of moral reasoning involving 'the moral point of view'; second, a set of beliefs affirming the reality of moral retribution; and third, a series of 'transmoral' beliefs that suspend moral judgment and retribution when this is needed to overcome moral paralysis and despair."[2]

Green is right to stress the importance of retribution in religious accounts. However, this aspect of religious ethics is a problem for many in the West. The first difficulty is derived from Kant who thought that morality must be disinterested. To be good simply to avoid hell is not moral. Don Cupitt, a contemporary philosopher of religion from Cambridge, has argued that a truly moral Christianity needs to disentangle itself from any sense of retribution, which he suggested would involve denying the objectivity of God.[3] He argued that to be moral simply because one is fearful of hell is less adequate than to behave morally because one is persuaded of the intrinsic appropriateness of the moral obligation. The second difficulty is that many sociologists believe that hell has lost its power on the western imagination. The majority of people in the West are not sufficiently sure that hell exists to deter them from bad behavior.

Having identified these shared assumptions about the nature of ethics, and some of the difficulties with them, it is now necessary to describe the different sources for ethics that are found within the different religious traditions. There are five sources that different strands of different religious traditions have recourse to when making ethical judgments: these are sacred texts, institutions and traditions, human reason, natural order, and religious experience. We shall now look at each in turn.

The first is sacred texts. All religions make "revelation" central. Keith Ward in his study *Religion and Revelation* has documented the ways in which revelation is central to religion.[4] The theistic traditions agree that knowledge of God depends on God revealing Godself to us. For many traditions, God is also the source of the moral order and has revealed God's will in Scripture. In certain strands of Judaism, the Torah preexisted the creation and provided the blueprint for the order of creation. All Christians accept that the Bible is the "Word of God," however, reformed Christianity describes it as the sole source of authority. Some fundamentalist Christians describe the Bible as the infallible guide to human behavior. Similarly Islam has a strong commitment to revelation as the source of morality. Islam cannot understand the western separation of the sacred and secular: the whole world (including society) should be ordered according to the infallible word of God. The eastern traditions make much of revelation. Certain schools of Hinduism talk about the Vedas as eternal, and the Laws of Manu provide guidance about the ordering of human society. The Buddha describes the Four Noble Truths as a discovery, which are now embodied in the texts that comprise the scriptures of Buddhism.

The second source of moral guidance is the institutions and traditions of each religion. Often these are seen as secondary (or supplementary) to the first source – Scripture. In Christianity, the Roman Catholic tradition believes that the Church is the mechanism provided by God to interpret the scriptures. Pope John Paul II has made this a central theme of his pontiff. *Veritatis Splendor*, for example, cites as authority both the Bible and the tradition of past papal pronouncements and Church Councils. In Islam the hadith (traditions and stories about the prophet and his immediate followers) is extremely important in the formation of Islamic law. Generally, some strands of Judaism do acknowledge the authority of a chief Rabbi. A good example is Hasidism: a Jewish movement founded by the Baal Shem Tov (1698–1760) in Volhynia and Podolia in the eighteenth century, from which the Lubavicher dynasty, which settled in America, developed. All Jews acknowledge to some degree the authority of the traditions that have developed in the Mishnah and the commentaries on the Mishnah known as the Talmud. Some forms of Mahayana Buddhism do have an institutional authority and many strands of Buddhism use the history of monastic practice as an authoritative source for ethical insight.

The third source of moral guidance is human reason. Both Judaism and Islam have a fairly optimistic view of humanity. They share the conviction that the gift of human reason, which distinguishes us from the animals, is a God-given resource that should assist us in arriving at the right moral judgment. Christianity complicates this picture with the doctrine of original sin. For Martin Luther (1483–1546), the Fall was so severe that sin distorted the capacity of human reason to see moral truth. We need to be saved from our sin and have our original righteousness restored through grace. However, the major religious traditions share a sense that although sin has deformed the capacity of humans to use their reason properly, it is still operational. As we saw in an earlier chapter, it is this idea that lies behind the Roman Catholic doctrine of natural law. Natural law assumes that all humans everywhere, without explicit aid of Biblical revelation, are able to discern partially the moral truth. For this reason all people are without excuse.

This leads to our fourth source for moral knowledge, which is the natural order. We have already described the Roman Catholic use of the natural world in natural law. Equivalents to Natural law are found in strands of other religious traditions. For example, the Hindu notion of dharma (right action) is grounded in the eternal law of the universe. Zaehner, a contemporary scholar on Hinduism, defined dharma as "the 'form' of things as they are and the power that keeps them as they are and not otherwise."[5] In Judaism there has been some debate whether the Torah can be seen as revealing natural law. Philo (20 BCE–40 CE) was probably the first Jewish scholar to think in this way, and certainly the Noachite Laws (those laws required to be observed by the righteous Gentile) have been interpreted as a Rabbinic attempt to incorporate natural law.

The fifth and final source for moral values is religious experience. There is, of course, a sense in which this source underpins all others, as it is the human awareness of God that generates all religion; but for this awareness no religious ethics would exist. However, this source is identified separately because some religious traditions make direct awareness of God much more central to their ethical system. Some traditions talk about discovering what God wants through religious experience and prayer, which can sometimes run counter to conventional ethics. One of the most striking illustrations of this is story is in Genesis 22, where Abraham is told by God to take his son Isaac and sacrifice him on a mountain. This narrative fascinates all three of the Abrahamic traditions (although Islam has Ishmail as the victim not Isaac). Kierkegaard (1813–55), the Danish philosopher, thought the story illustrated the obligation of obedience and the willingness to become the "solitary individual" willing to transcend the conventional understanding of morality.[6] Here the immediate experience of the transcendent can challenge everything we assume at the most fundamental level.

Shared ethical insights

Generalizations about religious traditions are very difficult for two reasons: first, there are very few generalizations that are true for every adherent in a tradition; second, there are very few ideas within a tradition that are not found in a different religious tradition. So it is important to remember that it is not that all religions agree or disagree with each other, but that certain groups within one religion agree with some groups within another religion and they also disagree with many of their co-religionists as well as other groups in other religions.

Once this is seen one should be hesitant about attempts to create a global theology or a global ethic. Hans Küng has suggested that the world religions should converge around a global ethic – an ethical minimum on which we can all agree.[7] Although anything that constructs better relationships between the religions is good, the danger here is that the complexity can be overlooked. The thought exercise that started this chapter identifies a further problem: many of us (well at least the author and some of his friends) would not want to agree with the virtual universal teaching of many religious traditions on homosexuality. In my judgment, the religious traditions have a very poor record on such topics as homosexuality, patriarchy, and toleration.

So although we will avoid simply identifying ethical equivalents across the different religions, it is helpful to note that the orthodox traditions (i.e. the traditional ones) do share certain common themes. Let us now look at four such themes.

1. A commitment to love, compassion, and justice

First, there is a shared commitment to love, compassion, and justice. Although these qualities are understood in different ways within different traditions, there is undoubtedly a sense in which these are universally recognized virtues. The Talmud sets out Rabbi Hillel's famous summary of the Jewish law: "What is hateful to you, do not to your neighbor: that is the whole Torah, while the rest is the commentary thereof; go and learn it."[8] Jesus inherited this theme and summed up the law in the two commandments: "Hear O Israel: the Lord our God, the Lord is one; and you shall love the Lord your God with all your heart, and with all your soul, and with all your mind, and with all your strength; and the second, You shall love your neighbor as yourself" (Mark 12:29–31). When Mohammad was asked, "whose Islam is good?" he gave a similar reply. "One who feeds others and greets those whom he knows and those whom he does not know." In Hinduism one finds compassion in the third of the three Da's, which is the foundation of all Hindu ethical reflection.

Having worried about Hans Küng's global ethics project, this might look all very encouraging. However, there are difficulties here. First, this shared theme of love runs parallel with other themes that are much more problematic. Most religious traditions, have, at some time or other, found no problem with loving your enemy to death (i.e., deciding that death is preferable to the enemy rather than letting the enemy continue to propagate error). Second in some traditions, the loving involves individuals, while in others it is more corporate. We shall return to this issue later in this chapter. For now, we note that Islam, for example, does not separate out the individual from the group. One of the five pillars of Islam is almsgiving; it is a religious duty on all Muslims to provide for the servants of Allah and the poor. Generally, Islam is a social, community-orientated religion, while, at the other end of the spectrum, certain strands of Buddhism can be highly individualistic. To imagine that one should try to change the world is an illusion that one should detach oneself from.

Having said all that, the witness to love, compassion and justice is a theme that many religious traditions share.

2. The centrality of the family

The second theme that is found across the major traditions is the centrality of the family. The great creation myths often have the complementary nature of men and women at their heart. Genesis, for example, provides the foundation text for Judaism, Christianity, and, to a lesser extent, Islam. Eve (representative woman) was created to help Adam (representative man). Both are created in the image of God. Jesus in the Gospels describes the state of one man married to one woman as God's intention in creation (see Mark 10). It is for this reason that Jesus describes divorce as wrong.

The Law of Manu in Hinduism stresses the importance of roles: children should obey their parents and wives should obey their husbands. This is all linked with the caste system – each person is great in his or her place. It is the order of family life that can provide an effective bulwark against the potential disorder of samsara (the interconnected process of birth and rebirth). The Buddha also saw the importance of family as the resource that enables the rest of society to operate effectively.

Of course, there are numerous differences in detail. Divorce is permitted in some traditions, but not in others. Polygamy is allowed in some and forbidden in others. Attitudes to contraception vary considerably. Despite this disagreement, it remains true that the traditional family unit remains the ideal and basic form of human organization. It is also worth noting that there is also agreement on the patriarchal structure of the family. The New Testament writer of the epistle of Timothy (almost certainly not Paul) enjoins wives to obey their husbands. And the Laws of Manu clearly state that "In childhood a female must be subject to her father, in youth to her husband, when her lord is dead to her sons; a woman must never be independent." Despite the proliferation of female deities in Hinduism, it remains just as patriarchal in practice as Christianity.

3. Significance of ritual in ethics

The third shared theme across the traditions stresses the centrality of ritual in forming the virtuous person. Although at the edges some traditions have an ideological objection to too much ritual, most make it the heart of religious practice. Ritual is the mechanism that enables life to be religious. Rituals mark the start and end of life; weddings and the birth of children are marked by religious rituals. Days, weeks, months, and years are all organized around a religious calendar that involves certain rituals. Fasting on the holy days is common to most religious traditions. The dietary laws of Judaism and Islam turn the act of eating into a religious activity. It is precisely because one cannot eat anything that one is reminded of one's obligations before God. Rituals provide the disciplines that protect a person from evil.

Some contemporary commentators believe that ritual is the key to the moral life. The Chief Rabbi of the United Hebrew Congregations of the British Commonwealth, Dr Jonathan Sacks, has made this a central theme of his work. He writes, "Without holy times, there is no framework or architecture of time, merely the rush and press of random events. A civilization needs its pauses, its intervals, its chapter-breaks if it is to be a civilization at all."[9] In short, families, communities, and nations all need those vital pauses that enable one to think about life in the bigger perspective.

It is the habitual nature of ritual that makes it so helpful in supporting morality. For Sacks, the social ecology of a culture will break down once everyone starts to think consciously about the appropriate course of action. Telling lies, stealing, and seducing someone who is married should be unthinkable acts. The life lived in the context of constant reminders of God – through prayer, observing dietary obligation, keeping Shabbat – should be a life that will exclude the very possibility of behaving in ways that are inappropriate. Because our God-consciousness is heightened, so our opportunities to misbehave will be reduced.

4. Medical ethics

The fourth area of widespread ethical agreement is in the area of medical ethics. As we shall discuss later in this book, most religious traditions stress the centrality and importance of the human person. The sanctity of human life is considered a virtual absolute. This is not to say that under no conditions may human life be taken; most religious traditions have very ambivalent attitudes to war or capital punishment. But human life is given a special status in ethical reflection.

As we shall see in the chapter on medical ethics, for Roman Catholics, the sanctity of human life is a theme of *Evangelium Vitae* (*The Gospel of Life*). Pope John Paul II reiterates the teaching that human life begins at conception; and the deliberate killing of the unborn is murder. He talks about a "culture of death," one in which the unborn are disposed of because they are inconvenient, the elderly are under threat of euthanasia because of a growing anxiety about resources involved in keeping them alive, and even capital punishment, although permitted, is very problematic.

Although most religious traditions are sympathetic to these Roman Catholic positions, there is a little bit more flexibility. Most are opposed to abortion, although they do not necessarily talk about the sacredness of human life from conception. Judaism has always been clear that the viability of the fetus is important in determining its status. If the fetus is clearly able to survive outside the womb, then it would be murder. However, if that is not the case, then the situation is more complicated. Certainly if the mother's life is in danger, then abortion is permitted. Hassan Hathout in *Islamic Perspectives in Obstetrics and Gynecology* takes a similar line. He writes, "All jurists of all sects unanimously agree that abortion after 16 weeks is a grave and punishable sin. A small minority showed leniency before 16 weeks, and a small minority showed leniency before seven weeks."[10]

For Hinduism, the fetus is covered by the ideal of *ahimsa* (non-injury). You should reverence all life, including the young and unborn. Likewise, one of the five precepts in Buddhism is that one should not kill and this is normally considered to extend to the unborn. The same principles also operate at the other end of life. Although death is not feared, it is not to be anticipated either. The gift like quality of human life (a gift from God) means that one should not refuse the gift before it is time to do so.

Differing ethical outlooks

Having briefly examined four areas of agreement, it is now necessary to turn to those areas that provoked disagreement. Although there are many areas that could be discussed, the four outlined below are probably the major ones.

1. The significance of the individual

In the early Buddhist texts one finds the Buddha depicted as a person who discovered the way and can show others how they must obtain the way for themselves. In this respect, at least, Theravada Buddhism is individualistic. Although it is good to be part of the *Sangha* (the community), it is not essential. It is possible to be lay and make significant progress to Enlightenment.[11] In this respect it resembles certain strands of Protestantism, which stress the importance of individual salvation and how unnecessary intermediaries (e.g. priests) are.

Orthodox Judaism is completely different. In the same way you cannot change your language, so you cannot change your Judaism. It is just part of you. A similar sense is found in Hinduism. With all the givens of birth – the family, occupation, and location – come all the givens of your previous karmic lives. Islam is similar. Being a Muslim in private is impossible; the five pillars embrace a social dimension. You cannot give alms to the poor unless you are part of the community.

Many historians of ideas have noted how the Protestant concept of individual salvation was important for the emergence of modern western democracy. It is as the idea of an individual became important that the whole concept of each individual having his or her own and equal say in government becomes intelligible. With individualism comes romantic love, the entitlement to marry whom one pleases, and an abhorrence of arranged marriages. With individualism comes a sense that one is entitled to pursue one's own aspirations rather than surrender these aspirations for the sake of duty or the community. Perhaps one of the reasons why Buddhism is so attractive to the West is this powerful individualist message.

2. Attitudes to the environment and ecology

Lynn White in his seminal article published in 1967 argued that it is the anthropocentricism (the human centeredness) of Christianity that is largely responsible for the ecological crisis. He suggested that it was the doctrine that humans are created in the image of God that led to the privileged status of the human. If everything non-human is there for the use of humans, then there is no obligation to worry about the exploitation and abuse of the environment.

It is true that humans have a higher status in Judaism, Christianity, and Islam. Every tradition gives the human a more significant role than animals, but in the Abrahamic traditions the difference is greater. For the main schools of Hinduism and Buddhism, the human is the only creature capable of cumulating more good or bad karma. However, many in the Green movement have found Buddhism especially, and to a lesser extent, Hinduism, an inspiration to their ecology. For both traditions tend to locate the human on a wider plane than the Judaeo-Christian tradition. Within the Judaeo-Christian tradition, the world started recently and apocalyptic expectations mean that the world is not expected to go on much longer. Each individual is a unique soul that has one life. While Hindus and Buddhists work on a much bigger perspective: the world is ages old, possibly eternal, and it will continue for ages to come. Each person has already lived many lives and, probably, has many more lives to come. With this outlook, the non-human world becomes much more important. It is not temporary, but instead religiously significant.

Whether in practice one's metaphysical assumptions about the world actually make a difference to the way the world is treated is a moot point. Granted, the Christian West has bigger and better tools that can reap more destruction, but environmentalists have to admit that damaging the environment is a global phenomenon, which is not unique to Christians.

3. Attitudes towards wealth

Once again, although religious people disagree about the appropriate attitude towards wealth, it is a disagreement found both within traditions and across

75

traditions. Judaism embodies the tension. The Deuteronomist (the writer of the book of Deuteronomy) implies strongly that those who are faithful in observing the laws of the Torah can expect material prosperity:

> I call heaven and earth to witness against you this day, that I have set before you life and death, blessing and curse; therefore choose life, that you and your descendants may live, loving the LORD your God, obeying his voice, and cleaving to him; for that means life to you and length of days, that you may dwell in the land . . .[12]

Although the Deuteronomist was not thinking directly of wealth, one can see how it led to an affirmation of wealth as a sign of God's providence. However, the eighth-century prophets of Israel found themselves denouncing the rich because they exploited the poor. One strand celebrates wealth as a sign of God's favor; the other condemns it as a sign of exploitation.

The same tension is found in Christianity. In the teaching of Jesus, the prophetic strand dominates. And with the early Church expecting the imminent end of the world, then possessions were shared within the community (see Acts 4:32). The monastic tradition retained the same radical emphasis and suspicion of wealth. Yet some evangelical Christians in the United States advocate a "prosperity theology" (God will bless you – literally with wealth – if you are faithful to Christianity).

In Hinduism, wealth is more clearly a sign of karmic good fortune, although of course the way one uses that fortune is the test for the current life. To be wealthy and completely indifferent to suffering would bring bad karma upon one.

The Buddhist attitude is harder to summarize succinctly. The fifth aspect of the eightfold path (right livelihood) stresses the need to work appropriately and in a way compatible with the best quality of life. E. F. Schumacher (author of *Small Is Beautiful*) saw in Burma an ideal, which is called "Buddhist economics." Schumacher argued that the West sees the ideal for industrialists is "output without employees" while for employees it is "income without employment." Instead, Schumacher argues, "the Buddhist point of view takes the function of work to be at least threefold: to give a man the chance to utilize and develop his faculties; to enable him to overcome his egocentredness by joining with other people in a common task; and to bring forth the goods and services needed for a becoming existence."[13]

At the heart of the disagreement between and within the world faiths is whether wealth and work are distractions from the greater task of salvation or Enlightenment. Much depends on one's general attitude to the world and to life. For those more affirming of the world, wealth can be a legitimate delight within it; for those suspicious of the world, withdrawal from the temptations of wealth can be important.

4. Ethics and liberal religious outlooks

One of the interesting features of current religious debates is the way that modernity has created alliances across traditional hostilities. With the rise of liberalism and related qualities such as toleration and feminism, we have seen the emergence of different forms of each religious tradition. In short, the situation now is that conservatives in each religious tradition have a great deal more in common with conservatives in other traditions than the liberals in their own.

Toleration has been a particular problem. Historically, religious traditions have been forced to find ways of coexisting in the same city and country. However, they did so with suspicion and fear. For Christians and Muslims, the commitment to the truth of their own divine revelation entailed an opposition to all those in error. Given that one's eternal destiny depended on being a Christian, one can understand the hostility shown to those who would lead others to damnation. Islam has an explicit obligation to make sure that the "People of the Book" (Christians and Jews) are free to worship, despite this, the desire to ensure that the young are not misled did lead to significant legal restrictions to their freedoms.

For the eastern traditions, the history is more complex. Given the diversity of view within Hinduism, it is difficult to see how anything could be considered unacceptable within it. Hinduism has an amazing capacity to embrace a different tradition within its own rich story; so Jesus can become yet another guru or even an incarnation of Vishnu. Nevertheless, because Hinduism is tied very closely with the aspirations of the people of India, it has found certain religions at certain times very problematic, especially Islam and Christianity. Buddhism, as it spread into China and Japan, shared the Hindu capacity to find ways of including certain indigenous practices into its belief system. However, Buddhists too had moments when they saw another tradition as threatening and found it difficult to tolerate.

Thus, toleration is a problem. Most religious traditions justify it pragmatically. Once in power, most traditions find it difficult to resist the temptation to censor its rivals to some degree. It is the liberals in most traditions who make the theological adjustments and welcome a complementary viewpoint as intrinsically worthwhile.

A similar story can be seen in respect to feminism. Again all religious traditions have strands and arguments that are opposed to patriarchy. Almost all the founders of most religious traditions are affirming of women. Mohammad insisted that women could inherit property and denounced female infanticide (a common practice then) in the strongest possible terms. Jesus taught women and had women followers. The Buddha permitted women to join monastic communities and discover the way to Enlightenment. In all these cases the founders of these traditions seem to be at odds with the overwhelming patriarchy of the religions they founded.

Once again, it is the liberals in most traditions that are finding ways to address the concerns of contemporary feminism. Reform Judaism disagrees sharply with Orthodoxy over the question. The movement for the ordination of women priests remains one of the most divisive issues in Christendom. Comparable movements can be found in most religious traditions.

The overwhelming impression of most scholars of religion is that these two issues (toleration and feminism) determine whether one is basically liberal (i.e. willing to adapt the tradition to a changing world) or conservative (inclined to see such change as a betrayal of the truth of the revelation).[14]

Conclusion

It is imperative that our ethical journey includes a diverse range of religious perspectives and voices. This chapter has explored, all too briefly, some of the key similarities and differences across the major religious traditions. There is much more that could be said.

There are two key issues that need to be taken from this chapter into the rest of the book. The first is this: should we take especially seriously areas of agreement between religious traditions? On the one hand, these areas of agreement include much that is constructive – the centrality of love, compassion, and justice. On the other hand, they include areas that are much more contentious, for example, the assertion that homosexuality is wrong and that patriarchy is acceptable. One tempting ethical methodology is to support the "majority" – that which the majority of people think is ethically right is ethically right. The thought exercise was intended to raise the question as to whether this is acceptable. As we shall see in chapter 9, the West has an entirely different understanding of sexuality from that which has been held for centuries by most religious traditions.

The second issue is the secular humanist challenge. In the next chapter we shall look at the argument of the secular humanist that religion has been a constant opponent to moral development. Insofar as liberals are emerging in the religions traditions, the secular humanist would say that it is only because of the lessons they are learning from modernity. The question is then: are secular humanists right to say that religion has been a movement for bigotry and oppression in the world?

In the next chapter we shall look at this argument with secular humanism in more detail.

Notes

1 This chapter is a slightly amended version of my article called "Religion and Ethics" in *Encyclopedia of Applied Ethics*, vol. 3 (San Diego, CA: Academic Press 1998) pp. 799–808.

2 Ronald M. Green, *Religion and Moral Reason* (Oxford: Oxford University Press 1988) p. 3.

3 See Don Cupitt, *A New Christian Ethic* (London: SCM Press 1988).

4 See Keith Ward, *Religion and Revelation* (Oxford: Oxford University Press 1994).

5 R. C. Zaehner, *Hinduism* (Oxford: Oxford University Press 1966) p. 2.

6 S. Kierkegaard, *In Fear and Trembling: Repetition*, edited by H. V. Hong (Princeton, NJ: Princeton University Press 1983).

7 See Hans Küng, *Global Responsibility* (London: SCM Press 1991).

8 I. Epstein (General editor), *The Babylonian Talmud* (London: The Soncino Press 1938). Shabbath, vol. 1, translated by H. Freedman, p. 140.

9 J. Sacks, *Faith in the Future* (London: Darton Longman and Todd 1995) p. 128

10 H. Hathout, *Islamic Perspectives in Obstetrics and Gynaecology* (Cairo: Alam al-Kutub / Islamic Organizations for Medical Sciences 1986) p. 69.

11 For a good discussion of this see R. Gombrich, *Theravada Buddhism* (London: Routledge 1988) pp. 72–8.

12 Deuteronomy 30:19–20.

13 E. F. Schumacher, *Small Is Beautiful* (New York: Harper and Row 1975) p. 51.

14 I have argued elsewhere that this model must be challenged. Given the vast majority of religious people in the world are conservative, it is important to find reasons for traditional Christians, Jews, Muslims etc. to be tolerant. In addition, I argue that for reasons hinted at in earlier chapters; religion is the only true safeguard for liberal values. See Ian S. Markham, *Plurality and Christian Ethics* (Cambridge: Cambridge University Press 1994).

8

Humanism: do we need God to realize that people just matter?

Thought exercise

Imagine you are sitting in the middle of a large room. Around the edge of the large room is one representative of all the major religious traditions in the world. Along with the major traditions – Hindus, Buddhists, Sikhs, Jews, Christians, and Muslims – some of the smaller and more recent traditions – Ba'hais, Mormons, and New Age advocates – are represented. Each person is given half a day to present his or her tradition. Your task is to decide which one is true. Each person is a superb and effective communicator; so each tradition has an equal chance. How would you decide which one is true?[1]

One idea underpinning this discussion of ethics is that we must recognize the importance of religion. In chapter 2, we looked at Nietzsche's attack on the "transcendent" assumptions that seem to underpin ethical discourse. In chapter 3, religion was often implicitly present as the strongest framework to locate moral facts. In chapter 5, the traditions of the virtues and natural law, which developed in the Christian tradition, were described sympathetically. Religion in general, and Christianity in particular, is getting a sympathetic hearing in this book.

So in the interests of balance it is time to explore an alternative tradition. One that insists it is deeply offensive to imply that only the religious can be virtuous. In addition, this tradition wants to claim that there is a strong moral case against locating moral values in God. This conceptual argument against a religious framework compliments the historical argument: too often religion plays an oppressive role in the society, with women the chief victims. Add to this the religious propensity to intolerance and cruelty and one has a rich cocktail of arguments for secular humanism.

Before we develop this argument, it is necessary to define our terms. The word "secular" we have met before. It is a term that describes the "non-religious space" in society; the "secularization process" describes the decreasing authority of religious institutions in the west. Humanism is a harder word to describe. Originally it was used by Christians to describe their religiously grounded commitment to humanity; however, since the Enlightenment it has taken on a different meaning. It is increasingly used to describe the post-Enlightenment conviction that "people simply matter because they are people." Our commitment to humanity does not need any further justification. Indeed once one gets rid of God and metaphysics (i.e. the ultimate explanations beyond physics), all that remains is this world, this life, our planet, and our fellow humankind. It is this tradition of "secular humanism" that we shall explore in this chapter.

The assumptions of secular humanists

Secular humanists are not very sympathetic to religion. The main reason is simple: they do not think it is true. The main arguments against faith are well known; so all we shall do is briefly summarize them here.

First, there is the general objection to all metaphysics. It was David Hume (1711–76) who couldn't understand how anyone can be confident about the ultimate answers to ultimate questions. This is the point of the thought exercise. Given the diversity of religions in the world, how can anyone be so confident that a particular tradition has the entire truth. We cannot get outside our limited and finite human experience and find out precisely what is responsible for "everything." Given this, Thomas Huxley (1825–95) in 1869 suggested, we should all be "agnostics," by which he meant "it is impossible to determine the truth of metaphysics."

Second, there is the rise of science. For secular humanism, the persecution of Galileo (1564–1642), who dared to challenge the cosmology accepted by the Roman Catholic Church, followed by the fierce antagonism to Charles Darwin's (1809–82) theory of natural selection, are ample evidence of the conflict between religion and science. The explanation for this conflict, secular humanists explain, is due to the displacement of religious explanations for the material world by scientific ones. In other words, planets were sustained in their orbit by the hand of God, now we know it is due to gravity. Or natural disasters (such as hurricanes) were the judgment of God, now science explains how these things arise without reference to God. The English biologist, Richard Dawkins, makes the point extremely well when he writes:

> We know approximately when the universe began and why it is largely hydrogen. We know why stars form, and what happens in their interiors to convert hydrogen to the other elements and hence give birth to chemistry in a world of physics. We know the fundamental principles

of how a world of chemistry can become biology through the arising of self-replicating molecules. We know how the principle of self-replication gives rise, through Darwinian selection to all life including humans.

It is science, and science alone, that has given us this knowledge and given it, moreover, in fascinating, overwhelming, mutually confirming detail. On every one of these questions theology has held a view that has been conclusively proved wrong. Science has eradicated smallpox, can immunise against most previously deadly viruses, can kill most previously deadly bacteria.

Theology has done nothing but talk of pestilence as the wages of sin. Science can predict when a particular comet will reappear and, to the second, when the next eclipse will occur. Science has put men on the moon and hurtled reconnaissance rockets around Saturn and Jupiter. Science can tell you the age of a particular fossil and that the Turin Shroud is a medieval fake. Science knows the precise DNA instructions of several viruses and will, in the lifetime of many present readers of *The Independent*, do the same for the human genome.

What has 'theology" ever said that is of the smallest use to anybody? When has "theology" ever said anything that is demonstrably true and is not obvious? I have listened to theologians, read them, debated against them. I have never heard any of them ever say anything of the smallest use, anything that was not either platitudinously obvious or downright false.[2]

The third argument against religion is the problem of evil and suffering. The standard statement of the problem runs thus: if God is all-powerful, then God must be able to abolish evil; if God is all-loving, then God must wish to abolish evil; but evil exists, therefore God cannot be all-powerful and all-loving. The problem, argues the secular humanist, exposes a fundamental contradiction in theism. Evil is an ever-present reality – from the abducted child who is then raped and murdered to the attempted genocide of the Jewish people in the Second World War. A God with the traditional attributes would not permit such evil; therefore, the argument goes, this type of God does not exist.

Secular humanism, then, is assuming that religion is not true. For Bertrand Russell (1872–1970), there is no option to atheism: therefore we have no option but to start constructing our ethical understanding in this context. In this famous passage, Russell provides a marvelous summary of his assumptions that underpins his ethical system:

Amid such a world, if anywhere, our ideals henceforward must find a home. That Man is the product of causes which had no prevision of the end they were achieving; that his origin, his growth, his hopes and fears, his loves and his beliefs, are but the outcome of accidental collocations of atoms; that no fire, no heroism, no intensity of thought and feeling, can preserve an individual life beyond the grave; that all the labours of the ages, all the devotion, all the inspiration, all the noonday brightness of human genius, are destined to extinction in the vast death of the solar system, and that the whole temple of Man's achievement must inevitably be buried beneath the debris of a universe in ruins – all these things, if not quite beyond dispute, are yet so nearly certain, that no philosophy which rejects them can hope to stand. Only within the scaffolding of these truths, only on the firm foundation of unyielding despair, can the soul's habitation henceforth be safely built.

How, in such an alien and inhuman world, can so powerless a creature as Man preserve his aspirations untarnished? A strange mystery it is that Nature, omnipotent but blind, in the revolutions of her secular hurryings through the abysses of space, has brought forth at last a child, subject still to her power, but gifted with sight, with knowledge of good and evil, with the capacity of judging all the worlds of his unthinking Mother. In spite of Death, the mark, the seal of the parental control, Man is yet free, during his brief years, to examine, to criticise, to know, and in imagination to create. To him alone, in the world with which he is acquainted, this freedom belongs; and in this lies his superiority to the resistless forces that control his outward life.[3]

Four arguments for secular humanism

For most secular humanists, Russell is right. We live in a world that is devoid of objective meaning. It is up to humanity to create meaning for ourselves. Religious people have for centuries felt that morality would be in trouble if we stop believing in hell or God. John Locke, for example, the famous father of the secular society insisted that atheists could not be tolerated because society cannot trust the word of an atheist. (He also, incidentally, had a problem with Roman Catholics: his difficulty here was they acknowledged the authority of a foreign power.) We will come back to Locke at the end of this chapter. But for now, we note that secular humanists disagree with all this hysteria: instead, they suspect that it is not secular forms of morality that are problematic but religious forms.

So the first two arguments are arguments against the religious basis for morality. The first argument, then, is this: conceptually a religiously grounded morality is impoverished and inadequate. It was Plato who famously posed the Euthyphro dilemma. This claims that either morality is beyond God and not arbitrary or that morality is determined by God and is arbitrary. If it is the former, then morality is not grounded in God because there is a standard of morality beyond God by which God's actions are judged. And if it is the latter then God is not good or loving because those words, by definition, describe a certain set of actions that would limit the capricious command of God. The point of the Euthyphro dilemma, explains the secular humanist, is that grounding morality in God doesn't help because it would only be moral if God too is judged by it.

In addition to the Euthyphro dilemma, secular humanists are disturbed by many religious practices. Immanuel Kant was horrified by the thought of a human on his or her knees 'worshipping" this big invisible ego in the sky. Worship, thought Kant, was very problematic. If God is who Christians claim God is, then why would God need all these creatures to spend all their time telling God "how big and great God is." It sounds like a massive ego trip on the part of God. Rush Rhees, the Welsh philosopher, put it rather succinctly, when he said, "If my first and chief reason for worshipping God had to be a belief that a super-Frankenstein would blast me to hell if I did not, then I hope I should have the decency to tell this being, who is named Almighty God, to go ahead and blast."[4] Worship, Rhees implies, is morally dubious. It was Feuerbach (1804–72) who argued that worship is the projection into the skies of all the best human values leaving us groveling around in sin and failure. In short, from the perspective of morality, the practice of worship looks very dubious. Combine this argument with the Euthyropo dilemma and you have a strong argument against a religious basis for morality.

The second argument against religion is the destructive nature of religion; the campaign for the toleration of religious diversity or the rights of women were not, on the whole, furthered by traditional Christians and Muslims. Indeed religious institutions were the main opponents of such campaigns. And, briefly, we need to examine why this is the case.

Most religions make a certain set of truth claims about the nature of ultimate religion. (I say "most" because it is true that there are certain strands – the mystical or certain aspects of Buddhism – that are much more "agnostic," but these strands are in a minority.) Coupled with these truth claims is the insistence that those who do not concur with this or that tradition is in error. And in many traditions, those in error are heading for some form of judgment, for example, to hell. When it comes to religious diversity, then, the problem many religious traditions find is this: their commitment to their truth claims, coupled with the very serious implications facing those in error, makes it impossible for them to be blasé about the close proximity of other faith traditions. Often they are not that happy about faith traditions further away, but at least distance makes it harder for a "religious war" to start. For the secular humanist, it is bizarre that a person can be so certain about the nature of the metaphysical realities that they are willing to slaughter – sometimes thousands – adherents of a different religion. Still, both historically and today, such slaughter remains commonplace.

Coupled with this inability of different faith traditions to get along with each other, there is the religious instinct to side with patriarchy against feminism or with homophobia against gay rights. It is remarkable how the religious texts of most traditions are opposed to the rights of women.[5] The Laws of Manu in Hinduism asserts the following:

> By a girl, by a young woman, or even by an aged one, nothing must be done independently, even in her own house. In childhood a female must be subject to her father, in youth to her husband, when her lord is dead to her sons; a woman must never be independent.

St Thomas Aquinas (1225–74), the greatest theologian of the Roman Catholic Church, asks the question whether "woman should have been made in the original creation of things?" And he answers:

> It was absolutely necessary to make woman, for the reason Scripture mentions, as a help for man; not indeed to help him in any work, as some have maintained, because where most work is concerned man can get help more conveniently from another man than from a woman; but to help him in the work of procreation.

Even the Buddha (who often gets a good press in feminist circles) still insists that even the youngest male monk can expect deference from the oldest nun: so the Buddha explains, "A priestess of even a hundred years' standing shall salute, rise to meet, entreat humbly, and perform all respectful offices for a priest, even if he be but that day ordained."

It is remarkable how it is almost the universal witness of all the faith traditions that women are second-class citizens. And it is not surprising that the majority of "orthodox" traditions have real problems with the affirmation of women. It is still a lively debate, for example in the Roman Catholic Church, whether women are holy enough to be in the sanctuary. The battle for women's rights over the last 300 years in the West is a battle that most religions have only belatedly joined and even then only the liberal forms of those religions.

The third argument is that one is more likely to affirm the significance of human life if one denies certain religious beliefs. It was Karl Marx (1818–83) who suggested that belief in life after death becomes a drug that enables those who are poor and oppressed to cope with their suffering and pain. In addition the doctrine that hell awaits those who sin and rebel against God's determined hierarchy is a major deterrent against any rebellion. It does seem, then, that belief in life after death can have the consequence of reducing the significance of this life.

One theme of the earlier chapters is that defending the objectivity of moral value requires a belief in God. Although it might be true that conceptually a belief in a transcendent being makes objective moral talk easier, it is still perfectly possible for an atheist to opt to affirm the value of humanity and the importance of goodness and love. Perhaps this morality will lack the sanction of an eternal being that orders us to behave in a life-enhancing way, but the decision to opt in to such a morality can, perhaps, be seen as even more moral. For the secular humanist, we are being called to behave in a life-enhancing way for the simple reason that this is a good way to behave. There is no God commanding this ethical commitment; there is no hell that will punish us if we choose to do otherwise; all we can do is plead and in pleading witness the good as simply good in itself.

Ultimately for the secular humanist the basis of the appeal is this: all there is in the universe is our moments here on earth with each other, rather than opt for despair, we should opt to affirm hope in the face of hopelessness. We only have each other; so we need to take care of each other. In a world without God, the work that God use to do, we are now required to do.

The fourth argument is that it is imperative that secular humanism should triumph in the public square. The consequences of religion controlling the public square have been deeply damaging for social cohesion and toleration. People are different: and difference is not handled very well by religious authorities. The public square needs to be neutral; no single religion should be allowed to dominate. If individuals want to believe in metaphysical entities, then that should be permitted; but for an individual to insist that everyone else should affirm their private metaphysical beliefs is wrong.

The concept of the secular has its roots in Enlightenment thought. After the so-called "Religious Wars" in Europe (1560–1715), during which Europe only had 30 years of peace, there was a desperate need for a new model for society. John Locke (1632–1704) was a pioneer in this respect. He was amongst the first to suggest that a nation need not be uniform in religious belief. It is possible to tolerate some religious diversity. Admittedly, his diversity was confined to Protestant dissenters unhappy with the English established church for he did not think that toleration could extend to Roman Catholics or atheists. He thought Roman Catholics were a problem because they acknowledged the authority of a foreign power; and atheists were a problem because their lack of belief in God meant that their oaths could not be trusted. However, leaving to one side for a moment these limitations, Locke set out the basis of a modern liberal society by his talk of the possibility of toleration grounded in a distinction between the public and private spheres of human life.

In *Two Treatises of Government*, Locke attempts to set out an alternative account of "political obligation" – one that was not grounded in the Bible.[6] Locke's alternative ran as follows: humans are by nature free and independent. They can, however, acquire obligations to obey political authorities that restrict their freedom, by consenting to them. The founding of political society is an agreement of all the members to accept restrictions on their freedom. From then on those members are required to comply with the rules of their society because they have consented to do so in the original contract. The original members give their explicit consent and all subsequent generations give their tacit consent. It is in this context that the liberal elevation of the individual is developed. Each person opts into society, relinquishing certain individual rights for the benefit of living in community. The implications are clear (although Locke did not entirely see them): you only relinquish the minimum required for social living and security of your property. On this account, one concedes that murder and theft would be anti-social, but (in a modern, rather than a Lockian, example) homosexual relations in the privacy of one's own home are the concern of the individual, not of society. In private, individuals are free to behave as they wish provided it does not infringe the rights of other individuals in society.

John Locke's achievement is to provide a framework for society that entrenches human liberty. The individual is "king" (literally, the monarch is conceptually overthrown). Society is not allowed to infringe personal liberty anymore than the minimum for social cohesion requires. A popular analogy that captures this idea is the image of society as a hotel. The hotel is a testimony to human freedom. The presumption is that one can do practically what one wishes in the privacy of one's own room. However, in the public spaces one should observe the appropriate conventions, for example, one should be suitably attired. For example, the fact that in a hotel bedroom the businessman is with another man's wife is irrelevant to the other hotel guests. Naturally rape would be completely wrong, even in private; the adulterous wife must have exercised her freewill and have given her full consent. However, provided the illicit affair meets this condition, it is not the business of anyone else in the hotel. The fact that others in the hotel believe in a religious text that declares the adulterous woman should be stoned is irrelevant. On the Lockean model, the belief in the authority of a religious text is a private personal belief, which the individual is entitled to hold, but it should not be imposed on anyone else. After all, they do not share that personal belief.

Conclusion

There is no doubt that the tradition of "secular humanism" is responsible for significant ethical discoveries. For centuries, religion coexisted with patriarchy, exploitation of the weak and poor in society, and deep social intolerance. The

European Enlightenment created a new mindset in the world that challenged religion on these matters. The net result is a world much more sensitive. It is not surprising that the discoveries of feminism and social toleration have attracted widespread acceptance.

However, in addition to this historical achievement, this chapter has stressed the conceptual challenge to religion. Secular humanists pose legitimate and difficult questions to religious people about the precise ways in which religion is supposed to support moral discourse. Not only is there the matter of the legitimacy of worship from a moral standpoint, but also the insight that moral action grounded in a fear of "hell" or the "command of God" sounds a less adequate basis for morality than the simple injunction "do what is right simply because it is right."

Many strands of most religious traditions view the secular humanist tradition as an important conversation partner. Many secular insights can be accommodated by the faith traditions. Many Christians and Muslims, for example, recognize the justice of feminism and are willing to revisit their sacred books and tradition in the light of feminism. This should not be viewed as a betrayal of the faith tradition, but as the inevitable and appropriate modification of that tradition in the light of new moral insight and discovery.

This concludes the theoretical conversation at the start of this book. We now move to the applied dilemmas as we encounter them in every aspect of our lives. As we do so, we will often discover that the exploration of the practical or applied issues in ethics need the frameworks we have outlined in the first half of this book.

Notes

1   This thought exercise is taken from my introduction to "Secular Humanism" in Ian S. Markham (ed.), *A World Religions Reader*, second edition (Oxford: Blackwell Publishing 2000).

2   Richard Dawkins, letter to *The Independent*, published March 20, 1993, reproduced in Ian S. Markham (ed.) *A World Religions Reader* (Oxford: Blackwell Publishing 2000).

3   Bertrand Russell, "A Free Man's Worship" reprinted in Bertrand Russell, *Mysticism and Logic*, third impression (London: Longman 1919).

4   Rush Rhees, *Without Answers* (London: Routledge and Kegan Paul 1969) p. 113.

5   The quotations that follow are all taken from Ian S. Markham (ed.) *A World Religions Reader*, second edition (Oxford Blackwell Publishing 2000).

6   What follows is adapted from my description of Locke's views in my *Plurality and Christian Ethics* (Cambridge: Cambridge University Press 1994) pp. 14–15. The entire book is a critique and ultimately an attack on the Lockian structure and justification for toleration. However, this critique and attack is not needed here.

Part Two

Ethical Dilemmas

9

Dilemmas in bed

Thought exercise

Consider the following argument:
Sexual experiences are very pleasurable. The sensible attitude to pleasurable experiences is to try to accumulate as many as possible. If you enjoy playing golf, then you do not confine oneself to one partner on the same course; instead you play with many partners on different courses. Now part of the pleasure of sex is the consenting and non-coercive nature of the relationship. Seeking as many consenting, non-coercive sexual experiences is a rational way to behave. To confine sexual activity to one person in the context of marriage is a needless limitation.

It was, perhaps, in the 1960s when this argument became culturally explicit in parts of western society. The rule that all sex must be consenting and non-coercive was always recognized. No one thinks that a healthy person can have a satisfying sexual relationship with a non-consenting person, much less with an animal; everyone (everyone, that is, who is morally serious – an idea we will discuss further in chapter 15) recognizes that it is wrong to take young children into the mysterious domain of sexual intimacy. Yet recognizing these important rules does not preclude a variety of sexual partners.

In the western world, the variety of sexual relationships is considerable. Starting with the world of heterosexuality, we have "casual sex" (i.e. the intimate relationship formed, perhaps, at a nightclub for one evening), "cohabitation" (i.e. two people who live together without getting married), "open marriages" (a couple who permit each other to have partners outside the relationship), "marriages" (two people who commit to being exclusively for each other), "polyamory" (groups of people who have a non-monogamous commitment to each other) and "affairs" (a married person who forms a sexual relationship outside the marriage). Then there is the world of bisexuality and homosexuality. A bisexual is a person who has sexual urges towards both men and women; a homosexual is a person who has an orientation towards their own gender. The transgender person recognizes a need to reconcile their identity with their physical gender, which might lead to an operation where the sexual identity of the person is changed.

Collecting data on precisely how people are behaving is very difficult. We do know, however, that there is a twilight world where married men make frequent use of prostitutes and others, or in a more tragic and less constructive way, go in for "cottaging" (i.e. seeking out casual sexual encounters with men – often around public restrooms). We also know about the non-conventional stories of individuals as they cope with their sexual impulses. For example, there are men who become women and then discover they are lesbians.

The libertarian view

A libertarian would largely accept the argument that started this chapter. It is, as we have already noted, essential to have mutual, voluntary informed consent. The libertarian would agree that it is wrong when (a) one of the parties is not in a position to give consent (e.g. the under-age, mentally impaired, or non-human) or (b) there is explicit duress (threats or extortion) or (c) fraud (e.g. you claim to be madly in love). However, provided the relationship involves mutual, voluntary, informed consent, then the libertarian would say that the relationship is ethically appropriate.

This worldview often runs parallel with a concern that traditional patriarchal marriage is a problem. An unhappy marriage can easily become an unhappy prison. Economic dependence makes it difficult to leave such a marriage. And where there are children involved, the problems become a hundred times greater. It is difficult to penetrate beyond the public face of a marriage: only the couple involved knows what happens late at night. Even close friends will find it difficult to know what precisely is happening.

It was the Marxist Engels who argued in *The Origin of the Family, Private Property, and the State*, that marriage was an institution intended for bourgeois families to protect their wealth and power. He believed that the roots of marriage are in capitalist anxieties concerning property. The problem for a man is simple: how can I make sure that I pass on my property to a blood relative? It is always obvious who the mother of a child is, but it is less obvious who was involved nine months beforehand. Engels argued that to guarantee the property line, marriage was invented. The prison of the family guarantees the succession of property, from father to son. It also provides a cheap form of labor that can be exploited. Wives are legally validated domestic slaves, who can keep a clean house, provide meals, and offer a child-rearing service. In effect sex within marriage is just a form of respectable prostitution: in exchange for lodging, women are domestic servants who satisfy the sexual needs of their husbands.

It is this latter point that feminists fastened upon. Alison Jaggar, in *Feminist Politics and Human Nature* (1983), stressed the problem of patriarchy in marriage. Marriages are often very patriarchal institutions (i.e. ruled by and in the interests of men). The man is in control: he is, to use Biblical terminology, the head of the household. Marriage serves male needs: the woman is left at home to serve the male. The place of the woman is in the bed (providing sexual satisfaction for the male) and the kitchen (providing meals), with permission to clean the rest of the house en route between these two rooms. Jagger points out that these are socially constructed roles – there is nothing intrinsic to women that makes it necessary that in the vast majority of homes they are the only ones to give the bathroom a good clean. As a result of these socially constructed roles, women do not get the space to develop their own needs. It is not surprising that many women are now opting for cohabitation (they have seen the damage that marriage did to their mothers) or getting divorced (they finally realize that escaping the prison is a condition for a full healthy life).

Some feminists have argued that women need to challenge patriarchy by excluding men from the sexual realm. Jill Johnston, wrote *Lesbian Nation*, which became a key text for lesbian separatists. True liberty and choices for women will only happen when women assert themselves sexually. So she writes:

> It just isn't possible any more to overlook the feminist analysis of the heterosexist institution by which women are oppressed. The new definition of lesbian emerges from this analysis. The choice of mate can no longer be regarded as a purely personal one . . . The purpose of feminist analysis is to provide women with an awareness of their servitude as a class so that they can unite and rise up against it. The problem now for strictly heterosexual conditioned women is how to obtain the sexual gratification they think they need from the sex who remains their institutional oppressor . . . The lesbian is the woman obviously who unites the personal and the political in the struggle to free ourselves from the oppressive institution . . . The lesbian argument is first and foremost withdrawal at every level from man to develop woman supremacy, which does not necessarily mean the diminution of the man the way male supremacy has meant the diminution of women as though one can't be up without the other being down, but it does mean the (re)-development of the moral physical spiritual intellectual strengths of women whatever the social consequences of that may be.[1]

Such is the pervasive and damaging influence of patriarchy that any compromise with heterosexuality will not succeed.

One does not have to go as far as Jill Johnston to see that marriage has been (and often still is) hard for women. Even in homes where both the husband and the wife are working, one finds the pattern continuing of "men read the paper after supper" and "women clear up and prepare the coffee." A pervasive sense that domesticity (ironing, cleaning, and cooking) is a women's role and men might agree to periodically reciprocate with masculine work (yard work and car maintenance) continues to shape many marriages. One factor behind the cohabitation and divorce rates is that women are increasingly choosing not to tolerate such a demarcation of roles.

It is now time, however, to revisit a more traditional view of marriage. For this, I shall take the Roman Catholic Church as representative of a traditional view of marriage.

Roman Catholic position

Unlike the libertarian position, the Roman Catholic view of sexuality is grounded in the creation story. The assumption is that there is a God who has created the world for certain purposes. In the *Catechism of the Catholic Church* (recently revised, 1994), part 3, which is called "Life in Christ," we find the following argument.[2]

The Catechism starts by reflecting on the nature of God as affirmed by Christians. Part of the idea lying behind the doctrine of the Trinity (that God is three "persons" in one) is that God's own internal life is one of "personal loving communion."[3] When Christians talk about humanity being created in the image of God, this means that men and women have been imprinted with the capacity to live in communion and love. The libertarian view tends to stress the biological aspect, while the Catholic view starts with a much more elevated view of the basis of love.

Next the Catechism acknowledges that sexuality is a central part of the human person; it affects all aspects of the human soul. Furthermore, it acknowledges the equality of the sexes, although it then goes on to stress the different and complementary roles for men and women. Marriage is a gift, given out of the generosity of the creator to humanity, which provides the space for the complementary nature of the two sexes to express itself. At this point the Catechism invokes Jesus' views on adultery in the Sermon on the Mount. Jesus wants a pure inward life, where even lustful thought is forbidden. So God wants marriage to be an institution for life. Moreover, its purpose is not only relational but also procreative: it is the basis of the stable continuance of human society.

Given this elevated view of sexuality, it is not surprising that the Catechism expects people to be chaste. Chastity is defined as follows:

Chastity means the successful integration of sexuality within the person and thus the inner unity of man in his bodily and spiritual being. Sexuality, in which man's belonging to the bodily and biological world is expressed, becomes personal and truly human when it is integrated into the relationship of one person to another, in the complete and life-long mutual gift of a man and a woman.[4]

Those who are single, engaged, or homosexual, or those called to a special religious vocation should all be chaste. There are seven offenses against chastity:

1 *lust* – a disordered desire for or inordinate enjoyment of sexual pleasure
2 *masturbation* – an intrinsically and gravely disordered action. It is the use of the sexual faculty outside marriage, although the Catechism does suggest that pastors should be gentle in understanding the problem, especially for the teenager.
3 *fornication* – undermines the dignity of the human person
4 *pornography* – creates a fantasy world which exploits and damages
5 *prostitution* – the Catechism describes as a "social scourge"
6 *rape* – always an intrinsically evil act
7 *homosexual acts* – the Catechism does concede that for many it is not a matter of choice; and the homosexual person should be accepted with respect, compassion, and sensitivity. Yet it does insist that such people are called to chastity, i.e. abstinence from the acts and dispositions just described.

The net result is that sexual expression is only permitted in marriage between a husband and a wife. The Catechism then goes on to argue that, given the gift of sexuality concerns the innermost being, then it should be expressed in a context which lasts until death. There are two purposes for sexual intimacy: the first is the good of the spouses themselves (yes, it is recognized that sex is indeed a delight); and the second is the transmission of life.

It is this latter point that leads to the distinctive Roman Catholic view on the importance of procreation (marriages should express themselves in children) and the prohibition on contraception. Planned parenting, explains the Catechism, should make use of the natural infertile days during the course of the monthly cycle.

Given all this, the Catechism is clear in its condemnation of all that violates the covenant (solemn agreement between the husband and the wife) – adultery, divorce, polygamy, incest, free union, and trial marriages. Adultery is an injustice, transgressing the covenant – i.e. the rights of the other spouse. Divorce is a grave offense against natural law. A divorcee, explains the Catechism, should not remarry: the remarried spouse is in a situation of public and permanent adultery.

Polygamy is not in accord with the moral law. Incest is a grave offence, which is often coupled with a manifest abuse of power by the elderly on the young. Free union is a practice that offends against the dignity of marriage; it destroys the very idea of the family and weakens the sense of fidelity. Trial marriages, explains the Catechism, are incompatible with human love, which demands a total and definitive gift of two persons to one another.

It is worth noting that this view of marriage is grounded in a very elevated view of human love, suggested by Biblical texts. Furthermore the other important feature is the recognition that sexual intimacy is linked to children and that children need to be born into a secure and committed environment.

Homosexuality

There are many places where the views of Roman Catholics and Libertarians collide: divorce is commonplace; cohabitation is increasingly the norm; and sexual experimentation and promiscuity, especially while single, are widespread. However, the most contentious social question of our time is homosexuality, especially homosexual marriage; so this will be the focus of attention between these two positions. Abortion dominated the "culture wars" (to use Hunter's phrase about the battle in America between social conservatives and social liberals)[5] in the latter part of the twentieth century; and it will be homosexuality that will dominate the next 20 years. Thinking clearly on this question is vitally important. As we have just seen, the Roman Catholics believe that the homosexual person is called to chastity, while the Libertarian believes that there is no reason why homosexuals cannot express their sexual feelings. And as we shall now see, for coherence and consistency the Roman Catholic position makes sense; almost everyone else, who wants to be morally consistent, will have to concede the legitimacy of homosexuality.

Let us start with a few facts. Now facts in this area are extremely difficult to establish. Collecting data is difficult (people are not entirely honest when it comes to answering questions about their sexual practice). However, the following picture is starting to emerge amongst "sexologists" working in this field.

First, humans are "given" a sexual orientation, and so a sexual predisposition. We don't choose our sexuality. It is true that we can experiment (it is amazing what students at university discover having consumed copious quantities of alcohol), but "experimenting" isn't the same as recognizing our fundamental orientation. This orientation can be heterosexual (certainly for the majority), homosexual, or bisexual (i.e. one is attracted to both sexes). It is clear that the concept of sexual orientation is a relatively late discovery. Although the culture of Ancient Greece did involve the male teacher, for example, inducting the male student into the realms of sexuality as almost a rite of passage, this made no assumptions about fundamental orientation. And when St Paul, writing in the Letter to the Romans in the Bible, says that "their men in turn, giving up natural relations with women, burn with lust for one another," he is probably talking about what we might call "experimental homosexuality." He is assuming that a basically heterosexual society has individuals within it who decide to willfully sin and experiment with homosexuality. The idea that certain individuals have a certain non-heterosexual disposition does not occur to him.

The second aspect of this picture is slightly at odds with the first. This point recognizes the fluidity of sexual practice within individual lives. It was Alfred Kinsey (in an American study reporting in 1948) who argued that we should not think in terms of two opposing groups, hetero- and homo-sexuals, but two tendencies present in at least half of us. His scale ran as follows:

0   fully heterosexual, with no homosexual experience
1   predominantly heterosexual, with incidental homosexual experience
2   basically heterosexual, with significant homosexual experience
3   bisexual, with significant heterosexual and homosexual experience
4   basically homosexual, with significant heterosexual experience
5   predominantly homosexual, with incidental heterosexual experience
6   fully homosexual, with no heterosexual experience.

His studies suggested 50 percent of people had homosexual experiences at some stage; 37 percent had such experiences to the point of orgasm. This means that across a lifetime virtually half of us find ourselves in a situation where we are attracted (perhaps momentarily) to someone of the same sex.

The third aspect to this picture is that we are no nearer providing an explanation for the causes of homosexuality. In the nineteenth century, many theories talked about the disposition as an illness. One of the most popular views was that it was partly caused by excessive masturbation. Although there are still some social conservatives that use such terminology, most specialists in the field have moved beyond such an analysis.

One of the most influential critiques of the causes of homosexuality came from the psychologist Frank Lake. He argued that children pass through a homosexual stage as a normal part of growing up (for example, the crush on a same-sex teacher or the quest for physical contact in a setting of sport). However, he argued that in the normal course of events, the child should grow through this phase, thereby implying that adult homosexuality was a form of "retarded growth." In a similar way, other psychologists have argued that homosexuality is a result of unsatisfactory relationships in childhood or unsatisfactory – failing – relationships in adulthood.

The quest for a biological cause continues: for a long time homosexuals were those with an excess of the wrong hormones: an excess of the female hormone estrogen causes homosexuality; a lesbian has an excess of the male hormone androgen. Some have implied that it is all linked with fetal development.

Although the quest for a cause will continue, the ethical question is what the significance of such a discovery would be. It is true that if it could be shown to be analogous to "blindness" (a human organ not working properly) or "pedophilia" (a disposition often arising from abuse in childhood), then the causation would have ethical significance. But the debate is definitely moving beyond both these models. When one reads Andrew Sullivan's excellent book *Virtually Normal*,[6] where he describes his fairly settled homosexual feelings since childhood, one can see that the models of physical impairment or environmental abuse do not make sense of his story. And along with Andrew Sullivan there are thousands of other homosexual men and women who have similar stories. What these stories teach us is that from a very young age, many people just have an underlying gay disposition.

Everyone who is morally serious recognizes that homophobia (a prejudice against homosexual men and women) is wrong. Even the Catechism of the Catholic Church accepts that homophobia is wrong:

> The number of men and women who have deep-seated homosexual tendencies is not negligible. They do not choose their homosexual condition; for most of them it is a trial. They must be accepted with respect, compassion, and sensitivity. Every sign of unjust discrimination in their regard should be avoided. These persons are called to fulfill God's will in their lives and, if they are Christians, to unite to the sacrifice of the Lord's Cross the difficulties they may encounter from their condition. (paragraph 2358)

Even though Roman Catholics do not believe that homosexuals should express their feelings in an act of sexual intimacy, the Catechism does make it clear that abuse, insult, and intimidation are wrong.

At this point it might be objected that it is all so "unnatural." At this stage in the book, one should now understand what is meant by that term. The term "unnatural" doesn't mean "it doesn't happen in nature." There is a vast variety of practices in the animal and plant world. The black widow spider eats its mate; and certain monkeys are very imaginative in their relationships. So it is not "unnatural" as in "not in nature." Instead the expression has its roots in natural law, the tradition described in chapter 5, which has been so influential in the Roman Catholic Church.

As we saw earlier, the sexual act has two main purposes – the unitive (the bringing of two people together in the act of love) and the procreative (the means of transmitting life). To use a sexual organ for any other purpose is unnatural because it is going against the Creator's intentions for the sexual act. The reason why the Roman Catholic Church is not going to shift its viewpoint on contraception is because it has no intention of decoupling the connection between procreation and the sexual act. Even though Roman Catholic teaching in the area of contraception is increasingly disregarded (especially in the West), the Vatican feels the price of conceding that the procreative possibility is not essential to sexual intimacy would be the potential legitimizing of same-sex intimacy.

The Vatican is, in my view, logical in seeing the issue in these terms. Other grounds for opposing same-sex intimacy are not strong. Some evangelical Christians want to insist that the Biblical prohibitions are sufficient. However, the references to homosexuality are few and many are opaque. The story of Sodom (from which we get the delightful expression – sodomy) in Genesis 19 is extraordinary. Two guests arrive in Sodom and stay at Lot's house. All the men in the town then converge on Lot's house calling on Lot to bring the men out to be "gang raped." Lot declines to do so, offering his virgin daughters instead. The two guests then save the situation by smiting all the men of the town with blindness and enabling Lot and the family to flee. It is very difficult to insist that this text should be used as the reason why a 30-year-old man cannot express his love to his close male friend.

The texts most often cited against homosexuality are Leviticus: 18:22 and Leviticus 20:13: "You shall not lie with a man as with a women: that is an abomination." This is part of the so-called Holiness Code. It was probably written in the eighth century to ensure that Israel retained a distinctive ethic against its neighbors. The problem of accepting this ethic as binding on us in the twenty-first century is that consistency would require us to accept the rest of the Holiness Code as binding. Along with many very worthy exhortations – "you shall not pervert justice, either by favoring the poor or by subservience to the great" (Leviticus 19:15), which one hopes are still binding on us now, there are many that most of us would find problematic. "You shall not put on a garment woven with two kinds of yarn" (Leviticus 19:19) is, I suspect, widely ignored. Even in the sexual realm, we might find that the abomination of homosexuality is joined by the equally vehement condemnation of practices that are now commonplace (albeit tragically).

> When a man reviles his father and his mother, he shall be put to death. He has reviled his father and his mother; his blood shall be on his own head. If a man commits adultery with his neighbor's wife, both adulterer and adulteress shall be put to death. (Leviticus 20:9–10)

Now reviling and adultery are both significant sins, but one might feel in the modern period that the death penalty is a tad excessive. If one is condemning homosexuality on the basis of authority (namely, the authority of this text in

Leviticus), then consistency requires that every assertion in the Holiness Code (not to speak of the rest of the Old Testament law) must have the same authority. It is an exacting set of expectations that, fortunately, few fundamentalist Christians are observing.

The only consistent argument, then, against the affirmation of sexual intimacy amongst homosexual men and women is the Roman Catholic argument that sexual intimacy must be open to the procreative possibility. The Roman Catholic Church is ethically consistent: it continues to teach that masturbation and contraception are inappropriate. And given that lesbians and many gay men (especially in this "safe sex" age) are simply practicing mutual masturbation, then it is important for consistency that the Roman Catholic Church continues to teach that masturbation and contraception are inappropriate.

Now this exercise in exploring the ethical worldview of Roman Catholics poses each of us a simple question. Do I believe that the sexual act must always be open to the procreative possibility? If so, then one can continue to argue that homosexual sexual intimacy is a misuse of the God-given gift of sexual intimacy. However, if not, then ethical consistency requires that we open up the possibility for social affirmation of the homosexual relationship. In short, if you think it is OK to use condoms and enjoy the unitive joy of sexual intimacy, then it must be OK for gay men and women to enjoy the unitive joy of sexual intimacy.

We are now starting to think ethically. We have explored two beautifully clear and consistent ethical worldviews. The Libertarian takes a certain view of sexual activity and consistently sets out an expectation and criteria for a permissive attitude to sex; the Roman Catholic (and others who think similarly) grounds sexual activity in a certain narrative (a story that shapes a tradition and frames a total worldview) and thinks through the implications of a position with some clarity.

Most of us are probably closer to Rome on this issue than to the Libertarian. And that is right. Love should shape our decisions about sexual intimacy. We should recognize that occasionally the sexual act leads to children and that implies the couple need to be committed to each other in an open-ended way. (Children, needless to say, are a life-long commitment; so the relationship that creates them needs to be equally committed.) However, there is no contradiction in insisting that more often the gift of sexual intimacy will not lead to procreation, it is instead the expression of love between two people. The sincere giving of love in a committed relationship is good, whatever the marital situation or the sexual orientation of the couple.

Looking ahead

It can be dangerous to look ahead. Sometimes those closer to the Roman Catholic – traditional – end of the spectrum look ahead in ways that are deeply offensive. To say for example that "recognizing that two men, who love each other, might want to express their love physically will lead to bestiality" is wrong, absurd, and insulting. However, it is true that debates about sexual questions do move on. Divorce and (for some parts of America) interracial marriage were questions that dominated the 1950s and the 1960s; cohabitation and homosexuality became the issue that dominated the 1970s onwards. So the question is this: can we identify the emerging issue for sexual ethics in the twenty-first century?

It seems likely that the transgendered will continue to challenge contemporary sexual ethics. Magnus Hirschfeld (1868–1935) was the first to coin the term "transvestite" – which is the technical term for a "cross-dresser." Then there is the "transsexual," who is a person who feels that they do not have the right gendered body. There is a growing community of individuals who receive the operation and change their sexual identity.

However, it is the polyamorous community on which I shall focus. With mobility and the emergence of urban life, humans have more opportunities than ever before to explore options. One aspect of this is the growing number of people who simply "fall in love" with others outside a committed monogamous relationship. For most individuals, this is an affair, but for some this evolves into something more. It could be argued that for the bisexual wife, the loving female companion need not be a threat to the relationship with her husband. There is growing evidence that the affair is evolving into a committed relationship. And this committed relationship is being tolerated by the spouse. And so a polyamorous relationship comes into being.

The Churches are beginning to have to face the issue. The Unitarian Universalists are leading the way. This growing US denomination has taken consistently progressive positions on key social issues. So a society has formed – the Unitarian Universalists for Polyamorous Awareness (UUPA). At the 41st General Assembly of the Unitarian Universalists Association, held in 2002, the UUPA succeeded in becoming an affiliate member of the Association. The UUPA explains polyamory in the following way:

> *Polyamory* is the potential for loving more than one person within a given period of time. Here we'll define "love" as a serious, intimate, romantic, stable, affectionate bond which a person has with another person or group of people. *Responsible non-monogamy* is another way of saying polyamory, and it is used to distinguish polyamory from "cheating."
>
> Polyamory is a general term covering a wide variety of relationship styles, including group marriage (polyfidelity), open marriage, expanded family, intimate network, and some kinds of intentional community.
>
> Polyamory is a relationship choice available to people of any sexual

orientation. Sometimes language familiar to lesbian, gay, bisexual, and transgender people is used to describe aspects of living as a polyamorous person (such as "coming out" as polyamorous). However, there are polyamorous people of all sexual orientations, just as there are monogamous people of all sexual orientations.[7]

As with all such campaigns, there is a social justice dimension. When it comes to placing children, the US courts have been inclined to view with suspicion households where there are "irregular" relationships amongst the adults. So the "poly" welcoming individual wants the law to recognize the legitimacy of this lifestyle choice. This evolving movement has learned much from the gay and lesbian campaign. When the UUPA offers some practical tips for poly welcoming individuals, the website explains that one should:

> Say "partner or partners" instead of "couple."
> Support multiple-person commitment ceremonies.
> Ask a poly person about his or her life. Ask about the person's partner(s) as a way of affirming the importance of those relationships.
> Speak up if someone reveals an irrational fear of polyamory. Be aware of subtle and institutional forms of discrimination against polyamorous people.
> If polyamory brings up strong negative emotions for you, gently explore those feelings by talking with someone you trust.[8]

It is important to note that each debate about a sexual activity has a different set of characteristics. In the 1960s, homosexuality was a privacy issue. So the argument ran: it is not the business of society to legislate about the activity of two consenting adults indulging in their own private sexual activities. In the 1990s, homosexuality wanted public recognition, hence the campaign for same-sex marriages. Polyamory seems to be taking a similar route: where many individuals have arrived at private understandings for centuries, this is now a campaign for public recognition and affirmation.

Conclusion

Sex definitely matters. We have seen two consistent ethical worldviews in this chapter: the libertarian takes a permissive attitude; and the Roman Catholics celebrate the importance of monogamy between one man and one woman. If I am right in my claim that polyamory might be the new social issue, then these two groups will have no problem taking a view. However, for many other people, less committed to one of these two options, forming a view will be a real challenge.

Notes

1   Jill Johnston, *Lesbian Nation: The Feminist Solution* (New York: Simon and Schuster 1973) pp. 275–6.
2   The *Catechism of the Catholic Church* (Mahwah, New Jersey: Paulist Press revised 1994), part 3, "Life in Christ," section 2, chapter 2, article 6.
3   Ibid.
4   Ibid. paragraph 2337.
5   See J. D. Hunter, *Culture Wars* (New York: Basic Books 1991).
6   Andrew Sullivan, *Virtually Normal* (New York: Vintage 1996).
7   Taken from the website for the UUPA at http://www.uupa.org/Understanding.htm
8   Ibid.

10

Dilemmas in business

Case study

It is the late 1960s. The American car industry is facing major competition from Japan, especially in the small car sector. The CEO of Ford, Lee Iacocca, decides that he wants a new car, which weighs less that 2000 pounds and can be priced at under $2,000. He wants the car available for sale in 1971. The design and production teams had 25 months instead of the normal 43 months. The Pinto was created. Owing to the reduced time for design and production, the Pinto was not tested for rear-end impact until it was finished. Although this test was standard procedure, there was no statutory obligation to do the test prior to making the car available for sale. The car was tested. The results were not good. The position of the fuel tank meant that if the car was hit from the rear at a speed over 20 miles per hour, then the fuel tank could be punctured by a bolt in the bumper and might ignite. To rectify this problem, the Pinto would need a baffle between the bumper and the gas tank (which estimates thought would cost between $6.65 and $11 per car). Ford did a cost-benefit analysis and decided that the cost of the baffle weighed against potential lawsuits from "excess" deaths made it uneconomic to install the baffle. From 1971 to 1978, the design of the Pinto was not changed. In addition Ford did not inform customers that the car was less safe than other comparable cars nor did it provide the option of purchasing the baffle. From 1976 to 1977, Pintos ignited from rear-end collisions on 13 separate occasions (more than twice the number for comparable cars). Ford paid out over $50 million in lawsuits, which far exceeded the $20.9 millions saved by not including the buffer in the original design.[1]

If you had worked at Ford during this period and knew about the internal debates around the safety of the Pinto, then would you have a moral obligation to inform the authorities or the media? Would you have done so?

It was probably Michael Douglas in *Wall Street* who made one of the best speeches ever in favor of unethical business. He defended the basis of business as "greed"; he insisted on the entitlement of capital to work exclusively for its own interest regardless of human and social cost. There is this great moment when Gordon Gecko (the Michael Douglas character) explains the value of greed:

> The point is, ladies and gentleman, that *greed* – for lack of a better word – is good. Greed is right. Greed works. Greed clarifies, cuts through and captures the essence of the evolutionary spirit. Greed, in all of its forms – greed for life, for money, for love, knowledge – has marked the upward surge of mankind.[2]

It was a movie of its time: Hollywood was nervous about the 1980s enthusiasm for the market. In the same way that Charles Dickens had provided a damning critique of the legal system and business in *Bleak House* in the middle of the nineteenth century, *Wall Street* articulated a comparable critique of free market economics for the twentieth century. Both *Wall Street* and *Bleak House* see business as fundamentally opposed to ethics.

The genius that articulated the case against business and capitalism most clearly was, of course, Karl Marx (1818–83). His best work was written in London, where he lived from 1849 onwards (the London of Charles Dickens's *Bleak House*). Influenced as a young man by the thought of Hegel, he argued that the forces that shape history are the key to understanding human life and progress. However, unlike Hegel, history was not being shaped by ideas but rather by economics. The economic relationships between people shape human behavior; and most ideas (e.g. law, religious, philosophical) in any particular society will reflect the economic arrangements between people.

Contrary to popular perception, Marx did see the positive side to capitalism. As feudalism collided with industrialization, it was capitalism which was the synthesis of the two. Capitalism emerged as the creative way forward out of the entrenched battle between medieval feudal society and the dynamic forces of industrialization. However, capitalism, argued Marx, was built on a fundamental injustice. His theory of surplus value identified the gap between the amount that the laborer gets paid and the value of the laborer's work. So when a person starts work at a factory at 9 am in the morning, she has probably earned her day's salary by 10 am. For the next few hours, she might be covering the cost of the materials and infrastructure that enables her to work. However, for the last five hours, she isn't getting paid for her labor. This is the surplus value. Instead the bourgeoisie (the capitalist) will be claiming this as "profit" and living the good life off the back of his exploited workforce.

Since the 1989 Eastern European Revolution, Marx has gone out of fashion.

However, let us concede that there are insights here. He is, surely, right in stressing the significance of economic relationships on society. Mrs Alexander, the famous hymn writer, included in her original composition of "All things bright and beautiful" this verse:

> The rich man in his castle,
> The poor man at his gate,
> God made them high and lowly,
> And ordered their estate.

This theology of divinely ordained places in society clearly serves the interests of the rich and powerful. Marx is right to challenge us and suggest that economics rather than God is behind such a theology. He is also right to insist that a "just wage" is a necessary obligation of a successful company. The workforce should enjoy and share in the economic benefits of success.

However, while conceding these insights, his negative view of the entrepreneur who takes the risk with his own capital is mistaken. The challenge of business is to satisfy the needs of society. Identifying those needs, producing your service or product, and informing everyone of your service or product are difficult challenges. There is no guarantee of success. Capitalism does indeed reward the risk-taker, but that is necessary otherwise no one will take the risk.

The other problem with Marx is that he has distorted the history of business. Capitalism actually depends on ethics; and it has its roots in an ethical worldview. The achievement of Max Weber, the brilliant German sociologist, was to demonstrate this.

The ethical roots of business

The truth is that historically business only flourishes in an ethical environment. It was Max Weber (1864–1920) who made the case that capitalism was a child of Calvinism. Marx was wrong to assume that ideas have no impact on history. Weber's argument starts from the obvious question: why did the factors that generate capitalism coincide in northern Europe in the seventeenth century? Weber's answer was that the Reformation had given birth to a distinctive attitude to wealth creation. It started in the work of Martin Luther who insisted that the term "vocation" should not be applied exclusively to those "called" into the priesthood or to a holy order. Instead all Christians have a vocation: wherever God had placed a person – from garbage collection to sporting star – was his or her vocation. Therefore that work should be done to the "glory of God" with as much energy and commitment as one can muster. John Calvin then came along and explained that the only way one can have confidence that one is part of the chosen is to ensure that the fruits of the Spirit (patience, perseverance, hard work, good stewardship, etc.) are reflected in one's life. This combination gave birth to an industry and focus that the world had never seen. The Protestant work ethic (make your labor as your gift to God and in so doing provide the evidence that you are chosen for redemption) became the defining quality of the West. Weber summarizes thus:

> One of the fundamental elements of the spirit of modern capitalism, and not only of that but of all modern culture: rational conduct on the basis of the idea of the calling, was born . . . from the spirit of Christian asceticism . . . The Puritan wanted to work in a calling; we are forced to do so. For when asceticism was carried out of the monastic cells into everyday life, and began to dominate worldly morality, it did its part in building the tremendous cosmos of the modern economic order.'[3]

Weber's thesis has provoked an entire industry of commentary and analysis. And it is easy to challenge the details. It is not clear, for example, that his description of Calvinism is entirely right. However, with the exception of Marxist commentators, the idea that capitalism depended (and continues to depend) on a certain set of ethical dispositions has been accepted.

Upon reflection, this is not surprising. Capitalism needs the "rule of law." It needs a strong judicial framework to ensure that trade agreements are observed. So many agreements assume "trust." I walk into a restaurant and consume a delightful meal; the owner of the restaurant needs to assume that I will pay for the meal that I have just consumed. If a significant minority of the customers in restaurants refused to pay for the meal, then it would not be long before restaurants ceased to exist. Alternatively if the restaurant insists on providing low quality yet very expensive meals, then they may make dramatic profits in the short term but will cease trading within a year. The long-term viability of a business needs to create a customer base of people who appreciate and trust the product.

The great and successful businesses are the law-abiding and ethical ones. The picture of all entrepreneurs cutting every cost to create wealth is false. Francis Fukuyama has made the case convincingly. In his impressive study *Trust*, he demonstrates the importance of social capital (of which trust is the key indicator) and spontaneous sociability as the necessary and key factors in economic success. Trust, he explains, "is the expectation that arises within a community of regular, honest, and cooperative behavior, based on commonly shared norms, on the part of other members of that community."[4] Social capital, then, "is a capability that arises from the prevalence of trust in a society or in certain parts of it."[5] And the third key term – spontaneous sociability is a subset of social capital . . . The most useful kind of social capital is often not the ability to work under the authority of a traditional community or group, but the capacity to form new associations and to cooperate within the terms of reference they establish . . . Spontaneous sociability, moreover, refers to that wide range of intermediate communities distinct from the family or those deliberately established by governments.[6]

Fukuyama is stressing the importance of the culture underpinning economic activity. And ideally a strong economy needs a culture of trust, underpinned by strong organizations and associations in between the individual and the government (organizations such as churches or voluntary societies), which Edmund Burke called the "little platoons." The argument of Fukuyama's book is that "Japan, Germany, and the United States became the world's leading industrial powers in large part because they had healthy endowments of social capital and spontaneous sociability."[7] So then the point is that the prosperous parts of the world have a strong ethical framework in which to operate. Japan, for example, had centuries of Confucian ethical insights on which to build; and the United States had the combination of a strong tradition of non-governmental association that made the creation of large corporations a key to its success.

At this point someone might object: what about Enron? Enron was a vast company that submitted fraudulent accounting records, which distorted the share price. When it all turned sour, the fall of the company was swift. Only the senior managers anticipated this decline and sold their Enron shares; those who were not privy to the details about the extent of the company's problems (much of the workforce) not only lost their income but also their savings.

Enron is a major scandal. It was probably a significant factor in the US recession of 2002. However, it is worth noting the following. Its unethical practices were not, in the end, good business. Furthermore the free press and the regulative system did, belatedly, catch up with Enron corruption. And finally, there is an entirely appropriate campaign to ensure that such corruption does not happen again. Even Enron illustrates the importance of, and need for, business ethics.

Basic business ethics

Once one sees that business ethics has all to do with good business, then many of the basics are easy to grasp. The first is that one must have a good product or a good service. To create a child's toy that is going to damage the child or to set oneself up as an electrician with no qualifications is both unethical and bad business. To sell a shoddy toy once is no achievement. To succeed one needs to sell toys over and over again. The kids network needs to get excited about your toy; and the manufacturer needs the admiration of the parents. It is important not to mix up the "scam" with "business." A scam is a one-off fraudulent activity that operates with the goal of robbing another person; business is in for the long haul.

The second principle is that it is necessary to create a well managed, highly motivated workforce. The success of a business depends on the workforce. People are expensive to hire (costs include advertising, staff time in interviewing and training) and fire (costs include observing legal practice, severance pay, staff morale, and management supervision). Therefore it is good business sense to recruit the right people and do everything one can to enable them to work effectively.

Keeping people occupied in a satisfying and interesting job is a difficult task. Employers can easily forget how long a work week is – in most cases at least 35 hours; it is amazing the number of employees who have insufficient to do. Conversely, it is also easy to forget that it takes time for a person to learn how to do a certain task. And it is possible for a significant percentage of a week to disappear on learning that task. Time management skills require both good supervision and good judgment on the part of the employee. Staff development is also important. No one wants to do precisely the same job for 20 years. Everyone wants a sense that one is progressing. Therefore it is not a "waste" of company money to encourage a workforce to improve their skills. Internal promotion opportunities are good. Regular staff appraisals are now good business practice. Ensuring that at least once a year, the employee can sit with her line manager and discuss the achievements and difficulties of the position is a good process.

The insight that the employee matters is now accepted as good business practice. However, it is true that free market theory needs to catch up with this basic insight. Robert Solomon identifies the problem very clearly when he writes:

> In traditional free market theory, the employee's labour is itself just one more commodity, subject to the laws of supply and demand. But whereas one can sell at "firesale" prices or simply dispose of pins or parts of machinery that are no longer in demand, the employee is a human being, with very real needs and rights quite apart from his or her role in production or in the market. Cramped uncomfortable working space or long, gruelling hours for employees may reduce overhead or increase productivity, and paying subsistence wages to employees who for one reason or another cannot, dare not or do not know how to complain may increase profits, but such conditions and practices are now recognized by all but the most unreconstructed "Darwinian" to be highly unethical and legally inexcusable.[8]

Solomon is right to say that the attitude to these practices has changed significantly in the last 50 years. However, Solomon is a little too sanguine about the business advantage of such practices. It is true that there are certain groups where exploitation is very easy. The illegal immigrant, who is desperate for work, is in the perfect position to be saddled with long hours and low pay. However, a mobile workforce, which is increasingly well educated, will not tolerate such treatment. Therefore the gain in treating the employee badly is very short term and very limited. It is possible for a few weeks, perhaps months, to exploit an employee, but then the employee will start searching for another position and the company is left with a problem.

Two reasons for the changed balance of power between the employee and the employer have already been noted above. These are mobility of labor and education. Business demands a mobile labor force; and increasingly, the workforce is willing to be mobile. It is common for people to be willing to move, often vast distances, for the right job. An employee is no longer constrained in the way she might have been 50 years ago by the limitations of opportunities in a certain region. Business also increasingly demands an educated workforce. With technology largely displacing the traditional manual positions, the need now is for a workforce that is highly skilled. Skills involve education; and the educated will not tolerate crude exploitation.

The third principle is that the business should care for the appropriate stakeholders. The term "stakeholders" captures the range of obligations on a business. The stakeholders will vary from company to company. However, in many cases, the stakeholders will include: the public (after all that this the group it seeks to serve), the consumers (those who will actually benefit from the product or service), the region (the location in which one works), and the shareholders (those who have risked capital to make the company work).

Some commentators insist that the shareholders are the primary group that needs to be served. Milton Friedman in a famous article called "The Social Responsibility of Business Is to Increase Its Profits" argued against the concept of corporate social responsibility. Those who advocate such a concept, Friedman argued, are "unwitting puppets of the intellectual forces that have been undermining the basis of a free society."[9] Friedman cites the fiduciary responsibility of a company to maximize their profits for shareholders. Any expenditure elsewhere (e.g. to a charitable cause) is equivalent to theft from the shareholders.

Friedman was writing in the 1970s and there is already a very dated feel to the arguments. The success of the company does depend in part on the success of the region in which the company works. Charitable giving to alleviate difficult social problems can help the region survive and thrive. In so doing, the public perception of the company is helped; and the employees benefit from being in a more desirable region. Stakeholder language has made companies more aware of the fragile nature of the social ecology. (Social ecology draws a helpful analogy with nature: in the same way that humans must learn to live in harmony with nature – ecology, so humans need to live in harmony with each other – social ecology.) Robert Bellah, Richard Madsen, William Sullivan, Ann Swidler, and Steven Tipton in their masterful study *Habits of the Heart* put the problem of social ecology like this:

> Today, social ecology is damaged not only by war, genocide, and polit-
> ical repression, but also by the destruction of the fragile ties that bind
> human beings to one another, leaving them frightened and alone. It has
> been evident for some time that unless we begin to repair the damage
> to our social ecology, we will destroy ourselves long before natural eco-
> logical disaster has time to be realized.[10]

Business has a major interest in social ecology. As Fukuyama has already shown us earlier on in this chapter, capitalism clearly depends on a strong social ecol-ogy. People need to be able to trust the basic social structures. For banking to succeed, for example, trust is essential; all banks presume that those who deposit savings with them will not all try to withdraw those savings on the same day. It enables the bank to lend money and thereby pay expenses and earn the interest that is paid to the saver. Supporting the region with chari-table giving is a small way in which a business can contribute to the region's social ecology. It recognizes that the region is a stakeholder to whom a com-pany is responsible.

We have already touched on some of the other stakeholders (e.g. the employee) earlier in this chapter. However, this movement from a preoccupa-tion with the shareholders to the recognition that there are many stakeholders that need attention is good business. Companies sensitive to the range of inter-ested parties are much more successful than those who confine their attention simply to the shareholders.

At the macro level described above, the obligations on businesses are increas-ingly clear. However, at the micro level (the level of the employer and the employee), there are a different set of ethical dilemmas and decisions. It is to this level that we turn to next.

Difficult ethical questions

The chapter started with a micro dilemma. If you had been working at Ford during the late 1960s and early 1970s, then would you have a moral obligation to "whistle-blow"? This is one example of the sorts of difficulties that the work place can pose. It is mirrored, to a lesser extent, a thousand times a day in offices

111

and factories around the world. The work place does indeed generate a whole host of difficult ethical questions.

The term "whistle-blowing" is used to describe a range of different activities where an employee attempts to hold either an individual or the company to account. Richard De George helpfully distinguishes between different types of whistle-blowing. He starts by distinguishing between internal and external whistle-blowing. The most common form of internal whistle-blowing is probably "personal whistle-blowing." This is when "an offence is not against the organization or system, but against oneself."[11] The classic example is sexual harassment. Indecent, suggestive, flirtatious behavior is very unpleasant for the victim. To report the culprit to the line manager is often the only way to make it clear that such behavior is unacceptable. The other form of internal whistle-blowing is "impersonal whistle-blowing"; this is when you are concerned about the behavior of others in the company, e.g. you report to the company that fraudulent expense claims are being made by the sales team.

Good companies should have established processes to cope with internal whistle-blowing. Companies want to provide healthy and honest environments in which people can enjoy their work. Encouraging a culture of "whistle-blowing" can be a good internal check on improper behavior. The best way to ensure a healthy work environment is to create a culture that makes the alternative unacceptable. Clear company expectations coupled with the commendation of appropriate internal whistle-blowing are effective ways to do this.

External whistle-blowing, however, is harder and more serious. In the case of Ford anyone expressing displeasure with the decision about the Pinto might well be jeopardizing his or her position. De George divides external whistle-blowing into two types: governmental whistle-blowing and non-governmental whistle-blowing. With the former, the organizations are part of the government structure (civil service). So, for example, it is governmental whistle-blowing when a police officer reports evidence of corruption to the governmental authorities. Although this can be difficult, De George thinks that non-governmental whistle-blowing is even harder. This is when you are working for a private company and decide to go to the authorities or the media. A key issue here is under what circumstances are you morally obliged to do that?

Generally, companies are entitled to expect loyalty from their employees. Many companies have established disciplinary procedures for those employees who decide to make an internal argument public. In a battle over budget priorities in a university, for example, Junior faculty might be tempted to encourage the local press to write a story on the "President's extravagant travel plans" as a strategy to put pressure on the administration to shift priorities. Such strategies are often damaging to the public perception of an institution and tend to undermine the established due process of budget setting. When there are appropriate processes for the participation in the decision-making of an institution, it is wrong to distort that process by "planting a story" in the local media. Good companies have a process of consultation and review; the company is entitled to expect that those processes should be used and the results tolerated. To go public with an internal argument is an act of disloyalty and perhaps disobedience that might provoke certain disciplinary procedures.

However, if one had been working for Ford in the early 1970s and had knowledge of the lethal potential of the Pinto, then one might feel that there is an obligation to "go public." De George argues that there are two conditions for such whistle-blowing. The first is: "The whistle-blower must have, or have accessible, documented evidence that would convince a reasonable, impartial observer that one's view of the situation is correct, and that the company's product or practice poses a serious and likely danger to the public or to the user of the product."[12] The second is: "The employee must have good reasons to believe that by going public the necessary changes will be brought about. The chance of being successful must be worth the risk one takes and the danger to which one is exposed."[13] De George's conditions are a whistle-blowing variation on just war conditions, which we will look at in chapter 12. You need a just cause, evidence that would persuade others, and confidence that you will succeed.

Whistle-blowing is probably the most acute ethical dilemma you might face at work, which is fortunately fairly rare. Issues such as "the awkward employee" or "the unreasonable manager" arise more often. Keeping a workplace harmonious is a challenge both for the manager and the employee. Good business practice has established certain key principles that help such harmony.

The first is institutional transparency. Everyone assumes that power is located in a group of which they are not a part. The hierarchy committing to transparency and consultation can alleviate this. If a group does not understand the impending budget crisis, then it is not surprising that they resent the elimination of certain perks and privileges. If the group is informed that there is a short-term budget squeeze, then the temporary removal of such perks and privileges becomes a small contribution to keeping their monthly income. The combination of paternalism (protecting others as a parent would) or elitism (assuming that only the senior can cope with the information) is lethal to workforce morale. It can create resentment and lead to a rapidly deteriorating workplace.

The second is the need for good and consistent practice. Resentment rapidly emerges if there is evidence that some are privileged over others. A personnel office in a company tries to ensure that all employees in like situations are treated in the same way. The idiosyncratic manager who insists on treating her staff differently can create significant workplace difficulties.

The third is to think "long term." Many of us are working in institutions that have significant histories. Others in the past had the idea and took the risk to create the company that provides the incomes of the current workforce. One duty that is incumbent on us all is to do our best to ensure that we pass the business or organization on to future generations. This is the vocation of institutional care.[14] Thinking long term should not necessarily imply a structural or fiscal conservatism. Insufficient change or risk-taking can often be as damaging as too much. The marketplace changes rapidly; and the obligation of a good company is to be always on the cutting edge. Imagination and anticipation are as important as a balanced budget. Leadership, of course, has a particular responsibility in this regard. But the obligation does apply to everyone in the institution. Organizations need everyone to play their part. Baring's Bank was 233 years old when it was forced into bankruptcy in 1995. The Board of Executives were not aware of the investment decisions and risks being taken by Nick Leeson and his immediate line managers that finally led to the downfall of the company. The Board was, of course, still responsible: it is an obligation of the Board to have systems in place that prevent such institutional vulnerability. However, the point is clear: the responsibility to take what we have been given (an organization or business), and ensure that we work sufficiently well so that it is available for others who come after us, is a responsibility that everyone in an organization should share.

Business and marketing

Thus far we have looked at the basics of business ethics and some of the ethical difficulties that the workplace can generate. In this concluding section of this chapter, we shall examine briefly some of the ethical issues surrounding business and marketing.

You can have an excellent product and lead an ethically sensitive company, but all of this will fail unless those who need your product are informed. Advertising – the most common form of promotion – might annoy, but without it a company is doomed to failure. Advertising is the essential lubricant of the market economy.

The temptation is for a company to opt for "any" strategy that might create a sale. The more pressure a salesperson can employ is justified, so the argument goes, by the sale that increases the company's profits. However, as this chapter has attempted to show in other respects, unethical advertising does not work in the long run. The classic illustration is "timeshare." Timeshare is a good and imaginative product; it promises high quality accommodation for your vacation: you buy a week in a timeshare complex and your accommodation is guaranteed. However, owing to the now notorious strategies of salespeople to get your sale, the whole industry has had to work extremely hard to survive, let alone flourish. The suspicion of timeshare has not only made it harder to sell the weeks in a complex, but it has also led to a range of intergovernmental regulations and the whole "brand image" was damaged. Unethical selling does not benefit the company in the long run.

Advertising can take two forms. The first is "service or product sales"; this is where a particular service or product is sold. The second is "brand advertising"; this is where one is creating a certain set of associations for a product that stimulates interest and loyalty. For the first, the important expectations are that the adverts should be "decent" and "truthful." Adverts should be decent because, by definition, an advert is intrusive. One has rarely been asked beforehand whether one wants to look at this advert. The flyer falls out of the newspaper; or the commercial appears on television; or your eye is drawn to the picture as you turn over the pages of a newspaper in quest for a particular news story. There is no reason why anyone should have to tolerate a deeply offensive advert. Naturally what offends is relative. The practice in the UK is that the Advertising Standards Authority (ASA)[15] insists that "relevance" is a key factor. A naked woman draped across a car is understandably offensive (as well as very dated); the semi-naked woman for underwear or toiletries is relevant. The market requires that advertisers must be able to inform in an attractive and interesting way and to forbid the portrayal of any woman in an advert would violate this convention.

Truthfulness is important because the key justification for advertising is that it informs; and an informed consumer needs accurate and truthful data. One can mislead in a multitude of ways: credit can be sold with a focus on the monthly repayments and not on the total amount of interest paid over the lifetime of the loan, or the promise of a "sale" price when the product is hardly ever available at a different price. Both the ASA in the UK and the Federal Trade Commission in the US are extremely critical of such practices. Adverts must be "truthful" and all deception (by omission or by being misleading) is condemned.

A famous example of this was the May D&F Case in the US. The Federal Trade Commission 1964 Guides Against Deceptive Pricing had insisted that an item can only be marked as "on sale" provided the product had been at an original higher price "for a reasonably substantial period of time . . . honestly and in good faith and not for the purpose of establishing a fictitious higher price."[16] May Department Stores, Inc., in June 1989, was charged on three counts, namely printing inflated prices on the product tickets, inflating prices to make the markdowns look larger, and keeping certain product lines on continuous sale. De George explains the outcome:

> May D&F claimed that its policy was to offer an item for sale for at least ten days at the beginning of each six-month period. That would establish the original price. Few items sold at that price, which was usually not competitive. The store would then place the item on sale for the remaining 170 days, sometimes offering special short-term reductions from that price. At the end of the 180-day cycle, it would raise the price

to the original price for ten days and then repeat the cycle . . . On June 28, 1990, Judge Larry J. Naves of the Colorado State Court decided the case against May D&F, stating that "The clear expectation of May D&F was to sell all or practically all merchandise at its 'sale' price." He fined the company $8,000.[17]

This is a correct ruling. A significant factor in purchasing a product is the price. The perceived value of the product is important. To distort that impression by a particular pricing strategy, is unethical.

Brand advertising is perceived as less unethical. But the Roman Catholic Pontifical Council for Social Communications on February 25, 1997 issued *Ethics in Advertising*, which was very critical of brand advertising. The report explains:

> The practice of "brand"-related advertising can raise serious problems. Often there are only negligible differences among similar products of different brands, and advertising may attempt to move people to act on the basis of irrational motives ("brand loyalty," status, fashion, "sex appeal," etc.) instead of presenting differences in product quality and price as bases for rational choice.[18]

Brand advertising provokes suspicion because it seems to be creating inappropriate associations for the consumer. So a shirt from a major store becomes linked with the beautiful woman and the fast car, although in reality these associations are unlikely to exist.

However, at this point we can push our ethical expectations too far. Given that the market is about competition and given that competition will inevitably lead to different companies producing similar products, then brand advertising is an inevitable part of the market. Take, for example, the proliferation of cola cans: along with Pepsi Cola and Coca Cola, we have numerous other supermarket brands. As a result of this competition, we can buy cheaper cola. And although price will be one factor in the advertising, it cannot be the only one. To sustain the competition, the market needs the "brand advertising" based on non-rational factors. Unless there is a degree of image association, for example, "Coca-Cola means life," then the choice will cease. In mature economies, such as the UK and the US, there is very little evidence that this "brand advertising" creates any problems for the consumer.

Conclusion

Most of us spend more hours at work than in any other category of activity, including sleep. Learning to be "ethical" at work should not be viewed as a potential problem for business success but rather a necessary condition for it. Ethical reflection about one's work is often the application of just plain good common sense.

As we saw with Max Weber's argument, the realization of this is a return to the conditions that gave birth to capitalism. A condition of the success of the market is a strong legal environment and a set of ethical dispositions shaping both consumers and businesses. Marx predicted the inevitable demise of capitalism because of the growing inequalities between the rich and poor. However, business rapidly spotted that a well paid workforce is not only a better-motivated workforce but also in turn it provides more affluent consumers who benefit from the fruits of business. The real risk to business is not the Marxist vision, but the danger of some businesses believing that the short-term unethical gain is worth it. If other businesses opt for the Enron strategy of misleading audit reports to inflate share price, then the audit reports will cease to be trusted and the stock market will stop attracting new investors. The survival of business and free market capitalism depends on the triumph of ethics in business.

Notes

1 This case study is adapted from Richard T. De George's description in Richard T. De George, *Business Ethics*, fourth edition (Englewood Cliffs, NJ: Prentice Hall 1995) pp. 221–2.

2 The speech is helpfully reproduced at http://www.americanrhetoric.com/MovieSpeeches/moviespeechwallstreet.html

3 Max Weber, *The Protestant Ethic and the Spirit of Capitalism*, translated by Talcott Parsons, foreword by R. H. Tawney (New York: Charles Scribner's Sons 1930) pp. 180–1.

4 Francis Fukuyama, *Trust* (New York: Free Press Paperbacks 1995) p. 26.

5 Ibid.

6 Ibid. p. 27.

7 Ibid. p. 150.

8 Robert N. Solomon, "Business Ethics" in Peter Singer (ed.) *A Companion to Ethics* (Oxford: Blackwell Publishing 1991) pp. 362–3.

9 Milton Friedman, "The Social Responsibility of Business Is to Increase Its Profits," *The New York Times* September 13, 1970 as discussed in Robert Solomon, "Business Ethics" in Peter Singer (ed.) *A Companion to Ethics*, p. 360.

10 R. N. Bellah, R. Madsen, W. M. Sullivan, A. Swidler, and S. M. Tipton, *Habits of the Heart* (Los Angeles, CA: University of California Press 1985) p. 284.

11 Robert T. De George, *Business Ethics*, p. 223.

12 Ibid. p. 235.

13 Ibid. p. 236.

14 I used this expression originally in Ian S. Markham, "The Reconstruction of Theology" in John Elford (ed.) *The Foundation of Hope* (Liverpool: Liverpool University Press 2003) p. 110.

15 As a former council member and Director of the Advertising Standards Authority in the UK, perhaps I might be permitted to commend this organization. The fact that it is funded by the advertising industry, whose members sign up to a demanding code and then accept the rulings of the ASA is a credit to the advertising industry in the UK. Along with decent and truthful, the code also requires that adverts are legal and honest.

16 FTC 1964 Guides Against Deceptive Pricing as quoted in Richard T. De George, *Business Ethics*, p. 243. This summary is taken from De George's discussion of the case.

17 Ibid. p. 244.

18 *Ethics in Advertising* – Pontifical Council for Social Communications, paragraph 10. I discuss this report in detail in Ian S. Markham, *A Theology of Engagement* (Oxford: Blackwell Publishing 2003). Aspects of what follows are taken from that discussion.

11

Dilemmas in medicine

Thought exercise

"You wake up in the morning and find yourself back to back in bed with an unconscious violinist. A famous unconscious violinist. He has been found to have a fatal kidney ailment, and the Society of Music Lovers has canvassed all the available medical records and found that you alone have the right blood type to help. They have therefore kidnapped you, and last night the violinist's circulatory system was plugged into yours, so that your kidneys can be used to extract poisons from his blood as well as your own. The director of the hospital now tells you, 'Look, we're sorry the Society of Music Lovers did this to you – we would never have permitted it if we had known. But still, they did it, and the violinist now is plugged into you. To unplug you would be to kill him. But never mind, it's only for nine months. By then he will have recovered from his ailment, and can safely be unplugged from you.' Is it morally incumbent on you to accede to this situation? No doubt it would be very nice of you if you did, a great kindness. But do you *have* to accede to it?"[1]

The world of medicine is beset with dilemmas. With the vast and exciting developments in technology, the medical options facing the human race are considerable. Unlike our ancestors, we can tell with confidence the sex of the baby while the child is in the womb; our genetic testing can provide a probability assessment of Alzheimer's in old age; and we place a 26-week embryo into an incubator and enable that child to live.

We are going to start our exploration of these dilemmas in medicine with two of the most socially contentious. The first is abortion (this is the decision to terminate a pregnancy); and the second is euthanasia (this is the medical termination of a person's life in response to a request from that person). We will then move on to consider some of the dilemmas posed by the discoveries that we are making in the Human Genome project.

Abortion

Inevitably one important battleground for ethical debate is the law. Both in the United States and the United Kingdom, the debates over abortion have been heated. Although both countries permit abortion, the reasons for the permission are very different. And the contrast reveals much about the relationship of law to ethics. So this section will start with a brief summary of the current legal position over abortion in these two countries.

In the United States, it was Jane Roe (now Norma McCorvey) in 1973 who took her case to the Supreme Court. The issue was simple: Texas law prohibited abortions, unless an abortion was the only way to save the mother's life. The Fourteenth Amendment to the Constitution provides protection of the citizen from undue influence of the state in a person's private affairs. It reads:

> No State shall make or enforce any law which shall abridge the privileges or immunities of citizens of the United States; nor shall any State deprive any person of life, liberty, or property, without due process of law; nor deny to any person within its jurisdiction the equal protection of the laws.

This implies a "right to privacy" – a concept that the Supreme Court had already articulated in *Griswold v Connecticut*. It was on this basis that the Supreme Court determined that the states are not permitted to interfere with the private decision of a woman to have an abortion; instead, in the first trimester, at least, this is a private decision between the mother and her physician.

The Supreme Court did, however, recognize that the states did have an interest as the fetus passed the point of viability. Viability is the moment when the embryo can survive outside the womb (albeit with the help of medical technology). So it introduced three different spheres:

1 For the stage prior to approximately the end of the first trimester, the abortion decision and its effectuation must be left to the medical judgment of the pregnant woman's attending physician.
2 For the stage subsequent to approximately the end of the first trimester, the state, in promoting its interest in the health of the mother, may, if it chooses, regulate the abortion procedure in ways that are reasonably related to maternal health.
3 For the stage subsequent to viability, the state in promoting its interest in the potentiality of human life may, if it chooses, regulate, and even proscribe, abortion except where it is necessary, in appropriate medical judgment, for the preservation of the life or health of the mother.[2]

It does mean that for the first trimester the US permits "abortion on demand." The legal justification is grounded in the context of privacy: the court has ruled that the state has no interest in the medical discussions between a woman and her doctor during the early stages of pregnancy. It is only as the fetus grows that the state starts to have an interest and therefore limits the options for the woman.

In the UK, the legalization of abortion occurred earlier. It was Liberal Party Member of Parliament, David Steel, who pioneered the bill through parliament. He was fortunate in having a very sympathetic Labour Home Secretary – Roy Jenkins – who helped the bill past the many obstacles. In 1967 the Abortion Law passed. The approach and arguments contrast markedly with the approach in the United States.

The first major difference is that the Abortion Law in the UK retains the prohibition on Abortion. However, it then permits the abortion procedure, up until 28 weeks (this at the time was the age from which a fetus may survive outside the womb – the moment of viability) for the following reasons:

- The continuance of the pregnancy would involve risk to the life of the pregnant woman greater than if the pregnancy were terminated.
- The termination is necessary to prevent grave permanent injury to the physical or mental health of the pregnant woman.
- The continuance of the pregnancy would involve risk, greater than if the pregnancy were terminated, of injury to the physical or mental health of the pregnant woman.
- The continuance of the pregnancy would involve risk, greater than if the pregnancy were terminated, of injury to the physical or mental health of any existing children of the family of the pregnant woman.
- There is a substantial risk that if the child were born it would suffer from physical or mental abnormalities as to be seriously handicapped, or in emergency, certified by the operating practitioners as immediately necessary.
- To save the life of the pregnant woman.

Two doctors were required to give consent to the procedure. Although technically this is not abortion on demand, the provisions that permit an abortion if it can be shown there is a risk of injury to the physical or mental health of the pregnant mother or any existing children does mean that a doctor somewhere will agree to abort the fetus.

In 1990 the Abortion Law was amended. By this time it was clear that medical technology had made it possible to keep a fetus alive at 24 weeks. So the Human Fertilization and Embryology Act reduced the upper limit for abortion down from 28 weeks to 24.

In the UK the argument is not grounded in a constitutional entitlement to privacy. Indeed the opposite is true: the woman must persuade two doctors that she meets one of the conditions for an exception to the legal prohibition to abortion. One further issue is worth noting: American abortion law is very preoccupied with the relationship of the federal law to the laws in the individual states. A crucial issue is whether each state is allowed to frame a particular law which will apply in that state. One might presume that this is not an issue in the UK. However, Northern Ireland was always exempt from the provisions of the 1967 Abortion Law. And with the introduction of devolution to Scotland and Wales, this might well become an increasing issue in the Kingdom.

The net result is that both in the United States and in the United Kingdom, some form of abortion is permitted. We now turn to the ethical debate underpinning the law: is it ethically right to permit abortion?

Arguments for the legalization of abortion

The major argument for the abortion option is that the difficult decisions about "bringing a child into the world" reside with the potential mother of that child. It is, in short, a woman's right to choose. This is the point behind Judith Jarvis Thomson's famous thought exercise. The violinist represents the fetus; so Thomson is conceding, for the purposes of the thought exercise, that the fetus is a human being. She writes,

> I am inclined to think . . . that we shall probably have to agree that the fetus has already become a human person well before birth. Indeed, it comes as a surprise when one first learns how early in its life it begins to acquire human characteristics. By the tenth week, for example, it already has a face, arms and legs, fingers and toes; it has internal organs, and brain activity is detectable.[3]

In this case the violinist was kidnapped (so perhaps the thought exercise is closer to rape than voluntary sexual intercourse); however, the point is that in terms of justice and rights, the violinist is not entitled to have his life protected by law. As Jarvis Thomson develops the argument, she insists that the justice and rights issue does not change even if the sexual activity is voluntary. So she illustrates with another thought exercise:

> If the room is stuffy, and I therefore open a window to air it, and a burglar climbs in, it would be absurd to say, "Ah, now he can stay, she's given him a right to the use of her house – for she is partially responsible for his presence there, having voluntarily done what enabled him to

get in, in full knowledge that there are such things as burglars, and that burglars burgle." It would be even more absurd to say this if I had had bars installed outside my windows, precisely to prevent burglars from getting in, and a burglar got in only because of a defect in the bars. It remains equally absurd if we imagine it is not a burglar who climbs in, but an innocent person who blunders or falls in.[4]

The culmination of the argument is that in terms of justice and rights the dependent life on the mother does not have an entitlement to life. However, a good Samaritan disposition (i.e. someone who is willing to inconvenience themselves to help others) might mean that the mother ought to carry the child to term. Jarvis Thomson writes,

> [W]hile I do argue that abortion is not impermissible, I do not argue that it is always permissible. There may be cases in which carrying the child to term requires only Minimally Decent Samaritanism of the mother, and this is a standard we must not fall below. I am inclined to think it a merit of my account that it does not give a general yes or a general no. It allows for and supports our sense that, for example, a sick and desperately frightened fourteen-year-old schoolgirl, pregnant due to rape, may of course choose abortion, and that any law which rules this out is an insane law. And it also allows for and supports our sense that in other cases resort to abortion is even positively indecent. It would be indecent in the woman to request an abortion, and indecent in a doctor to perform it, if she is in her seventh month, and wants the abortion just to avoid the nuisance of postponing a trip abroad.[5]

Linked to this argument that the decision should reside with the mother is the fact that the full impact of the pregnancy is felt by the mother. After all, it is the woman who will carry that child for nine months; and it is, almost always, the woman who will have the primary childcare responsibilities. Men are pretty good at providing the sperm (perhaps after a great party, induced by the excess of alcohol) but less good at sticking around as the sperm fertilizes the egg and grows into an embryo (let alone a child). The world is full of absent fathers.

Opponents of the so-called "right to life" lobby complain that this lobby is extremely concerned about the fetus but relatively indifferent to the child. Male priests, male legislators, male judges might collaborate to insist that the mother has the child; but the same legislators do not collaborate to ensure that the child then has her basic needs met so that she grows up into a healthy, well adjusted woman.

The second argument introduces an important distinction between a human

organism and a person. The Fourteenth Amendment of the United States Constitution reads: "nor shall any state deprive any person of life, liberty, or property."
Now does a small human organism of 12 days after conception (the point at
which twinning is no longer possible) really constitute a person? If one had to
sit down and list the qualities of a person (ignoring for the moment the abortion
debate) as opposed a pig, then the following might be important: the capacities
for language, relationship, moral judgment, and abstract thought. If these are
the qualities of a person, which are protected by the Fourteenth Amendment,
the argument goes, then the fetus is not a person and therefore not protected by
the Fourteenth Amendment. Michael Tooley in *Abortion and Infanticide* writes
that an entity "cannot have a right to continued existence unless he possesses
the concept of a subject of experiences, the concept of a temporal order, and the
concept of identity of things over time."[6] Now this does not mean that the fetus
is morally insignificant. It has the potential to become human. But, the argument
goes, it is morally acceptable for the woman to decide to abort the fetus if she
considers it necessary.

The third argument is that the alternative to legalized abortion is the use of
"back-street" abortion operations. Where there is a need, one can be pretty sure
that someone will step forward to provide the service. In a situation where abortions are illegal, the operators stepping forward are not reputable with the result
of a potential risk to the mother's life.

The fourth argument is linked with the argument over euthanasia. It is simply
this: where there is no obvious harm to other living human beings, then the law
should permit options for those who want to avail themselves of them. Even if
a majority morally disapproves of an action, this is not a good reason to make
it illegal. Divorce, for example, might be tragic and sad, but the judiciary should
not be making the decisions for the couples that want to avail themselves of this
option. So in a similar way, those opposed to abortion are not being required to
have an abortion. The argument goes that the purpose of law is to make available to those who feel (after appropriate counseling and support) that it is the only
way forward. The law should not be used to impose a certain moral approach
on everyone.

Arguments against the legalization of abortion

The major argument against abortion is that we are killing a weak, powerless
human being who ought to be protected by law. The status of the embryo is a
key issue in this debate. When does human life begin?

The traditional Christian view is that life starts some 40 to 80 days after fertilization (fertilization is when the egg meets the sperm). Augustine, the Bishop
of Hippo (354–430), believed that the soul was implanted in the womb after 40

days for men and 80 days for women. However, a key difficulty in this debate is that there is a seamless link between the child that appears and the fertilized egg. Everyone would agree that the 9-month embryo is identical with the baby. And as we move back through the months there is no moment that becomes the "defining moment." *Roe v Wade* makes much of "viability" (i.e. the moment the embryo can survive outside the womb). But this is endlessly moving back in time as technology advances. And given that many people need technology at some time or other to keep them alive (e.g. after a major car accident) then it would be wrong to deny the technical possibility to sustain human life to an embryo. It does seem odd to intentionally kill a life (e.g. a 20-week fetus) which in 10 years time, perhaps, technology will be able to save.

It is for this reason that in the nineteenth century the Roman Catholic Church took the view that life starts at conception. Once the fertilized egg exists, there is a human life, which in the normal course of events will grow into a child. If life starts at conception, then it is an act of murder to take another human life.

The purpose of law is to protect those who are most powerless. Children need many legal protections (for example, from sexual or physical abuse); a baby needs protection, along with the unborn child. The eradication of a human life simply because the 17-year-old wants to go to college or the mother already has three existing children significantly reduces the value of human life.

There is an obvious irony in modern political discourse. We are increasingly sensitive to the rights of all people. The campaign for "civil rights" from women to African Americans has been a result of growing moral sensitivity. Yet the growth in the language of rights has run parallel with a willingness to take and eliminate certain groups. Pope John Paul II draws attention to this irony in his encyclical *Evangelium Vitae* (1995). He writes,

> On the one hand, the various declarations of human rights and the many initiatives inspired by these declarations show that at the global level there is a growing moral sensitivity more alert to acknowledging the value and dignity of every individual as a human being, without any distinction of race, nationality, religion, political opinion or social class. On the other hand, these noble proclamations are unfortunately contradicted by a tragic repudiation of them in practice. This denial is still more distressing, indeed more scandalous, precisely because it is occurring in a society which makes the affirmation and protection of human rights its primary objective and its boast. How can these repeated affirmations of principle be reconciled with the continual increase and widespread justification of attacks on human life? How can we reconcile these declarations with the refusal to accept those who are weak and needy, or elderly, or those who have just been conceived? These

attacks go directly against respect for life, and they represent a direct threat to the entire culture of human rights.[7]

The Pope is identifying a contradiction. The language of rights implies an entitlement regardless of your power or perceived worth in society. Yet so much discussion about human life at the start, where we assume that it would be better for the unborn child if the child were dead; at the end, where we imagine that the elderly have nothing to give human community and it would be more sensible if they were gently put to sleep; for the disabled and handicapped, where we assume that their lives are a drain on our limited resources; and even for the poor and uneducated, where talk of eugenics is quietly whispered: in all these respects, the Pope is worried that there is a potentially dangerous contradiction in our modern discourse.[8]

This argument from Pope John Paul II illustrates that there is a cluster of concerns underpinning the lobby against abortion. The first and main concern is the rights of the unborn child; if this is a person, then the woman is simply not entitled to decide to terminate that life. The second is what the Pope calls "the culture of death." We are becoming a culture in which "convenience" is considered more important than "respect for life." Where the fetus is endangering the life of the mother then perhaps as a consequence of protecting the mother's life, one may have to sacrifice the life of the unborn child. But where the 17-year-old will be inconvenienced by a few more years at home rather than going to college or where society will be inconvenienced by being obligated to provide sufficient social support for a poor struggling family cope with an additional child, "respect for life" demands that we cope with the inconvenience.

Additional arguments often emerge in the literature. The psychological damage of abortion (as the body often continues to prepare for the arrival of a child) is a problem, which so-called "pro-life" advocates insist is not often mentioned. The slippery slope argument is often brought forward. If you are willing to abort, sometimes very late in the pregnancy, then it will not be long before we have infanticide. If there is a social sense that the fetus should not have lived, then why should the baby? To counter the argument that society should permit the option for those who want it, the lobby responds that law cannot permit the option of murder. It is a little like the argument from slave owners who insisted that a legal option for slavery does not compel everyone in society to have slaves. This is, of course, true, but if slavery is an evil, then the law should not provide legal options for evil acts.

To conclude this discussion on abortion, it might be helpful to anticipate the likely future trends. Although in both the United States and the United Kingdom there are significant lobbies that want to repeal the abortion law, they are unlikely to succeed. It looks like the legal option is here to stay. However there are continuing pressures to control the numbers of abortions and perhaps reduce the number which are in the third trimester. For most people, abortion should remain a last resort; one that is invoked only when all other options are exhausted.

Euthanasia

The word "euthanasia" comes from the Greek, which means literally "good death" or "dying well." There are two crucial distinctions that need to be made right at the outset when thinking about euthanasia. The first is the distinction between "voluntary" and "non-voluntary." Here the difference is whether the person, who is the possible subject for euthanasia, is competent to make the decision herself. If, for example, Ann is in the terminal stages of cancer and asks the doctor to end her life, then that would be voluntary euthanasia. If, however, Ann was a victim of a traffic accident who is in a persistent vegetative state (the stage often after a coma, when a person has lost cognitive neurological function, which will be discussed further in a moment), then a doctor's decision to terminate care would be non-voluntary euthanasia. The second distinction which is important is the difference between active and passive euthanasia. Active euthanasia involves a "direct action," for example, by using a lethal injection; passive euthanasia is the decision to withdraw or withhold medical treatment.

Now there are many different ways into the euthanasia debate. Let us start with the case of Theresa (Terri) Marie Schiavo (1963–2005), which came to the attention of the American public in March 2005. In February 1990, Terri Schiavo's heart stopped; she suffered brain damage owing to oxygen deprivation. At this point the majority of neurologists believe she was in a persistent vegetative state. This means that while the brain stem might be operating (and therefore Terri Schiavo may have her eyes open and seem aware), the higher brain is not operative. To complicate matters further, there have been four patients who have been diagnosed with persistent vegetative state who have recovered within two years after the diagnosis. At the point the courts intervened (at the request of her husband), there had been no significant change in her condition for 12 years. The legal issue was whether the feeding tube, which provides basic food and water straight into her stomach, should be removed. The Supreme Court has already ruled that a patient has a right to refuse medical treatment and food. So her husband argued that it would have been Terri's wish for her feeding tube to be removed; the parents argued that it was still possible she might recover (they contested the diagnosis) and that it would be wrong to kill her.

In an unprecedented move, Congress, the Senate, and the President of the United States got involved. They enacted legislation, by meeting over the weekend (March 19–20, 2005), which permitted the federal courts to consider and review the legal issues in this case. The assumption here is that issues relating to an individual are determined by the State courts not the federal ones. However, the federal courts concurred with the Florida state courts. On March 18, 2005, the feeding tube was removed. On March 31, 2005, Terri Schiavo died.

Embedded in this tragic case are many complex issues. First, we have the problem of diagnosis. Medicine is an approximate science: the subject works by eliminating options and then offering the diagnosis which is most likely to be true. Second, there are the debates around "living wills" (or advanced directives). The Roman Catholic Church is very nervous about the practice of "ticking boxes" to exclude certain treatments and certainly holds the view that "feeding" through a tube is not a medical treatment. Third, there is the role of the law. Many ethical issues end up in the courts; and in this case, the legislators got involved. Finally, many people looked at the whole episode and decided that they definitely didn't want to get into a position where they are attached to a machine for 15 years. This opens up the debate about physician-assisted suicide or voluntary euthanasia.

For the rest of this section, we shall concentrate on the last debate. But we do so recognizing that this is only a part of a wider set of issues that need thought and discussion.

The Voluntary Euthanasia Society (VES) in the United Kingdom wants legislation that permits "voluntary euthanasia" (i.e. a law that permits the terminally ill to ask a doctor to terminate their life). The campaign is confined to "mentally competent adult patients to have wider choice at the end of life."[9] There are four major arguments in favor of euthanasia.

The first is that patients should have complete control over their treatment. It is an appeal to "patient autonomy." Medicine is a very imprecise science: often prognosis is difficult and therefore the treatment is not obvious. For the pro-euthanasia lobby, the patient ought to be in control; the doctor should be the servant of the patient. Given the amazing advances in medical science, doctors have a vast array of technological and medical procedures that can keep life going almost indefinitely. Surely, the argument goes, the patient must be entitled at some stage to say "stop." In addition, we know that death may be accompanied with pain, so why shouldn't the patient have the option of deciding that he or she has had enough? Why should society insist that the patient must carry on? From this perspective it is viewed as part of the campaign for greater rights for patients.

The second argument is that it will prevent the current duplicitous practice of the medical profession and the secretive attempts of some to commit suicide or assist others to commit suicide. On November 15, 1998, *The Sunday Times* revealed that 15 percent of doctors admitted responding positively to a request from a patient to let them die. The VES claims:

UK law fails to prevent mercy killings and lonely, back street suicides. It fails to stop "death tourism," where people travel overseas to be helped to die. VES campaigns, always within the law, for a transparent legal framework to protect the vulnerable and provide guidance and support to doctors.[10]

Talk of "back-street suicides" is odd. The phrase is clearly intended to remind us of one of the key arguments used in favor of abortion. However, if it is a "suicide" without assistance, then of course that doesn't need to be (and rarely is) in a "back-street." The tragic lonely decision to take one's own life (whether from depression or physical illness) can be done from a bridge or in front of an underground train or from an overdose of medication. However, it is true that "death tourism" is becoming more widespread. Dignitas, for example, is a Swiss organization that can facilitate your death in a euthanasia-friendly country (such as The Netherlands or Belgium). So the argument goes: legislation that would permit voluntary euthanasia would prevent the unregulated doctor and death tourism.

The third argument is similar to the third argument in favor of abortion. In a free society, then the law should permit options for those who want to take advantage of them. VES is not arguing for involuntary euthanasia (that, they suggest, should be controlled by "living wills") but for euthanasia for those who are competent and able to ask for it. Why should those who think it wrong stop those who don't share their moral scruples?

The final argument is that we would save resources. We live in a world where medical demands are potentially unlimited. The death of those who want to die would save scarce medical resources. It seems very odd to insist that those who are terminally ill and want to die must continue to occupy a bed and use expensive drugs, when down the corridor in the same hospital might be a young child who needs the doctor's time and access to the same drugs.

Arguments against euthanasia

Most countries in the world are very hesitant about entrenching in law a legal option that one might get medical assistance to commit suicide, albeit under strict controls. The Netherlands has passed The Termination of Life on Request and Assisted Suicide (Review Procedures) Act, which came into force from April 2002. Five months later, the Assisted Dying Bill was implemented in Belgium. In Belgium the law permits a doctor to help an adult who is terminally ill (which must be confirmed by a second doctor), with unbearable suffering, and has made the request in writing to die. There have been attempts elsewhere in the world: the Northern Territory in Australia passed a Euthanasia Law in 1995, which was overturned by the federal government and finally repealed in 1997. And the State of Oregon in the United States has an Assisted Suicide Law, which the Supreme Court in January 2005 did not declare unconstitutional. For Oregon, patients must be terminally ill, have made repeated requests, be competent, and have the diagnosis confirmed by two doctors. In the United States, Oregon is the only state to have such a law. So although many countries are having the debate, there remains continuing hesitation about introducing a law. So why is this?

The first argument against is the growing science of palliative care. Palliative care is the science that treats the symptoms of a disease but not the disease itself. In other words, when it is clear that the illness is terminal and the patient is not going to be cured, palliative care is responsible for managing the pain during the last few weeks or months. Palliative care specialists estimate that in the vast majority of cases most of the pain of death can be alleviated. Naturally, there will still be the psychological pain of death, but the physical side can be managed very effectively.

At this point, advocates of voluntary euthanasia suspect that some doctors are managing pain so effectively that in effect lives are being shortened. Palliative care specialists disagree. Although it is common practice at the final stages to increase the pain relief to levels that make death inevitable, there is no way anyone can know whether this hastens death or not. Pain, of course, can kill as well: if the person did not have the appropriate levels of pain management, then that person might die sooner and in much greater pain.

Palliative care specialists are appealing to the principle of double effect, which actually goes back to Thomas Aquinas. When discussing self-defense, Aquinas distinguished between a directly intended primary end to an action and a merely foreseen consequence of an action. If a person attacks you and in the act of self-defense you kill that person, then you can invoke the principle of double effect. The intention was not to kill, but to defend oneself, which had the foreseeable possible consequence of killing that person. So in the same way, the goal of palliative care is the management of pain; sometimes the pain management needed will make death inevitable. But the intention is not to kill; rather it is to ensure that the patient is comfortable in their final days and hours.

There is a lively debate as to whether the science of palliative care has been impeded by the rush to a euthanasia law in The Netherlands. Many think it has been set back; doctors in The Netherlands have ceased being as imaginative as their counterparts in the rest of Europe. Rather than think about the appropriate levels of pain management needed, the temptation is simply to resort to the lethal injection.

The second argument is that a euthanasia law might create a mechanism that places the patient in a situation where they face undue pressure from family or other interested parties (perhaps the hospital). With all the complexities facing the end of life, to factor in the dilemma whether one chooses to die now or later adds a significant burden. Consider, for example, a college student who has a grandmother who is terminally ill. Although it is clear she will die in the next few weeks or months, there is no guarantee that this will be in time for the student to pay his college fees. It is obviously tempting for him to surreptitiously put some pressure on his grandmother and encourage that she signs the form. This is especially true given that many elderly people feel that they are a burden and might talk about "wishing they could die." As at other times in a life, we all have moments when we might talk in these morbid ways: and such talk is often a desperate message to others seeking love and affirmation. Death is going to come; the pain can be managed; to complicate the final weeks and months with an option that you sign a form inviting the doctor to kill you seems both unnecessary and potentially very risky. Defenders of euthanasia insist that the decision is the patient's alone and must be made without duress. However, of course, it is difficult to be sure that these conditions are met: duress can be applied very subtly at times.

The third argument is that many doctors do not want the power. When one goes into the medical profession, the primary goal is to make people well; they do not want to provide a suicide service. There is also an anxiety about the "culture" of hospitals. There is some evidence that individuals worry about donor cards for fear that a medical professional would not do everything she could for them after a traffic accident. The fear is that the kidney in my mangled body is needed by a patient down the hospital corridor and therefore I would not be treated properly. So if this is an anxiety around donor cards, think how much more the elderly would worry every time they went into hospital with an infection.

The fourth argument is the "slippery slope" or "domino" argument. It takes the following form: we will start with euthanasia for the terminally ill, then slowly the service will expand until it is available to other groups. Advocates of euthanasia are very critical of this argument: they see no reason why a carefully written law cannot confine the euthanasia option to certain limited groups. Helga Kuhse writes:

> In its logical version, the "slippery slope" argument is unconvincing. There are no logical grounds why the reasons that justify euthanasia – mercy and respect for autonomy – should logically also justify killings that are neither merciful nor show respect for autonomy. In its empirical version, the slippery slope argument asserts that justified killings will, as a matter of fact, lead to unjustified killings. There is little empirical evidence to back up this claim. Whilst the Nazi "euthanasia" program is often cited as an example of what can happen when a society acknowledges that some lives are not worthy to be lived, the

motivation behind these killings was neither mercy nor respect for autonomy; it was rather, racial prejudice and the belief that the racial purity of the *Volk* required the elimination of certain individuals and groups. As already noted, in the Netherlands a "social experiment" with active voluntary euthanasia is currently in progress. As yet there is no evidence that this has sent Dutch society down a slippery slope.[11]

Opponents of euthanasia are not as sanguine as Kuhse. They point to the abortion law; it was justified by the difficult cases (young teenage girls who are raped) and then in practice became abortion on demand. There is a pattern here: if you create a legal option, then do expect that those who take advantage of it will be greater than one anticipates. And the logic of the voluntary euthanasia position points to a wider circle of potential beneficiaries of the law. What is the ethical difference between a person who is terminally ill with cancer and wants to die and someone who is terminally ill with depression and wants to die? The anxiety here is less that everyone disabled will be marched into clinics and killed, but rather that the "definition" of terminal will become so elastic that in practice in 50 years time we could institutionalize a suicide service.

The fifth argument is that the vast majority of patients are able to commit suicide if they wish; if this is what the patient wants to do, then the patient can do it. Although of course leaping from the Golden Gate Bridge in San Francisco is not the easiest thing for everyone to do, at least the effort involved makes it clear that you really want to do it. And in making a decision of this magnitude such certainty is important. To insist that suicide must be made easy runs the risk that people who don't really want to commit suicide will do so. However, as it happens, the Internet provides a rich set of resources for those who want to end their own life. In this information rich age, it is no longer that difficult. Given this, the argument goes, we don't need a voluntary euthanasia law.

It is worth noting that all the arguments thus far have been legal, medical, and pragmatic. The last argument is an overtly religious one. For many religious people euthanasia is wrong because of the gift-like quality of life. The privilege of life, on this view, is not a right or entitlement. We are not entitled to be born; we just find ourselves with the privilege of breathing and living. Life is a gift from God. So we are not entitled to decide when to die. The giving and taking of life are not meant to be in human control. God is sovereign of those moments. We undermine our sense of gratitude for the privilege of being when we start to decide that we are allowed to terminate our life if we so choose. For Christians the problem of euthanasia is the same as the problem of suicide: suicide is forbidden because it is an ungracious act of rebellion by a creature towards to the creator, so to opt prematurely for death is a comparable act of ingratitude.

Other medical dilemmas

The focus of this chapter has been on two of the most contentious medical issues of our time. However, medicine is a rich arena for dilemmas; and medical ethics is a flourishing area of study. To conclude this chapter, there are three topics I will discuss briefly. The first is the growing area of "preventative medicine," especially screening. The second is the growing options around infertility treatments. And the third are what Simon Lee calls the "uneasy cases"; in this regard, we will look at the Jodie and Mary Siamese twins' case of the summer of 2000.

Preventative medicine

It seems obvious that rather than wait for the symptoms of a potentially life-threatening disease to emerge, we should do everything we can to prevent or detect it early. This has become a mantra in much public health policy in the western world. If fewer people smoked, the argument goes, then fewer people would die prematurely and fewer demands on scarce and expensive healthcare would be made. Encouraging a healthy lifestyle (regular exercise and a good diet) has become a key part of secondary school education. These public education programs are good: if we can encourage people to live good, healthy lives, then everyone will win: the individuals will have healthier lives and society will have to spend less on medical care of people following complex diseases.

An extension of the preventative medicine campaign is the question of screening.[12] It is now commonplace in America and in much of western Europe for women to be encouraged to have a cervical cancer smear and for men to be tested for prostate cancer. However, such programs are controversial. L. Russell, author of *Educated Guesses: Making Policy about Medical Screening Tests*, argues that the health services propagate the illusion that screening can lead to a longer life through early detection and treatment.[13] There is, however, a possibility of a wrong result. The cancer might be missed: abnormal cells might be present in the cervix, but may not be included in the scraping of the cervical tissue; or the abnormality may be missed by the technician responsible for examining the thousands of cells on the slide. To those who believe that these dangers can be mitigated by regular testing, another danger arises, that of borderline or false positives due to a non-cancerous inflammation or injury to the cervix. The odds for such false positive results will increase with the number of tests the woman has over her lifetime. To reduce the proportion of false positives in a screening program, all positive smears may be either repeated, or confirmed by procedures such as colposcopy, with attendant risks to the woman. Coupled with this potential problem of misdiagnosis, there is the cost. Russell, writing in 1994, suggests that screening all American adult women for cervical cancer would cost $6 billion a year. This means, Russell explains, that it costs $1 million for each additional year of life for each woman detected. Mant and Fowler cite a UK 1985 study which reported that 40,000 smears and 200 excision biopsies were required to prevent one death from cervical cancer in Britain.[14] Thus the cost involved per life could have been as high as £300,000. Russell's view is that, given the limited resources available for healthcare, it is not obvious that this is the best use of such resources.

Prostate cancer is equally controversial. At first sight this seems a wholly legitimate area for screening: our aging population has led to a significant increase in mortality from this cancer. We have a fairly reliable means of screening, namely the measurement of serum levels of prostate specific antigen. However, there is a significant ethical difficulty. The fact is that autopsy studies show that many men die *with* prostate cancer but not *from* prostate cancer. The danger is obvious. A screening program might well identify slowly developing prostate cancer, which will not be responsible for the person's death. This, coupled with the fact that radical treatment can be highly invasive and have unpleasant side effects (e.g. incontinence and impotence) makes one question the value of the screening program.

Now at this point it is important for the author to add a caveat: just because there is a lively debate about screening, doesn't mean that you (the reader) should not get screened for these cancers. Current medical advice is encouraging such screening and the technologies are always improving. However, one should know (an informed and consenting patient is an important concept in medical ethics) that such screening has its problems and drawbacks.

These debates around cervical and prostate cancers are nothing compared to the potential screening issues arising as a result of the Human Genome Project. This project started in 1990 with the goal to map and sequence the entire human genome. Progress has been dramatic. We are already in a position to diagnose, with much greater accuracy, those who are affected by the fragile-X syndrome. Progress has been made in the battle against cancer, the Human Genome Project having enabled us to identify the genes involved in certain of its forms. Clinical trials of gene therapy are underway (i.e. the augmentation of the bad gene with a normal gene). In addition, it is now possible to identify those who have a susceptibility to developing diabetes, arthritis, hypertension, and heart disease. In short, over 3,000 genetic disorders have been identified.

We already have a potentially lucrative source of genetic information about newborn babies. The blood specimen taken from each newborn infant to test for conditions such as phenylketonuria is an obvious source of DNA. We are already in a position to screen comprehensively every newborn baby for a large number of genetic disorders. The question is: should we do so?

The first difficulty is that the information generated by such screening needs considerable interpretation. Most often, it is a probability judgment: there is a percentage risk that this might happen. In addition, for chronic conditions or ones that have very different levels of severity between different affected individuals (such as cystic fibrosis and sickle cell disease), it can be very difficult to present a single "truth" about the condition that screening might have detected. At present, we do not understand what contributes to variability and so, at an individual level, we cannot predict the likely level of severity. The second difficulty is that one might not want to know that in 40 years time there is a possibility that one will suffer from an incurable disease. Consider, for example, a newborn baby that is found to carry the gene for Huntington's disease, a progressive neurological condition manifesting in early adult life. This is a disease that cannot be prevented, treated, or cured; the potential for distress is considerable. In addition, the status of the baby is now, after the test, ambiguous. Prior to screening, the child was considered healthy, but now it has a potentially fatal illness. We have a "genetically ill person."

The third difficulty is that such screening of all newborn babies will generate additional information that can create significant ethical difficulties. Wertz and Fletcher discuss a case of false paternity, discovered inadvertently when evaluating a child with an autosomal recessive disorder for which carrier testing is possible and accurate.[15] When testing the relatives for genetic counseling, the doctor discovers that the mother and half the siblings are carriers, whereas the husband, who believes he is the father, is not. The consequences of disclosure could be traumatic. The husband's relationship with the child and mother could be changed dramatically for the worse. This is obviously an acute dilemma for the doctor, which would be multiplied many times over if we have genetic screening for all newborn babies.

The final difficulty is that there are many agencies who would love to have such information. Future partners might want to know about the genetic potential for reproductive purposes; employers are interested in the health of their employees; insurance companies would love to be able to levy premiums on the basis of reliable health information. And given that certain aptitudes, such as mathematical skills, may have a genetic base, educationalists might be interested in the result. For those who have a positive genetic report, such widespread dissemination is not a problem; but those who are not so fortunate might have to cope with significant discrimination and prejudice.

The world of reproductive medicine

Infertility can be very distressing. For most of us growing up, pregnancy is a major fear. One's sexual experiments are not always done as responsibly as they should be. And it can be a considerable relief when the monthly cycle finally reassures a young couple that parenthood is not happening in the immediate future. So it comes as a massive shock to a couple when trying for children proves difficult. The expectation is that one gets married and has children; one doesn't expect to find it impossible. Marriages have broken down on the discovery of infertility: it can be devastating. And the numbers involved are not small; it is estimated that in the United States 6.1 million people are affected by infertility.[16]

Space will not permit an extensive discussion of all the different forms of infertility treatments. So instead we shall examine four major ones, namely, artificial insemination by donor (AID), surrogate motherhood, in vitro fertilization (IVF), and cloning. The latter, of course, is an option possible only in the future: it is not currently available. We start with AID.

AID (artificial insemination donor)

This involves the injection of seminal fluid, which is obtained from a donor by masturbation, into the upper vaginal canal of the neck of the womb or into the cavity of the womb itself. With AID, the donor producing the semen specimen is not the partner and is usually anonymous. This method is mainly used to aid conception when the husband is infertile or when he has or carries a genetic disorder which has a high risk of being transmitted to his children.

On one level this seems a good satisfactory solution to the problem. However, there is one major difficulty here. It means that (as things stand) the child will not know who the genetic father is. Along with the lack of genetic history, there is a small risk that they might form an incestuous relationship as an adult.

Surrogate motherhood

This is when a substitute mother agrees to bear a child for another woman who cannot bear children herself, normally for a fee.

Again at first sight this looks like a very satisfactory solution to the problem. However, there are complexities. The body goes through certain changes as the baby grows inside the woman. What happens if the surrogate mother wants to keep the baby? And giving birth to a child can become complicated: what if the child has Down Syndrome, is it an option for the contracting couple to insist on an abortion or decline to take the child?

In vitro fertilization (IVF)

"In vitro" means "in glass." The procedure involves the mixing of sperm and egg in the laboratory. Once fertilization has taken place, the zygote (fertilized egg) will be either surgically placed in the woman's fallopian tube or allowed to develop further outside the body and then be introduced into the uterus. It is normal to place at least three zygotes into the woman on the presumption that some will not implant.

IVF is increasingly common. It is a reproductive technology that has developed considerably over recent years. Certain groups consider it very problematic: Roman Catholics believe that a unique human being exists from the moment of conception. So this is the doctor creating people, many of whom end up in a freezer only to be destroyed after ten years. The reason for this is that it is recommended that one collect sufficient eggs and sperm from the potential parents for several tries: there is still a high chance that the fertilized eggs will not implant in the womb. If the IVF is successful on the first time of trying, then the rest are frozen and then destroyed.

Reproductive cloning

This is currently illegal in over 30 countries. However, it is theoretically available and a small number of scientists would like to clone a baby. The procedure is as follows: one takes the genetic material in the nucleus of a human cell and transfers it to an egg, where the nucleus has been removed. The egg then grows into an embryo. At that point, if the procedure were permitted, it would be placed into a woman's womb. The net result is the creation of an identical twin of the person from whom the genetic material was taken.

There are several problems with cloning. The first is that with cloned animals, there have been serious health difficulties, for example, fetal disorders, overgrowth, and poor survival after birth. Lord May on behalf of the Royal Society in the UK said this:

> Research indicates that human cloning is a threat to the health of both the cloned child and the mother. Animal studies on reproductive cloning show a high incidence of fetal disorders and spontaneous abortions, and of malformation and death among newborns. There is no reason to suppose that the outcome would be different in humans. Given that, attempts at human cloning seem reckless and grossly irresponsible and arguably exploitive of vulnerable people who desperately want children.[17]

The second difficulty is social. If cloning became widespread then of course women could simply reproduce themselves, thereby making men surplus to requirements. Lesbian couples have been attracted to the possibility of reproduction without men. However, there is speculation that such cloning would adversely affect the gene pool and that creation of a child twin of one of the parents could create emotional difficulties.

Infertility options are continuing to change and develop. As we look to the future, it is clearly an area where medical dilemmas will multiply.

Uneasy cases

It was Simon Lee, a leading specialist in Jurisprudence in the United Kingdom, who coined the expression "uneasy cases." An uneasy case is one where "the moral dilemma is so acute that if you do not have some sense of unease, you have not fully understood the complexities involved."[18] He starts his book with the famous and tragic story of the Siamese or conjoined twins, "Jodie" and "Mary," who were born on August 8, 2000. Lee explains the problem thus:

> Their parents, a Catholic couple from Gozo, Malta's neighboring island, had sought expert care from a Manchester hospital. The medical team advised that Jodie and Mary would both die within months unless they were separated by an operation. One, Mary, would die as a result of the operation but the other, Jodie, would have a good chance of survival and flourishing. Their parents were reluctant to sanction the operation, citing religious reasons.[19]

This is an acute dilemma. The medical problem was simple: the girls shared one heart and one pair of lungs. Although Jodi was the stronger of the two, she would not be able to sustain the life of her sister on the shared heart and lungs. How can a parent choose to kill one baby so that another might live? Is it right to use the life of one child as a means to a possible end of saving the other child? A major complication was that the parents had expressed their views: both of their children are entitled to live; they did not want to kill one to save the other. Instead they wanted to trust God and allow "what God intends" to take its course. What right do the courts have to override the wishes of those who are closest to the children?

The result was that the courts did insist, over the wishes of the parents, that the operation should go ahead. Mary did die and Jodi survived the operation. The key ethical argument for the courts was the principle of double effect, which we discussed in the euthanasia section. The intent was to save Jodi, not to kill Mary. Jodi was entitled to defend herself against the "parasitic" impact of Mary. Whether this is right or not is a continued matter of debate.

Conclusion

It is in the medical realm that many of the hardest decisions are being made. The issues are literally matters of life and death. The ethical discourse in this area is extremely important. We need to reflect on the "appropriateness" of our behavior: this is the realm of ethics. There are options emerging which will create the *Brave New World* of Aldous Huxley. We are all required to participate in the conversation: the decisions that are being made may affect us all.

Notes

1 This famous case study is taken from Judith Jarvis Thomson, *A Defense of Abortion* as reproduced in Peter Singer (ed.) *Applied Ethics* (Oxford: Oxford University Press 1986) pp. 38–9.

2 Supreme Court Ruling, Roe v Wade (1973).

3 Judith Jarvis Thomson, "A Defense of Abortion" in Peter Singer (ed.) *Practical Ethics*, p. 37.

4 Ibid. p. 48.

5 Ibid. p. 55.

6 Michael Tooley, *Abortion and Infanticide* (Oxford: Clarendon Press 1983) p. 167.

7 Pope John Paul II, *Evangelium Vitae*, paragraphs 18.4–18.5.

8 For a more extended discussion of the Papal arguments see chapter 12 in my *Theology of Engagement* (Oxford: Blackwell Publishing 2003).

9 See the website of the Voluntary Euthanasia Society at www.ves.org.uk

10 Ibid.

11 Helga Kuhse, "Euthanasia" in Peter Singer (ed.) *A Companion to Ethics* (Oxford: Blackwell Publishing 1991) pp. 301–2.

12 Parts of what follows are taken from my article on screening called "Ethical and Legal Issues," *British Medical Bulletin* 54 (4) (1998) pp. 1011–21.

13 L. Russell, *Educated Guesses: Making Policy about Medical Screening Tests* (Los Angeles, CA: University of California Press 1994).

14 D. Mant and G. Fowler, "Mass Screening: Theory and Ethics," *British Medical Journal* 300 (1990) pp. 916–18.

15 D. C. Wertz and J. C. Fletcher, "Privacy and Disclosure in Medical Genetics Examined in an Ethics of Care," *Bioethics* 5 (1991) pp. 212–32.

16 See the very helpful website on IVF. www.ivf.com

17 Press release September 22, 2003 "Royal Society backs UN call for a ban on reproductive cloning" as found on www.royalsoc.ac.uk

18 Simon Lee, *Uneasy Ethics* (London: Pimlico 2003) p. 5.

19 Ibid.

12

Dilemmas involving violence and power

Thought exercise

"In 1939, after Hitler's occupation of Poland, Britain and France declared war on Germany, and the Second World War opened to a new type of air war, despite pleas from President Roosevelt for restraint. In particular, "under no circumstances [to] undertake the bombardment from the air of civilian populations or of unfortified cities." This diabolical form of warfare was already known to the world – the Italians had pioneered it against the peasant villages of Abyssinia, the German dive bombers had refined it in Spain.

But by May the following year, with Denmark, Norway, Holland, Belgium and now even France falling to the German advance, Britain reneged on the understanding and began to use the bomb. Churchill broke the conventions step by step. Initially, only "military targets" were bombed, but this allowed for what is now called "collateral damage" (civilian deaths) as the targets included things like railway stations and ports, and the bombs were only accurate to within half a mile. From June 20, 1940, the military targets included industrial centers. In September, the Germans launched the Blitz against English cities and civilians, and in October, Churchill allowed the new head of Bomber Command, Arthur Harris, to start "area bombing." These were raids designed to destroy whole cities – men, women, and children. The story goes that one night, "Bomber" Harris was caught speeding home from London to High Wycombe. The police officer chastised him: "Drive like that, Sir, and you could kill someone!" Harris replied: "Officer, I kill thousands of people every night."

Churchill described the changes as merely one of "somewhat broader interpretation" of the convention of seeking only military targets. Yet the "Valentine's Day" memo, Directive 22, from Sir Archibald Sinclair, Air Minister, to Bomber Command in 1942 said that bombing should aim to destroy "the morale of enemy civil population, in particular industrial workers," and that the bombers' aiming points were to be "built-up areas, not for instance, the dockyards or aircraft factories." Nonetheless, throughout the war, MPs and the British public were assured that bombing raids were always scrupulously confined to "military targets."

Hitler, of course, issued his orders to his troops with little mincing of words: "'Poland shall be treated as a colony . . . I have issued the order to my SS troops – for the time being only in the East – to kill mercilessly and without pity men, women, and children of Polish origin."

On May 30, 1942, in one of the most successful raids, a "big wing" consisting of 1,000 Lancaster bombers destroyed most of Cologne. A year later, the raid on Hamburg killed more people in one night than all the German attacks on England put together. Using clouds of aluminum foil to fool the city's defenses, the bombing was particularly accurate and the old wooden houses blazed in a firestorm, the like of which had never been witnessed before. The civilians huddled in their air raid shelters were often reduced to fine dust. Rescue workers after the raids could remove the remains of whole families in a single bucket.

One civilian clerk in Bomber command, Freeman Dyson (later a famous nuclear physicist), recalled years later, how it felt to collate all the reports on the bombing reports so carefully kept from the British people. "I sat in my office until the end, carefully calculating how to murder most economically another hundred thousand people." Dyson was sickened by the policy. Although he knew that Hitler's extermination squads were then in the process of killing unimaginable numbers (perhaps 12 million) of defenseless civilians, he could not believe that what Bomber Command was doing was so very different.

Dresden was the old cultural center of Germany – full of history and architectural and artistic masterpieces. It was also full of refugees fleeing the Russian advance, and effectively defenseless when the decision was taken to bomb it in February 1945. The firestorm that had been so successful in Hamburg, returned. A cauldron of flame consumed an estimated 100,000 people.

Did the ends justify the means?"[1]

The majority of human lives are lived in relatively uncomplicated and normal ways: men and women get out of bed, do a day's work, and climb back into bed at the end of the day. However, there is a significant minority of people whose lives are marred by violence. In certain parts of the world violence can, for a time, become a constant preoccupation. In this chapter we shall explore the problem of violence and power. At what point is it ethically legitimate to resort to violence? How does one prevent the cycle of revenge? Is it, perhaps, necessary to take a stand and exclude violence as a means to any end?

We start by describing the different forms of violence in this world, before concentrating on its social and political form. En route we shall look at the role toleration can play in society and the selective views of humanity we all have. The chapter concludes with a comparison between the pacifist and just war traditions.

Types of violence

Broadly, violence divides into two types – illegitimate and legitimate. Illegitimate violence takes a multitude of different forms: on the individual level, it includes rape, murder, mugging, assault, and pedophilia; on the group or national level, it includes the attempted genocide or the expansionist propensities of one country over another. Hitler in Germany provides a good illustration of illegitimate group violence.

In political theory, legitimate violence is identified as the use of power by a legitimate authority grounded in the consent of the people. So in a democracy, where an elected government makes laws (which are then implemented by a police force that is held accountable) against those who break the laws, we can see the legitimate exercise of power, which sometimes must take the form of force. (Force here is simply another word for "legitimate violence.")

Naturally, the extremes in each case are fairly easy to establish. A rapist and Hitler are good examples of illegitimate violence; and the work of a police force in a well run democratic country (note I hesitate to give an illustration of such a country) is an illustration of legitimate violence.

In the middle, however, there are endless dilemmas, which provoke considerable public argument. Consider an 18-year-old male who is found guilty of mugging. Consider further that this mugger was born to drug-addicted parents in an urban district where there is no social support and poor schools. Although the mugger is guilty of illegitimate violence – after all, the victim didn't deserve the violence – perhaps he is also a victim of violence: the violence of a social system that doesn't support the children of drug-addicted parents and provide the mechanism that enables the child to succeed. Or to take a different example, consider the action of the English police force at the height of the bombing campaign of the IRA in the north of Ireland and in England. Although the provocation was terrorism (interpreted, of course, by the IRA as the brave acts of freedom fighters), the willingness of the police to fabricate evidence and create certain injustices was clearly not the use of legitimate force. In both instances – the mugger and the English police response to the IRA – we find the line blurring: the mugger might also be a victim of institutional violence, while the police force might also be undermining its legitimacy by not respecting due process.

However, even with the middle posing some hard cases, the division between legitimate and illegitimate violence is a helpful one. There are clear instances of the use of illegitimate violence. It is because of the illegitimate violence that others have to respond with force. But this poses the obvious question: why are some people violent?

Views of humanity

One key issue in ethics is your view of humanity. There is a spectrum ranging from the optimistic to the pessimistic. Those at the optimistic end of the spectrum tend to stress that people are basically good. However, environmental and social factors spoil this goodness. The evidence for this is that if you surround a child with love, satisfy its basic needs, and encourage the self-confidence to grow, then it is unlikely that child will be violent. Alternatively if you abuse a child, do not satisfy the basic needs of shelter and food, and endlessly humiliate the child, then you can be fairly sure that the child will be violent and hostile.

At the pessimistic end of the spectrum, we find other philosophers and scholars stressing the human inability to be perfect and the almost perverse pleasure we get out of wickedness. The evidence for this position is the ease with which children can discover bullying or the fact that many of the prominent Nazis (and certainly their supporters) were refined, cultured, and educated people. On this view, violence is inside all of us: we all have the potential for the most evil of crimes.

This debate plays out in a variety of different forms. In Christian theology it expresses itself in the debate between the image of god and original sin. The belief that all people are made in the image of God, sees us as spiritual beings with a real capacity for good. Original sin stresses that our basic orientation from the moment we breathe is towards self and egoism.

In literature we find novels repeatedly revolve around this theme. William Golding's masterly novel *Lord of the Flies* takes the most privileged of children and places them in an idyllic setting. The novel then slowly descends into a breakdown of structure and order finally culminating in a murder.

In my view the truth is somewhere in the middle of the spectrum. In classical Roman Catholic theology, there is the recognition that we have potential for both good and bad. The image of God enables us to do good; the Fall into sin describes our potential for evil. All of us are both potential angels and devils.

It is also true that our capacity to do both good and evil is heavily shaped by the environment in which we find ourselves. We are all chameleons: we learn the culture of those around us and this becomes our world. Spend much of your time surrounded by street fighting gangs in Los Angeles and your language and code of behavior will start resembling that group. Alternatively spend much of your time in a Trappist monastery in France and your language and code of behavior will resemble that group. Environment isn't a determining factor in behavior but it is a key influence.

Once the influence of culture is recognized then one can start to understand why animosity between cultures is so widespread. So what we need to consider is why can't we all just get along?

From love and acceptance to hostility

Relationships between groups and individuals operate along a spectrum. This is a spectrum that moves from love and acceptance at one end, to hostility at the other. Sometimes we find it puzzling why everyone can't just love and accept each other. After all, we share a common humanity: and ultimately the peace of the world depends on positive relations between all people. So why is it so difficult for us to get along?

The answer to this is complicated. But it starts from the reality that love and acceptance (in most cases) starts within a family, which lives in a community, and will be part of a broader national and cultural setting. We learn love and acceptance in a context, and part of that which we learn to love and accept are those characteristics that make up a particular cultural identity. In short, we learn as children to love and accept that which is broadly similar and reliably stable and uniform.

The problem arises with difference. The difference may be ethnic (e.g. a different nationality) or religious (e.g. Christian and Muslim) or sexual disposition (e.g. gay) or moral (e.g. a believer in polygamy). Because of difference, we are instantly sensitive to a range of questions. What is the history of relations between my people and community and that from which this different person comes? What is the nature of the religious difference and can I reconcile this difference with the truth claims of my religion?

Outright hostility is a tempting starting point. It might indeed be justified if the differences are too great. As a person living in a liberal culture and a New York Times reader, I have real problems when I meet a "white supremacist." Let us admit that there are some people we just don't want to accept. And this is an important option in some cases.

However, there is an important halfway house between love and hostility. This is where we meet the concept of toleration. Toleration has its roots in the seventeenth century.[2] John Locke is a key person in the story. In his first Letter on Toleration, published in 1689, he argued that limited religious tolerance should be extended to "dissenters" who did not follow the practices and beliefs of the established Anglican Church. The limit of this tolerance was drawn up to protect the internal cohesion of the society. So Roman Catholics were excluded because they owed their allegiance to the Bishop of Rome, seen then as in part a political figure, and not to the king; and atheists were excluded because their oaths could not be trusted.[3] Although we today are not necessarily impressed with such a limited tolerance, we can still recognize in it a remarkable historical achievement. Locke takes a strong social conflict of his time, that concerning the virtual Anglican monopoly of legitimate religious allegiance and official authorization, and argues for a policy of official State tolerance. This was a new idea for the West:[4] the State could extend tolerance towards these groups, i.e. permit them even though the majority might strongly disapprove of them.

For a person or group to be tolerant, two conditions must be met. First, that person or group must be in a position of power to allow or to forbid the action or situation in question. Dilemmas involving the exercise of tolerance arise when the party in question has some degree of power. The landlady is in that position in respect of the couple seeking to rent from her. If the landlady decides to exercise her power by refusing to rent (or forcing them to move out), then she would be intolerant (if, for example, it was because she disapproved of homosexuality or unmarried cohabitation). This power can be either explicit or implicit. In our example the landlady has explicit power (i.e. she is in a position to decide who may be her tenants). When the white majority in the community makes life unpleasant for their recently arrived black neighbor, they are exercising implicit power (i.e. diffused power located in a community outlook). Many of the worst examples of intolerance are the result of implicit rather than explicit power.

The second condition is that one must disapprove, even if only minimally or potentially. The sense of disapproval or even antagonism is important. One does not tolerate that which is accepted or an object of love. If one is an ardent supporter of homosexual rights, then one is not being tolerant in letting one's flat to a gay couple. I do not tolerate my wife; I love her. No disapproval is involved; I am proud and fond of her. Nor does one tolerate that towards which one is indifferent. If you do not care about homosexuality, then you are not tolerating it. You are simply indifferent; it stands alongside other equally irrelevant issues such as the existence of the Loch Ness monster.

So at one of the end of the spectrum, we have love and acceptance; at the other, hatred and hostility; and, in between, we have toleration. It is good when some of the groups we just "tolerate" we learn to love and accept. There are many differences that shouldn't provoke either disapproval or mere indifference, but can be celebrated. Cultural diversity may be a delight. Cities that have learnt to appreciate cultural differences in terms of food, religion, music, and art are rich places in which to live. Cultural difference, in many ways, shouldn't be tolerated but celebrated.

However, there are cultural differences that need to be opposed. The culture of the Nazi or the white supremacist cannot be celebrated and probably cannot even be tolerated, but needs to be opposed. The question here is what form that opposition takes. Is it ethically appropriate for a legitimate authority to use power and war against illegitimate violent or intolerant opinions?

The pacifist response

One response is to forbid "violence" as a response to "violence." The twentieth century has two famous examples of the pacifist response. Mahatma Gandhi

(1869–1948) in India insisted that the nationalist movement in India was not allowed to resort to violence and terrorism to achieve its ends. The occupying power (namely the British) had to be forced to leave India by a campaign of civil disobedience. Gandhi believed in the power of non-violence. He explained:

> An armed soldier relies on his weapons for his strength. Take away from him his weapons – his gun or his sword, and he generally becomes helpless. But a person who has truly realized the principle of nonviolence has the God-given strength for his weapon and the world has not known anything that can match it.[5]

Gandhi made the Hindu-Jain notion of ahimsa (the principle of non-violence and non-injury to living creatures) central to his philosophy. This is the highest way of relating to others; and this Gandhi believed was the only way that peace and reconciliation between people will be realized.

It was the imperative for pacifism as the way to peace and reconciliation, which also resonated with the second famous pacifist of the twentieth century – Martin Luther King Jnr (1929–68). King led the civil rights movement in the United States. He explains his commitment to non-violence as the inevitable corollary of his commitment to the Christian doctrine of the image of God:

> Now let me say that the next thing we must be concerned about if we are to have peace on earth and good will towards men is the nonviolent affirmation of the sacredness of all human life. Every man is somebody because he is a child of God. And so when we say "Thou shalt not kill," we're really saying that human life is too sacred to be taken on the battle-fields of the world. Man is more than a tiny vagary of whirling electrons or a wisp of smoke from a limitless smouldering. Man is a child of God, made in His image, and therefore must be respected as such. Until men see this everywhere, until nations see this everywhere, we will be fighting wars. One day somebody should remind us that, even though there may be political and ideological differences between us, the Vietnamese are our brothers, the Russians are our brothers, the Chinese are our brothers; and one day we've got to sit down together at the table of brotherhood.[6]

Despite enormous provocation, Martin Luther King insisted that the mechanisms of social change had to be non-violent. So the bus boycott which was triggered by Rosa Parks and the campaign for voter registration were all non-violent strategies. In both cases Gandhi and King believed their message of social change depended on not resorting to violence.

There are four arguments for pacifism. The first is the simple axiom that killing is wrong. The taking of life for any cause does not further that cause. Jesus famously explained that: "You have heard that it was said, 'An eye for an eye and a tooth for a tooth.' But I say to you, Do not resist an evildoer. But if anyone strikes you on the right cheek, turn the other also."[7] The point is that you should not exercise your entitlement to the judicial principle that you may exact a punishment equivalent to the crime (one eye for one eye). Rather you absorb violence instead of escalating it. The cycle of violence provoking revenge, which in turn provokes more violence, is broken by the simple act of accepting the violence. The life of Jesus, which ends on the cross, illustrates the principle of non- retaliation.

From this starting point, the other three points flow. The second argument is that exercising a right to violence often makes the situation worse. Military solutions to complex problems are rarely found. The English attempt to find a military solution to the terrorist attacks of the IRA in the north of Ireland did not succeed; and it does not look as if the Israeli government is doing any better against Hamas. Sometimes in the short term, it looks as if a military solution has succeeded, only to find decades later the original problem returns in a new guise. The Allies at the end of the First World War imagined that the Treaty of Versailles (1919) was the solution to the problem of Germany; only to find in 1933 a key factor in the popularity of Adolf Hitler was the unpopularity and per- ceived injustice of this treaty.

The third argument is that the resort to violence has a degrading impact on all. Gandhi puts this well, when he explains:

> It is an unshakable faith with me that a cause suffers exactly to the extent that it is supported by violence. I say this in spite of appearances to the contrary. If I kill a man who obstructs me, I may experience a sense of false security. But the security will be short-lived. For I shall not have dealt with the root cause. In due course, other men will surely rise to obstruct me. My business, therefore, is not to kill the man or men who obstruct me, but to discover the cause that impels them to obstruct me and deal with it.
>
> I do not believe in armed risings. They are a remedy worse than the disease sought to be cured. They are a token of the spirit of revenge and impatience and anger. The method of violence cannot do good in the long run.'[8]

This quotation leads into the fourth argument for pacifism. There is an obliga- tion to solve problems at the underlying level. Violence, in the end, obscures the underlying conflict or disagreement. Often the extremist who resorts to vio- lence does so because of an underlying insecurity. The "white supremacist," who wants to lynch blacks, and the homophobic, who wants to persecute gays, are expressing their cultural and personal insecurity by lashing out in hatred and dislike of others, people different from themselves and therefore intolerably disturbing. To fight this violence with violence only exacerbates the insecurities; however, to fight this violence with love can be a way of transforming the damage that underlies the insecurities.

Pacifism is a vision: it is a potential way of life. It does assume that love can triumph and, in the end, bad people can and will be changed. Could a Gandhi or a Martin Luther King have defeated Hitler in Germany? This is less clear. And it is for this reason that many argue that there are occasions when the resort to killing is necessary. Naturally there must be rules. When two nations fight, the armies determine the result. The killing of children (or more broadly – non-combatant civilians) does not help the result of the war at all. These rules are now part of international law, recognized by the vast majority of nations in the world, as legitimate rules for combat. These rules developed from the just war tradition. It is to the history and nature of these rules that we turn to next.

The just war tradition

We have already seen that Jesus lived and died a pacifist. Even though the Romans were occupying Palestine, Jesus consciously rejected the option of violence. When Jesus was arrested outside in Gethsemane, Matthew's gospel reports that one of his disciples tried to defend him with a sword. Matthew writes:

> Suddenly, one of those with Jesus put his hand on his sword, drew it, and struck the slave of the high priest, cutting off his ear. Then Jesus said to him, "Put your sword back into its place; for all who take the sword will perish by the sword. Do you think that I cannot appeal to my Father, and he will at once send me more than twelve legions of angels? But how then would the scriptures be fulfilled, which say it must happen in this way?[9]

Historians agree that Jesus did not only teach pacifism, but was willing to die for his pacifist principles. The conscious rejection of pacifism continued to shape the early church for the first 300 years of its existence. It was not until the conversion of the Roman Emperor Constantine (c.340 CE) that Christianity started to try to find ways of justifying war. It was the Bishop of Hippo, St Augustine (354–430), who planted the seeds of the just war tradition. His immediate problem arose in 410 CE when Rome was facing defeat at the hands of the Visigoths and neighboring tribes. Part of the Empire's vulnerability was due to the reluctance of Christians to defend the Empire. Augustine found in the Hebrew Bible ample justification for war (see Exodus 15:1–18, Deuternomy 20:10–18, Joshua 6–7). As God was willing to command war, and as God is responsible for appointing the rulers of nations, then surely war, under certain circumstances, can be justified.

Augustine suggested two conditions. The first was that the war had to be authorized by a legitimate authority. Under no circumstances can the action of vigilantes be justified: individuals taking the law into their own hands can often lead to the cycle of violence – killing giving birth to revenge. Given he believed that God was responsible for the status of the rulers of the nation, then the legitimate authority was the God-authorized ruler. The second was that there must be a just cause. This can include self-defense or the protection of others, but it cannot include the expansionist ambitions of a particular ruler.

In the thirteenth century, the great Dominican Friar St Thomas Aquinas, whom we met in an earlier chapter on natural law, added a third condition. There has to be a right intention. You must intend to promote good not evil. In one sense this condition was clarifying the second condition – the cause must be just. Underpinning the clarification of Aquinas, we have the insight that the goal of waging war is to create a just peace. Aquinas believed that sometimes the way to arrive at a just peace is to wage war against the unjust ruler. The sort of picture emerging is that we are justified in occasionally resorting to war, if and only if, it is the only possible route to a just peace.

The just war tradition continued to grow and develop. In the sixteenth century, two Spaniards, Vitoria and Suárez, are responsible for developing the tradition and explicitly talking about 'international law." Franciso de Vitoria (1492–1546) is universally acclaimed as the founder of modern international law. He was a Dominican and for much of his career taught at the University of Salmanca. Two years after Vitoria's death, Francisco Suárez (1548–1617) was born. His extensive writings in theology (especially ecclesiology) and ethics (especially politics) made him prominent. Between Vitoria and Suárez three further conditions were added to the just war tradition. The first was that all other means of rectifying the injustice have failed. War really must be the last resort. All peaceful means must have been tried to rectify the wrong that has been done. The second was that there must be a reasonable hope of winning the war. Now this is an interesting condition: the tradition does teach that it is wrong for a ruler to lead a nation into an heroic fight, even if the cause is just, where there is certain defeat. Futile just wars are not commended. The point, of course, is that the tragedy of the many potential deaths always needs to be weighed heavily in the scales before embarking on the action. The third condition was that the manner of conducting the war must be legitimate. This is the challenge to the thought exercise at the start of this chapter. The presumption is that needless killing is always wrong. Death and misery must be kept to the minimum necessary to create a just peace. So, for example, Vitoria did think that taking weapons from those you conquer was legitimate, but despoiling their agricultural crops was wrong. Given many recent wars (e.g. the Bosnia-Herzegovina war) have involved the victors raping and burning the homes of the losers, leading to a considerable refugee problem, Vitoria had a moral insight here that the world still needs to learn.

As we enter the twenty-first century, the just war tradition remains as relevant as ever. To summarize the journey thus far, we find that we now distinguish between the appropriate conditions for waging war (*jus ad bellum*) and the moral conduct once involved in war (*jus in bello*). Almost anyone who feels that occasionally war is legitimate will affirm that the just war tradition is important. And the modern contemporary arguments are over three areas: first, is it possible to have a "just revolution"? Second, can one ever use nuclear weapons within a modern war? And if, ethically, one cannot use them, then in what sense are such weapons a deterrent? And third, in a world where the biggest fear is that a terrorist group may obtain access to a weapon of mass destruction, do we need to modify this tradition to permit "preemptive" warfare? Let us now list the just war criteria and explore these three issues.

The conditions for the waging war (*jus ad bellum*) are as follows:

1 *The need for a legitimate authority.* Although some have argued that a "just revolution" ought to be an option against an unjust ruler, the tradition wants to confine legitimate authority to an existing government. The problem with private individuals and groups is that violent action can easily merge into the world of gang warfare and the vigilante. Linked with this, there is a sense in which the vocation of leadership of a nation involves the responsibility of deciding when it is necessary to take up arms for a just cause. The leader is in a position to see the big picture and therefore best able to make the call that violence is necessary.

2 *The cause must be just.* The problem in practice with this condition is the extent of one's memory. The tradition wants to confine war to self-defense, a defense of another nation, the protection of innocents, or to regain that which should not have been taken. However, many battles (e.g. the wars between Serbia and Croatia) have tangled historical roots. The question whether a just cause extends to a preemptive war is difficult to answer. As a general rule, the tradition requires that an evil deed needs to have been committed. The problem with anticipating an evil deed is that one is never sure that the deed will have been committed; it is therefore easy to be unjust. The mere manufacture of weapons of mass destruction then appears a borderline case: they might be no more than a deterrent to possible enemies.

3 *The third condition is right intention.* Now this remains an important insight: a preemptive war with the goal of creating a just peace might be legitimate. If,

for example, the primary reason for the 2003 Iraq war was to depose a dictator who continues to threaten the state of Israel, thereby making it difficult for the Israeli government to forge a just peace with the Palestinian people, then perhaps this condition is being met. If on the other hand, the motive for the Iraq war was to control the oil supplies of the region, then that would not be compatible with this condition. The rule here is that the ultimate end of war must be to establish a just peace.

4 *War must be the last resort.* It is always a serious matter to embark on war. War dead are an inevitability. Indeed such is the "science" of war today, it is possible to estimate the numbers of dead (both combatants and non-combatants). Therefore, given the seriousness of war, the government must have exhausted all other diplomatic and non-military means for securing peace and justice. This is a key difficulty for anyone arguing for a preemptive war: it will inevitably seem that war has been chosen before all the other options have been exhausted.

5 *A reasonable chance of success.* We are living in an interesting historical moment. With only one superpower, it is clear that the government of the United States will always meet this condition. With its vast military might, the United States can secure a result within months of starting a conflict. The ambiguity here, however, is whether that is a sufficient definition of success. Establishing the subsequent peace is extremely difficult.

6 *Proportionality is an important aspect to the military* response. When the government of Argentina invaded the British-ruled Falkland Islands, then it would have been a violation of this condition of a just war for the United Kingdom to have used nuclear weapons against the major cities of Argentina. The response to an injustice must not create even more injustice. This condition poses significant difficulties for both the use of nuclear weapons and the concept of a preemptive war.

The conditions applying to the conduct of the war (*jus in bello)* are as follows:

1 *It is wrong to target non-combatants.* The major victims of a war are often the elderly, women, and children. These people are not in a position to determine the results of the battle. So the death and injury of a non-combatant is wrong. This again is a key difficulty with nuclear weapons. However, it is important to note that the latest generation of weapons is capable of being targeted very effectively. The Allies in the Iraq war were able to target a particular site with almost complete accuracy. It is worth noting that the tradition does recognize that "collateral damage" will occur (i.e. there are moments when tragically a non-combatant is hit); however, with the latest technology, we are in a position where this condition can generally be met.

2 *It is necessary to use proportionate means.* Proportionality is both an issue before one embarks on the war and during the war. Use of a nuclear weapon is almost always problematic. Whether, for example, the destruction of Hiroshima (let alone Nagasaki) met this condition remains one of the most contentious issues surrounding the conduct of the Second World War. Those who thought it legitimate argue that these two bombs ensured an earlier surrender of the Japanese to the Allies; those who think this illegitimate just point to the millions of non-combatants who were killed.

Conclusion

This is a key ethical question for us all. It is very difficult for a government to lead a nation to war without, at least, the tacit support of the people – this is true even in non-democratic regimes. Therefore responsible citizenship does require some thought about this issue – a theme to which we will return in chapter 15. The presumption in this chapter is that the slogan "all is fair in love and war" is wrong. There are, at least in respect to war, certain very important rules. The pacifist challenges us all: perhaps we need to be willing to die for the message and commitment to peace. It is remarkable that Jesus, Gandhi, and Martin Luther King Jnr all taught peace and all died violent deaths. The witness to the evil of escalating violence is not a cheap or easy one. The world has already insisted on several prominent martyrs; more will probably follow before we learn the lesson that war is always a very inadequate way of solving disputes.

Notes

1   The entire thought exercise has been taken from "The Good Fight" in Martin Cohen, *101 Ethical Dilemmas* (London and New York: Routledge 2003) pp. 112–13.
2   What follows is a revised version of material found in my *Plurality and Christian Ethics* (Cambridge: Cambridge University Press) pp. 10–14.
3   It is worth noting in defense of Locke that the Pope had issued an authority to depose Elizabeth I and had not revoked it; and the rule of law in England was not so stable that one could take risks.
4   There are other early examples, for example, sixteenth-century Poland, and free churches did have very limited rights before Locke.
5   Mahatma Gandhi, *The Mind of Mahatma Gandhi* as found on www.mkgandhi.org
6   Martin Luther King, "Christmas Sermon 1967" from James Melvin Washington (ed.) *A Testament of Hope: The Essential Writings on Martin Luther King, Jr* (San Francisco, A: Harper and Row 1986).
7   Matthew 5:38–9, New Revised Standard Version.
8   Mahatma Gandhi, *The Mind of Mahatma Gandhi* as found on www.mkgandhi.org
9   Matthew 26:51–54, New Revised Standard Version.

13

Dilemmas in government and leadership

Thought exercise

A leader is at a cocktail party attended by famous figures from throughout the ages. Over the course of the evening, Plato, Mother Theresa, and Niccolò Machiavelli all discreetly slip him copies of their résumés, each one greatly interested in serving as his chief adviser . . . Plato and Mother Theresa in this scenario receive only a polite letter of acknowledgment for their interest in this job. The leader picks up the phone and say "Mr. Machiavelli, I want you to be on my team."[1]

Do you agree with this decision?

Every morning, a relatively small number of men and women wake up to face a new day aware that their decisions during that day will affect thousands, perhaps millions, of people. This is called "power," and the most overt form of power is the leadership of a country. Power brings a highly distinctive set of ethical dilemmas. For most of us, those above us keep us ethically accountable. However, for those who are at the top, there is no one above who can keep them accountable. In mature democracies, the hope is that a combination of "checks and balances" coupled with "electoral accountability" ensures that those in power exercise appropriate "self-restraint." However, in a setting where civil society is less developed, perhaps owing to a history of rampant colonialism or poverty, the temptations of the misuse of power are often impossible to resist. Our task in this chapter is to explore the nature of government and sketch out the ethics of leadership.

The chapter will start with the different models that describe the role of the government in the State. We shall compare the "liberal" account with a more "communitarian or organic" account. Then we look at the achievement of democracy, before concluding with an exploration of leadership ethics. It is in this last section that we shall explore Steven Sample's claim that Machiavelli would be the best advisor for any leader.

The role of government in the State

The literature looking at the role of the government in the State is vast. So what follows is a brief sketch of the two main models that tend to dominate the debate. These are the "liberal social contract" approach and the more "organic, communitarian" approach. These approaches are not easily identifiable with the political "left" or "right" – labels that themselves are used differently in different countries and contexts.

The liberal social contract approach

It was Thomas Hobbes (1588–1679) who painted a gloomy picture of humanity without government. Life, explains Hobbes, was nasty, brutish, and short. In this state of nature, as Hobbes called it, there was anarchy and violence. Hobbes then goes on to defend a form of totalitarianism. A strong ruler is needed to impose order and rule. The argument of his book *Leviathan* is that we concede absolute power to this ruler because this is the only way we can enjoy the benefits of law.

John Locke (1632–1704), who we have already met in this book, developed this myth about the origins of the state in a liberal way. For Locke, Hobbes was right about the state of nature: everyone was behaving as they pleased – one could steal, murder, or more mundanely behave indecently; there were no controls on behavior. However, the movement from anarchy to law was caused by individuals opting to surrender certain rights for the privilege of living in society – under law. One surrendered the entitlement to murder or steal for a reciprocal agreement with others that they would not murder or steal. Locke believed that there was a historical moment when the "social contract" was made. The initial individuals made a decision to trade some of their freedom for order. Subsequent generations, explains Locke, exercised their "tacit consent," although it is unclear in Locke how exactly this happened. The concept that was developing here was that ruler (or government) was responsible for the rule of law that enabled those who have contracted into society to live together.

In this account, individuals have surrendered the minimum number of rights necessary to live together. Now this means that the ruler is dependent on the consent of the people – the idea of democracy was starting to emerge – and must recognize certain fundamental rights of the individual. Therefore the State, on this view, has an interest in those areas that enabled people to live together, it has no right to interfere in the private life of the individual.

As the tradition developed, it arrived at the minimalist view of the State. The State is responsible for organizing the minimum that enables individuals to live together. Adam Smith, writing in the eighteenth century, confined the work of the State to the following: internal law enforcement (i.e. a police force) and external security (i.e. a military).

A properly "liberal" State requires a minimalist government. Contrary to current American usage of the word "liberal," the government should not be involved in vast welfare programmes and initiatives. It should not be running the railways or manufacturing cars. In addition, the government has absolutely no right to intervene with the decisions of consenting adults in private (whether it is to smoke cannabis or to have sex together). Taxation should be low because the needs of the government are very limited.

The most popular analogy is the concept of a hotel. Raymond Plant describes the liberal society thus:

> In an hotel people come together under a set of rules which govern their interactions during their stay. The rules are meant to facilitate their private ends whatever they may be. Individuals are anonymous. If they wish to enter into group activities this is a matter of choice. The hotel does not itself, as a condition of being there, offer a sense of common purpose or identity. The guests at the hotel have no positive duties to one another unless they choose to assume such obligations. The hotel is focussed on anonymity, privacy, contract and rules, not on a common purpose or a common notion of human fulfilment.'[2]

This is a very helpful analogy. If you imagine a business hotel, then you will find an environment where the individuals come to the hotel with virtually no obligations to the other guests. The only rule is that in the public space, you should behave in a way that does not interfere or offend the other guests. There is no obligation to be friendly or interested in others – in fact such behavior is positively discouraged. And in the privacy of your own bedroom, you can behave largely as you wish: you can entertain your mistress, watch an adult movie, or just read your Bible.

The organic and communitarian approach

One problem with the liberal account is that there was, historically, no meeting when individuals surrendered certain rights for the benefits of living under law. Instead, then as now, individuals were born into families, which were part of preexisting communities, that, in turn, were part of a larger structure (a region or a country). Individuals were located in a culture which shared a language and religion. They did not pick this environment; they were simply born into it.

The organic account of the State starts by recognizing a close connection between culture and nationhood. It was Hegel (1770–1831) who made this point central to his understanding of nationhood. Edmund Burke (1729–97), when analysing the French Revolution, made the point that the State should grow with the culture and that the responsibility of the State varies from culture to culture. Richard Hooker (1554–1600), the Anglican divine, argued that the Protestant religion of the established church was identical with the nation of English people. The culture of England was Protestant and the State should uphold the Protestant culture.

Enoch Powell (1912–88) is a good illustration of this tradition. He represented Wolverhampton and then South Down in Ulster in the House of Commons.[3] Powell's views came to prominence when, in a speech to the West Midlands Area Conservative Political Centre in Birmingham on on April 20, 1968, he argued against free immigration from the former colonies and complained about the changing character of British cities.[4] He claimed that the 5 to 10 per cent of the British population who were from the Commonwealth represented an unacceptable threat to the stability of British cities.

For Powell, people do not opt into a nation, but are born into it. Nationhood is linked with a certain language, a certain religion, and a certain history. Now Powell admits that the combination of language, religion, and history that produces a particular sovereign nation State is a mystery.[5] Nevertheless, an entity emerges that identifies with a set of shared symbols and demands self-rule. Powell writes,

> Nationhood is an absolute. There is no such thing as semi-nationhood, or semi-nationalism . . . Nationalism, if it is real, cannot be brought off with less than the complete article. This is not because the nationalist is less reasonable or more greedy than his fellow men; it is because nationhood is the complete article.[6]

National cultural identity is the basis of a stable society. For Powell, to tamper with or destroy that cultural identity is treasonable. Therefore, anything that undermines the culture of a nation will destabilize that nation. With the growth of immigration during the 1950s and 1960s, different cultural outlooks were introduced into Britain. For Powell these people are alien:

> Of the great multitude, numbering already two million, of West Indians and Asians in England, it is no more true to say that England is their country than it would be to say that the West Indies, or Pakistan, or

India are our country. In these great numbers they are, and remain, as alien here as we would be in Kingston or in Delhi; indeed, with the growth of concentrated numbers, the alienness grows, not by choice but by necessity.[7]

He describes in graphic terms the fear indigenous English people allegedly feel as they watch their cities being "taken over."

For Powell, it is comparable to treason for a government to permit so much immigration. He denounces successive British governments when he writes,

It was not for them to heed the cries of anguish from those of their own people who already saw their towns being changed, their native places turned into foreign lands, and themselves displaced as if by a systematic colonization.[8]

For Powell, the government are guilty:

for no government has the moral right to alter, or permit to be altered, the character and the identity of a nation without that nation's knowledge and without the nation's will. It is a moral issue, and it is a supreme issue.[9]

Powell believed that the task for the government of Britain is to protect the Protestant Anglo-Saxon culture. Powell's equivalents can be found in all cultures. Israr Ahmed, for example, is his Pakistan equivalent. Ahmed was the founder of the Tanzeem-e-Islami – a movement dedicated to the propagation of the teaching of the Qu'ran and bringing about an Islamic state (initially in Pakistan, but ultimately throughout the world). Although Pakistan has a constitutional commitment to Islam, Ahmed believes that Pakistan functions as a secular state. For in an Islamic state, he explains, "only Muslims will take part in the process of legislation."[10] He goes on: "Though every adult Muslim male and female would have the right of vote for the legislative assembly, only Muslim males, whose character is above board, will be able to participate in the elections as a candidate."[11] Although he goes on to explain that the rights of non-Muslims to property, life, and religion will be protected, it is clear that non-Muslims are second-class citizens in Ahmed's vision of the Islamic state.

This disagreement over the nature of the State is a key issue in understanding the role of government in the world today. The liberal state tries to create a neutral centre that confines religious life to the personal and the private. The organic account recognizes that nationhood reflects culture; and different nations should therefore protect the purity of their culture.

The Hart–Devlin debate

Often the exercise of power involves passing laws. We have seen that the nature of the State will be reflected in the judicial system of the State. This is the realm of jurisprudence and the debate between the H. L. A. Hart and Patrick Devlin in the UK became the supreme example of these two contrasting views of the States expressing themselves in two contrasting approaches to law.

This debate was provoked by the report of the Wolfenden Committee on Homosexual Offences and Prostitution (1957). The heart of the report was that it was not the task of the State to legislate about morality. The role of law, the report explained was:

> to preserve public order and decency to protect the citizens from what is offensive or injurious and to provide sufficient safeguards against exploitation and aggravation of others, particularly those who are especially vulnerable because they are young, weak in body or mind, inexperienced, or in a state of special physical, official or economic dependence. It is not, in our view, the function of the law to intervene in the private lives of citizens.'[12]

This is the classic liberal position. We divide behavior into the public and private realms. We legislate on the former, but we leave the latter – as much as we can – to individual decision.

Now Lord Devlin was happy with the recommendations of the Wolfenden report, but unhappy with the reasoning. He wanted to argue that it was appropriate for the State to legislate on morals. Indeed it is important that the State does so, for the survival of society depends on such legislation. So Devlin explains, "If men and women try to create a society in which there is no fundamental agreement about good and evil they will fail; if, having based it on common agreement, the agreement goes, the society will disintegrate."[13] At this point we find the "organic" and "communitarian" view of the State being assumed. It is important that we keep our shared morality as a culture. If there are points at which we feel a deep sense of revulsion, then it is appropriate to make that act illegal.

H. L. A. Hart wrote a reply to Devlin. He is the straightforward liberal who invoked John Stuart Mill's famous "harm-to-others" principle. For Hart, Devlin is on dangerous ground. He feels that we must be able to distinguish that which "harms others" (public) from that which is simply "private." And he cannot see any justification for interfering in the latter realm. So Hart explains that Devlin's mistake is his

... undiscussed assumption. This is that all morality – sexual morality together with the morality that forbids acts injurious to others such as killing, stealing and dishonesty – form a single seamless web, so that those who deviate from any part are likely or perhaps bound to deviate from the whole. It is of course clear (and one of the oldest insights of political theory) that society could not exist without a morality which mirrored and supplemented the law's prescription of conduct injurious to others. But there is again no evidence to support, and much to refute, the theory that those who deviate from conventional sexual morality are in other ways hostile to society.[14]

For Hart then we can and should make the distinction between the public and private realms. For Devlin, he thinks this might undermine our shared cultural morality and in so doing undermine society. Hart has a classic liberal view of the State, while Devlin holds an organic one.

The remarkable achievement of democracy

On both accounts of the State, it is possible to have some form of democratic government. The word "democracy" comes from two Greek words that mean "rule of the people." Instead of a monarchy or rule by the clergy, the people determine their own future.

In the history of political thought, democracy has not had a good press. Plato (427–347 BCE), for example, in *The Republic* is deeply critical of democracy and sees it as the equivalent of mob-rule. Thomas Aquinas (1225–74) was a supporter of a limited monarchy. Karl Marx (1818–83) saw liberal democracy as the tool of the powerful that needs to be challenged before the creation of a genuine classless society.

Although Francis Fukuyama might have been a little optimistic in claiming that liberal democratic societies are the "end of history," he did have a point. He was writing at the end of the Cold War and the collapse of the Berlin Wall.[15] He meant that we cannot improve on this form of social organization: naturally wars, poverty, and political arguments will continue, but political organization around the principles of liberal democracy has triumphed. He was right in this respect. The idea of a peaceful transfer of power from one person to another, determined by the vote of the people, is the best way of proceeding. The people grant the leadership their power; and it is the people that hold the leadership accountable; and it is the people that can take that power away and give it to someone else.

When one commits to democratic principles, then it means that one believes in persuasion rather than force. We are opting for a certain vision of society. Our disagreements are not going to be resolved by resorting to violence, but by disagreement, exploration, and persuading the court of "public opinion."

These features of a democratic society make such good sense that it is not surprising that many cultures are opting for that form of government. It is true that all democracies are highly imperfect. The opportunity to persuade, in the United States, for example, does depend on vast resources. One needs literally millions of dollars to put on a campaign to become a senator, let alone a president. And Fox News – a key information provider for millions of people – offers a very limited view of the world. It is virtually unthinkable that an advocate for the Swedish model of the Welfare State would be given a fair hearing on that channel. The problem of resourcing a democracy so that the people have an appropriate sense of all the options remains a pressing difficulty throughout the western world.

It is important that we continue to make the argument for democracy. Not everyone is persuaded. Fresh movements will always rise up and suggest alternatives. Normally the form of the argument is this: our current democracy is imperfect for this or that reason; temporally we need an undemocratic government or to use force for these reasons; and at the end of the temporary stage, we will be able to usher in an authentic democracy. Such arguments are very dangerous. The key difficulty is that most leaders find it very difficult to recognize the end of the temporary stage; they start to imagine that they are indispensable. Robert Mugabe of Zimbabwe is a classic example. In a democratic state, we do see power passing peacefully from one ruler to another. One strength of the American constitution is the limit of two consecutive terms for the President. The United Kingdom has not necessarily been well served by Prime Ministers who seek a third or even a fourth term.

The point is that democracy is both a remarkable achievement, but also very difficult to realize. Leadership of anything (from the Boy Scouts to Microsoft to a country) can create a hubris that leads to the perception of indispensability. This is the biggest temptation of leadership. And this is the point at which leadership ethics is desperately needed.

Leadership ethics

We started this chapter with a thought exercise from Steven Sample. He suggested that Niccolò Machiavelli (1469–1527), the Italian civil servant and political analyst, should be the first choice for any leader searching for a chief advisor. So we shall start this section by identifying seven principles of leadership found in Machiavelli's *The Prince*. This is probably the first textbook ever produced on applied "leadership ethics"; it was an attempt to provide some advice to those who aspire to leadership. In each case I shall invite Machiavelli to explain the principle in his own words.

1   It is important to master the science of war. Machiavelli writes, "A prince, therefore, should have no concern, no thought, or pursue any other art besides the art of war, its organization and instruction. This is the art that those who command are expected to master. This art has such potency, that not only does it ensure that those who are born princes remain princes, but it often enables men of humble rank to rise to that position."[16]

2   It is better to tend towards a reputation for meanness rather than generosity. So Machiavelli writes, "A prince, therefore, should give little thought to being considered miserly if it means not robbing his subjects, being able to defend himself, not becoming impoverished and contemptible, and not being forced to become rapacious. For this is one of those vices which enables him to rule."[17]

3   It is better to be feared rather than loved. Machiavelli offers the following argument for this: "[O]ne can say the following about men: they are ungrateful, inconsistent, feigners and dissimulators, avoiders of dangers, eager for gain, and whilst it profits them they are all yours. They will offer you their blood, their property, their life and their offspring when your need for them is remote . . . But when your needs are pressing, they turn away. The prince who depends entirely on their words perishes when he finds he has not taken any other precautions . . . Men are less worried about harming somebody who makes himself loved than someone who makes himself feared, for love is held by a chain of obligation which, since men are bad, is broken at every opportunity for personal gain. Fear, on the other hand, is maintained by a dread of punishment which will never desert you."[18] He goes on to say, it is important not be hated, but to be feared is good.

4   Although it is important to appear good and trustworthy, one must be willing to do otherwise. Machiavelli explains to actually be good and trustworthy all the time "is harmful, but when you appear to have them [i.e. these qualities] they are useful, like seeming merciful, loyal, humane, upright and religious . . . But you must remain mentally prepared, so that when it is necessary not to have these qualities you are able, and know how to assume their opposites. It is essential to realize this: that a prince, and above all a new prince, cannot practice all those things which gain men a reputation for being good, as it is often necessary, in order to keep hold of the state, to act contrary to trust, contrary to charity, contrary to humanity and contrary to religion."[19]

5   In cases of conflict, it is better to avoid neutrality, and support resolutely one side or the other. Machiavelli writes, "Irresolute princes, in order to avoid current difficulties, normally assume the path of neutrality and are normally ruined as a result. But when you boldly declare your support for one side, if the person you back wins, although he is powerful and you are at his mercy, he is indebted to you and there is a bond of mutual support . . . But if the

person you back loses, he will grant you refuge, and in helping you as much as he can, your shared fortunes may improve."[20]

6 Pick the team around you wisely. "The choice of ministers," explains Machiavelli, "is a task of no little importance for a prince. Whether they are good or not depends upon the prudence of the prince. The first impression one forms of a ruler's intelligence is based on an examination of the men he keeps around him."

7 Invite a small inner team to be free to speak the truth to you. Machiavelli does not think it wise to let everyone speak critically to the leader, yet it is also wrong for the leader to surround him or herself with flatterers. Instead "a prince should therefore follow a third path, choosing wise men in his state who alone are given the freedom to speak to him truthfully, and only about those things he asks and nothing else."[21]

Now, returning to the thought exercise, the question is: do we think that Semple is right to invite Machiavelli to be his chief advisor?

Machiavelli's main achievement is to identify the main traits that are necessary for a ruler to succeed in a totalitarian (i.e. non-democratic) environment. In this environment, the model of leadership commended by Machiavelli makes complete sense. It is important that one knows the secrets of war and one is willing to do anything necessary to keep power: for in this environment, it is unlikely that power will pass peacefully from one Prince to the next. Your survival literally depends on your power; therefore doing everything necessary to keep power is the key to continuing to live.

However, the reason why modern democratic societies are so important is that such rule is less necessary. A free press will expose the duplicitous nature of a regime. Bill Clinton imagined that his adulterous affair was simply a secret between him and his lover, but such is the interest surrounding the President he was discovered; Richard Nixon was willing to do everything to keep power, but *The Washington Post* brought him down; and successive British governments have had to endure enquires about their integrity forced upon them by public pressure.

Those who live by Machiavelli's principles are much less likely to survive in a modern democracy than those who seek to serve with some integrity. In fact Machiavelli's principles are the temptation for the leader; one that must be resisted. Granted the principles that "one cannot expect to be loved all the time" and "seek advisors who in confidence are willing to tell you the truth" are insights that you can derive from Machiavelli's work, the underlying model is unhelpful. Instead the leadership principles need to start from the basics: why exactly does one aspire to leadership?

The best reason is that one has discovered that he or she has the vocation of institutional care. Now the word "institution" here is being used very broadly;

it includes organizations (such as churches or the Rotary Club), to companies, charities, and countries. It is a vocation because it is the utilization of a set of gifts (which include vision, the capacity to motivate, organizational skills, etc.) to progress an institution. It involves care because institutions are precious. Many institutions have been operating for generations. In most cases they are passed to a particular leader for safekeeping and development through the latest set of challenges and demands. One has a duty to set the simple goal that, at whatever point the leadership stops, the institution must be as strong as it was when one started to lead.

The concept of institutional care has underpinning it the concept of "service." Leadership properly understood is service. One must be ready to serve those who work for you. Institutions are as good as the people within them. Enabling and empowering are the key concepts that transform people and therefore transform institutions.

Finally, in a democratic environment, management should be done in a framework of transparency and accountability. Power often wants to restrict information. The problem with restricting information is that others are then puzzled why exactly this or that decision has been made. It feeds conspiracy theories; if people do not know why a decision has been made, then they will offer their own analysis and reach their own conclusions. Transparency facilitates accountability. When the people are informed, it is then possible for the people to make a decision about the appropriateness of the leadership.

Conclusion

This chapter started with the key debate in political theory. How do you understand the State and the role of government in the State? We concluded that section by reflecting on the achievement of democracy. It was in that context we revisited the leadership skills necessary for both the country and other institutions. Machiavelli's vision is a temptation. It feeds patriarchal instincts that power must be exercised in a ruthless and uncompromising way. This chapter wants to stress the alterative. Although sometimes Machiavelli's way seems to work (who knows exactly who escapes detection for abuse of power?), we need to create a culture where it "works" less and less often. By thinking of leadership as a vocation of institutional care, with commitments to transparency and accountability, it might be possible for a culture committed to the common good to emerge.

Notes

1 This thought exercise is taken from and adapted slightly from Steven Sample, *The Contrarian's Guide of Leadership* (San Francisco, CA: Jossey-Bass 2002) p. 91.

2 Raymond Plant, *Politics Theology and History* (Cambridge: Cambridge University Press 2001) p. 7.
3 For a fuller discussion of Enoch Powell see my *Plurality and Christian Ethics* (Cambridge: Cambridge University Press 1994). Some of the material that follows is adapted from there.
4 For the text of the speech see T. E. Utley, *Enoch Powell: The Man and His Thinking* (London: William Kimber 1968) pp. 178–90.
5 See J. E. Powell, *Still to Decide* (Kingswood: Elliot Right Way Books 1972) p. 170ff.
6 Ibid. p. 172.
7 Ibid. p. 190.
8 Ibid. p. 202ff.
9 Ibid. p. 204.
10 Israr Ahmad, *Khilafah in Pakistan: What, Why, and How?* (Lahore, Pakistan: Markazi Anjuman khuddam-ul-Qur'an 2001) p. 6.
11 Ibid.
12 The Report of the Wolfenden Committee on Homosexual Offences and Prostitution as quoted in Simon Lee, *Law and Morals* (Oxford: Oxford University Press 1986) p. 26.
13 P. Devlin, *The Enforcement of Morals* (Oxford: Oxford University Press 1968) as quoted in Lee, ibid. p. 27.
14 H. L. A. Hart, *Law, Liberty and Morality* (Oxford: Oxford University Press 1968) as quoted in Simon Lee, ibid. p. 28.
15 See Francis Fukuyama, "The End of History" in *The National Interest* 18 (Summer 1989), pp. 3–11.
16 Niccolò Machiavelli, *The Prince and Other Writings*, translated and edited by Stephen J. Milner (London: Everyman J. M. Dent 1995) p. 86.
17 Ibid. p. 91.
18 Ibid. p. 94.
19 Ibid. p. 97.
20 Ibid. p. 114.
21 Ibid. p. 117.

14

Dilemmas and the future:
the environment, animals, and plants

Thought exercise

"In an account of the Dutch voyage to the Mascarene Islands in 1598, under a rough sketch entitled 'the destruction of the Dodos,' is a verse on how to catch the dodo:

For food the seamen hunt the flesh of feathered fowl,
They tap the palms, the round-sterned dodo they destroy,
The parrot's life they spare that he may scream and howl,
And thus his fellows to imprisonment decoy.

The seamen were very hungry, the dodos were very easy to catch and there were an awful lot of them. At first. And if it were all right to catch the first one, then it must have been all right to catch the next one, and the next one, and the next. Well, who was to know when it became not all right? If indeed it ever was wrong. There are a lot of seagulls left."[1]

Moral reflection is not confined to the present, but also needs to take seriously the future. In this chapter, we shall reflect on some of the ethical demands that the future might make on the present. The focus will be the corporate, social, and political realms, namely the extent to which human social and political behavior today should be influenced by concerns about the future of the planet or other species. Our brief examination of the topic will focus on three issues: the first is the problems associated with economic growth; the second is the environment; and the third is animals.

Economic growth

Perhaps the key debate in economics about the future is the argument over the legitimacy of economic growth. Economic growth is the goal of virtually every economy in the world. This means that the economic planners want to see growth in terms of trade, jobs, and therefore wealth. In a growing economy, one hopes that everyone will get richer, although some get richer a great deal faster than others. The growing economy brings in more tax revenues that can be used to provide support for those who are struggling. To bring about a growing economy, governments often borrow money. This money is then invested in production, which provides jobs, and the wealth from these jobs is then spent on goods and services, which in turn leads to more jobs. That, at least, is the theory.

In 1967 E. J. Mishan produced a book called *The Costs of Economic Growth* that attacked this vision of economic management. His argument was that economic growth is treated as if it were a panacea; however, the costs of economic growth are so great that it has become detrimental to human welfare. Instead, argues Mishan, we need "a far more selective form of development which must include a radical reshaping of our physical environment with the needs of pleasant living, and not the needs of traffic or industry, foremost in our minds."[2] Mishan attacks many of the results of modernity and the quest for economic growth. For example, he describes the motorcar as:

> one of the greatest disasters to have befallen the human race. Given the absence of controls, the growth of populations and increased wealth and urbanization would, in any case, have produced overgrown cities. Commercial and municipal greed, coupled with architectural apathy, share the responsibility for a litter of shabby buildings. But it needed the motorcar to consummate these developments, to fill our days with clamor and fumes, to suburbanize the countryside and to subtropianize suburbia, and to ensure that any resort which became accessible should simultaneously become unattractive.[3]

For Mishan, the quest for endless economic growth is deeply damaging in its effects. It is a moral problem: we are constantly dissatisfied with the present, which makes us ill at ease in the moment. Mishan believes that much of our modern society is impoverished and destructive because it has undermined the sense of community. It has undermined certain social structures that existed in the past and therefore has made humanity less and less satisfied. He writes:

> In the ruthless transformation of our planet home we are concurrently destroying much that man's nature doted on in the past: a sense of inti-

mately belonging, of being part of a community in which each man had his place; a sense of being close to nature, of being close to the soil and the beasts of the field that served him; a sense of being part of the eternal and unhurried rhythm of life.[4]

And to the criticism that he is being a romantic about the past, Mishan responds:

It would be untrue to assert that in all past civilizations a feeling of security and contentment was experienced by all families as it would be idle to deny that many suffered from hardship, disease, and poverty. But wherever people lived comfortably, whether in town or village, or farm, their satisfactions were rooted ultimately in their closeness to each other and to the natural order of their lives.[5]

Mishan anticipates certain themes that became prominent in the "no-growth" movement that so influenced the Green parties in Europe. We shall look at the ethical demands of the environment later on in this chapter. However, for now it is worth noting the following. The main argument of the no-growth movement was that there is an environmental limit to growth. Growth depends on oil and natural gas, which are limited resources. Jonathon Porritt, a prominent sympathizer of the Green movement, explains: "It is no longer possible to manufacture abundance through making unsustainable demands on the world's resources and environment."[6] He then quotes the Greens' description of the economy:

The characteristics of such an economy are clear: reduced industrial throughput, greater self-reliance and sustainability through largely decentralized economic activity, maximized use of renewable resources and conservation of non-renewable resources, a far-reaching redistribution of wealth, land and the means of production, with the possibility of more fulfilling, personally satisfying work, all set within a more co-operatively based framework, and enhanced by the use of new technologies where they complement the above features.[7]

Naturally defenders of economic growth do not concur with this analysis. Although it is true we must recognize that some of the resources we are currently very dependent on are limited, there are others which are not. The sun and wind are two examples. In addition the combination of human ingenuity, technology, and regulation means that many of the environmental costs can be prevented or ameliorated. The air in many of our western cities is cleaner now than it has been for generations; fish are back in the River Thames running through London; and our garbage is in landfills that are now an aesthetic delight thanks to a careful landscaping of the area. Even the dire predictions about the lack of oil proved mistaken as technology enabled us to access oil in parts of the world that we always thought inaccessible (e.g. the North Sea).

Growth advocates point out that there is a sinister side to the Green agenda. The population explosion anxiety, for example, runs parallel with a belief that we need fewer people, which in practice leads to policy commitments involving anti-immigration and anti-development. The classic example of this argument was Garett Hardin's rather unpleasant article called "Lifeboat Ethics: The Case against Helping the Poor," which is worth looking at in some detail.

Hardin frames the problem thus:

> If we divide the world crudely into rich nations and poor nations, two thirds of them are desperately poor, and only one third comparatively rich, with the United States the wealthiest of all. Metaphorically each rich nation can be seen as a lifeboat of comparatively rich people. In the ocean outside each lifeboat swim the poor of the world, who would like to get in, or at least share some of the wealth. What should the life-boat passengers do?[8]

Hardin then goes on to make the case that the only way forward for the survival of those in the lifeboat is to forbid anyone else joining them on it. So Hardin writes:

> So here we sit, say 50 people in our lifeboat. To be generous, let us assume it has room for 10 more, making a total capacity of 60. Suppose the 50 of us in the lifeboat see 100 others swimming in the water outside, begging for admission to our boat or for handouts. We have several options: we may be tempted to try to live by the Christian ideal of being "our brother's keeper," or by the Marxist ideal of "to each according to his need." Since the needs of all in the water are the same, and since they can all be seen as "our brothers," we could take them all into our boat, making a total of 150 in a boat designed for 60. The boat swamps, everyone drowns. Complete justice, complete catastrophe.[9]

Hardin goes on to argue that even the spare ten seats should not be filled. We need them as a "safety factor." He then develops the argument that this is indeed our predicament by drawing on a combination of Green concerns and right-wing bigotry. The nations in the two-thirds developing world, complains Hardin, have disproportionate population growth and corrupt governments (who do not keep aside sufficient resources for the inevitable periodic famine – the Joseph principle). If we feed the people in these poorer countries, then we create an environmental problem. So Hardin explains,

Every human born constitutes a draft on all aspects of the environment: food, air, water, forests, beaches, wildlife, scenery and solitude. Food can, perhaps, be significantly increased to meet a growing demand. But what about clean beaches, unspoiled forests, and solitude?[10]

Hardin wants a complete stop to immigration into the richer nations, no overseas aid to poorer countries, and no famine relief campaigns in the crisis periods.

The assumption underpinning Hardin's article is that the economy is a cake whose size is determinate. Only a limited number of people can have a useful slice of that cake; and if you want a bigger slice of the cake then that must mean others go without or receive a smaller slice. The lifeboat has a fixed capacity, which Hardin thinks we have virtually reached. But in fact the economy is not such a cake and moreover prosperity needs population growth.

This is an important point. If you imagine a remote medieval village of 200 people, then it is likely it will be a poor village. There is a very small community of both sellers and buyers. You wouldn't be able to start a company which produces specialized toys because there are insufficient people to buy the product. This village wouldn't have the population to justify careers in law, accountancy, engineering, manufacturing, art, music, sport, and the academy. It would generate very small tax revenues or even a tax system, because there would be very little commerce. So there would be no tax base for welfare support and almost everyone would have employment around the agriculture land. The fact is that a wealthy economy needs a significant population: growth in trade needs more people. In comparison with our medieval ancestors, we have more wealth now than we have ever had before. Economic growth is dependent on population growth and bigger units of population.

A good illustration of this factor is the growing concern about the stable or declining populations in Europe. In many European countries the demographic trend of fewer children and more elderly people is creating real difficulties. Where is the tax base to support the increasing numbers of elderly people? It is not surprising that Canada and Sweden are both offering significant incentives to couples to have children. Now it is true that excessive population growth can create significant difficulties, especially around the supply of water and other amenities. However, as a general rule more people means more trade and consumption which means more growth. There is no reason why most parts of the world cannot be richer than they currently are. And the no-growth advocates can sometimes sound "anti people."

However, the Mishan worry remains: we live on a planet with a fragile ecosystem. The ozone layer, the rain forests, and the state of our rivers and oceans are important. We are morally obliged to ensure that we behave in ways that safeguard the future of the planet. Although I believe we should resist the Garrett

Hardin environmental ethic, there are other options that we do need to look at. It is to these options that we now turn.

The environment

Modernity has had a dramatic impact on our world. We live at a moment in history when the human capacity to change the world around us is remarkable, and much of this change has not been good. David Barnhill and Roger Gottlieb helpfully summarize the impact that humans have had when they write:

> Every tree and river, large mammal and small fish, now exists in relation to human action, knowledge, commerce, science, technology, governmental decisions to create national parks, international campaigns to save endangered species, and (God help us) leisure lifestyle choices about mountain bikes, off-road vehicles, and sports fishing. Cell phone towers sprout like mushrooms on mountain tops, grizzly bears wear radio collars, genetic engineering produces overweight, arthritic pigs, and the children of Los Angeles slums grow up with stunted lungs because of polluted air. The world's coral reefs are bleaching a sickly dead white; all of Japan's rivers are dammed; and the cod off Nova Scotia have been fished out.[11]

Given the sheer extent of our control and manipulation of nature, there is a need for an environmental ethic. We need some moral controls on our behavior as a species. The question is, what are those controls?

Robert Elliot helpfully distinguishes between three different types of "environmental ethics."[12] The first is a human-centered ethic. Here one worries about the environment because of its impact on human life: it is an anthropocentric (human-centered) ethic. When one takes a human-centered approach, one is interested in environmental issues because our survival as a race depends on the continuing effectiveness of our planet to sustain human life. So, for example, if we completely destroy the ozone layer, then the planet would be unable to sustain human life. Therefore, the argument goes, a concern for the ozone layer is in the long-term interest of humans. This position often takes a utilitarian form: what course of action will bring about the most happiness for the greatest number of people? Going back to the thought exercise, the extinction of the Dodo has not really affected human lives. So with this approach, it is arguable that the extinction of a particular species is not a problem.

The second type of environmental ethics is "animal-centered ethics"; this approach takes the impact on humans and non-human animals as morally relevant factors that should determine our decision-making. The assumption here is that we are called to "share" this planet with other species. It is an abuse of power to simply insist that as the brightest species, able to act with impunity, we should do so. Recognizing the "rights" of animals is important. From this perspective the death of a species is a tragedy and the suffering of a species is an injustice. We should be able to reconcile our need (and of course some would dispute whether it is a need) for animal meat with a care for the numbers of fish, deer, or, in the case of the thought exercise, the dodo. To plunder an entire species for pure "economic gain" is an unforgivable selfishness.

The third type is a "life-centered ethics." Elliot explains, "The class of living things includes more than humans and non-human animals; it includes plants, algae, single-celled organisms, perhaps viruses and, it is sometimes suggested, ecosystems and even the whole biosphere itself."[13] Here respect is accorded to all life, whatever form it takes. It starts from the simple ethical principle that all life is entitled to exist: there is no ethical reason why humans should be privileged. It is deeply critical of all anthropocentric justifications of environmental concern. The moral obligation is to shift the preoccupation from the human to the intrinsic value of all life.

This position is often associated with "deep ecology" – an umbrella term that embraces a range of radical environmental worldviews. *Shallow ecology* worries about the environment because humans have a vested interest in the ongoing survival of resources to enable further exploitation, whereas *deep ecology* is committed to the environment because it has intrinsic value. Value is not imposed from outside – from the human perspective – but each part of the environment in its own place and role, is acknowledged as equally significant and equally precious.

David Barnhill and Roger Gottlieb list 11 characteristics that distinguish those who identify with deep ecology. These are:

1 an emphasis on the intrinsic value of nature (biocentrism or ecocentrism)
2 a tendency to value all things in nature equally (biocentric egalitarianism)
3 a focus on wholes, e.g. ecosystems, species, or the earth itself, rather than simply individual organisms (holism)
4 an affirmation that humans are not separate from nature (there is no "ontological gap" between humans and the natural world)
5 an emphasis on interrelationships
6 an identification of the self with the natural world
7 an intuitive and sensuous communion with the earth
8 a spiritual orientation that sees nature as sacred
9 a tendency to look to other cultures (especially Asian and indigenous) as sources of insight
10 a humility towards nature, in regards to our place in the natural world, our

knowledge of it, and our ability to manipulate nature in a responsible way ("nature knows best")

11 a stance of "letting nature be," and a celebration of wilderness and hunter-gatherer societies.[14]

From this point of point of view, it is a human conceit to claim that humans are more significant than skunks or mountains. It is not only conceited, it is deeply damaging. Under the banner of "economic growth" humans use and destroy animals, plants, and mountains at their peril.

We can and should affirm the concern that underpins deep ecology, but there is a major difficulty with it. It has embedded within it a potential denial of human responsibility. To insist that everything is equally significant (has equal rights to expression) rapidly becomes a nonsense. The AIDS virus is a natural part of the environment, but no one would want to say it has as much entitlement to existence as a mountain. A carrot is important, but it is correctly seen as less important than a dog. Dogs have feelings and capacities for relationships which carrots do not. It is the complexity of a dog that entitles it to more rights and greater care. And for all the reasons that dogs exceed carrots, so humans exceed dogs.

This is important because we need to recognize that with human ability and privilege in nature (by virtue of our complexity as a species) comes responsibility. If there is no distinction between a human and a carrot, then why does it fall on the human to care about our impact on the environment? We don't require that of the carrot. The answer of course is that we must care about our impact on the environment because evolution has made us the most complex and powerful creature on the planet. And with that complexity and power comes responsibility.

Although the metaphysic of deep ecology might be problematic, it is spot on with its intuitions. Humans are privileged in nature, but this privileging is not an entitlement to assume that we are the only entity in this world that matters. Our privileged position should lead to a responsibility ethic for the rest of creation. We must find ways to coexist in a healthy and constructive way with other species. Many governments today talk of "sustainable economic growth." This is growth that seeks to engage constructively with nature and the environment. We use renewable resources; we recognize that a certain habitat is sacrosanct because it is the home for a range of precious species (even if they are bugs or insects) and should be left untouched; and we concede that our endless quest for "more" cannot always be satisfied because of wholly legitimate environmental limits on our behavior.

Animals

Many who are sympathetic to deep ecology are also sympathetic to animal rights. For many this is the next major rights movement. The nineteenth and early twentieth centuries belonged to the campaign for feminism; the twentieth century saw the campaign for racial equality and civil rights; the start of the twenty-first century will belong to gay, lesbian, and transgendered people; and the next movement needs to be a campaign for "animal rights."

Tom Regan in his now famous book *The Case for Animal Rights*[15] argues that animals do have "moral rights," which are universal and inherent rights, as opposed "legal rights" that are granted by a particular society in a particular place. His argument appeals to the concept of "inherent value." If it can be shown that animals have "inherent value" (i.e. a value that is independent of their goodness or usefulness to others), then the language of rights should be used to protect that value. So, for example, it is clear that my snow blower is simply a tool; its only value is its utility to me in a snowstorm. However, a dog does have inherent value; it is, to use Regan's terminology, a "subject to life," which is capable of beliefs, desires, and can conceive of the future. For Regan all mentally normal mammals who are at least a year old have inherent value and therefore moral rights.

Regan makes a good case that one should talk of animals as morally significant. However, his own problem, as he admits, arises in situations where rights conflict. Regan offers the following thought exercise:

> Imagine five survivors are on a lifeboat. Because of the limits of size, the boat can only support four. All weigh approximately the same and would take up approximately the same amount of space. Four of the five are normal adult human beings. The fifth is a dog. One must be thrown overboard or else all will perish. Whom should it be?[16]

Regan's own answer is right. We must, sadly, kill the dog. He explains,

> no reasonable person would deny that the death of any of the four humans would be a greater prima facie loss, and thus a greater prima facie harm, than would be true in the case of the dog. Death for the dog, in short, though a harm, is not comparable to the harm that death would be for any of the humans. To throw any one of the humans overboard, to face certain death, would be to make that individual worse off (i.e. would cause that individual a greater harm) than the harm that would be done to the dog if the animal was thrown overboard.[17]

Now it is not obvious that Regan is being consistent here. What is needed is the recognition that there is a hierarchy of rights. Carrots have fewer rights than dogs and dogs have fewer rights than humans. However, is this speciesism?[18]

It was Peter Singer who coined the expression "speciesism" to describe the vice of valuing one species over others for no good reason. The reasons that people normally cite for preferring humans to other living things are intelligence, moral awareness, language, and capacity for thought that humans possess. Not all humans, however, have all these attributes. Babies, the severely mentally ill, and the very old may not have the same power of speech or as much intelligence as other human beings. Adult non-human animals (especially the higher primates) have much better "speech" and powers of reasoning than human babies. We do not, however, exclude babies and include gorillas in our preferences because of this. Such choices, Peter Singer says, expose the affirmation of the human as a prejudice: humans are guilty of speciesism.

Singer is right to insist that some of the important characteristics of the human species are found outside the human community. Dolphins are highly intelligent, for instance; and the higher primates can, in some respects, mirror human communities. This is the reason why I propose a sliding scale of rights. According to this scale humans are more significant than any other form of life but gorillas and dolphins are more significant than say mice, while mice are more significant than daisies. Other animals and plants should be judged against these same criteria.

Singer, however, is wrong to insist that a definition of a species should encompass the less developed and mal-developed. To do that would be like defining an eye with respect to blindness, simply because for some people, tragically, their eyes do not operate properly. Babies have a potential that a gorilla does not. Elderly humans who deteriorate so much that speech becomes impossible or those who are born with severe Down Syndrome are, in part, analogous to those who are asleep. Keith Ward, the English ethicist and philosopher, makes the point well, when he writes:

> Just as a person who is asleep does not use his or her rational powers,
> so a mentally handicapped person is prevented from using such powers,
> often throughout a whole lifetime. The subject of their consciousness
> is not non-human, or that proper to an animal. It is human, belonging
> to the human species, but is deprived of its proper form of activity.[19]

Humanity should be defined by the characteristics true of humans in their normal mode; that is, developed, awake and well. When we are less developed or asleep or ill we are still human, even if we are unable to use and enjoy all the capacities and gifts of being human.

It is important from an ecological point of view to defend the significance of humanity. This, as we have already noted, in our discussion of deep ecology is what protects human responsibility. If humans have no greater value (and therefore no greater rights and responsibilities) than any other part of the environment, then to criticize and exhort humans to behave more responsibly becomes a nonsense. For the ecological crisis to be tackled, we need to persuade more people that we have the power to adjust our priorities and act justly towards other animals and the environment.

Having stressed the importance of humans, it is also important that we widen the circle. To kill a complex, sophisticated creature such as a dolphin is wrong. Because of their sophistication, the higher primates deserve respect. In the same way that the taking of human life can only be justified in very special circumstances (see the chapter on war and violence), so the taking of, for example, dolphin or gorilla life should be equally rare.

Rocks and mountains

The focus in this chapter has been our responsibilities towards different forms of life. However, the chapter will be incomplete unless we consider our obligations to inanimate nature. A mountain takes millennia to form. In our enthusiasm to quarry that mountain for minerals, we often forget the natural processes that created the geological structures. If "old age" deserves respect, vague term though that is; then at the very least the rocks, mountains, rivers, and sea on the planet are entitled to respect. They have been around much longer than humans.

However, should we go further? Consider a missile being tested on an unpopulated island, which causes significant damage to a waterfall; does this matter? A decision on this question is partly linked to decisions on other questions. If you decide reluctantly, that nations need weapons, then the testing of them is a military and even a moral necessity. It is better to test them on a waterfall, than a city. However, if you think the human propensity for violence needs to be prevented by principled pacifist witness, then the missile test becomes a supplementary argument for your position. It is wanton environmental damage that can be prevented by encouraging nations to relinquish the resort to war as the solution to disagreements. However, this argument does not in itself prohibit such damage in its own right.

Perhaps we can all agree that human "vandalism" is wrong. Destruction of a waterfall or a mountain just for "fun" would be wrong. And when we are making decisions about road construction or urban development, it is morally relevant to consider the need to damage a mountain or destroy a forest. We should do so reluctantly because we can damage so quickly that which took centuries to form. And our damage means that successive generations of animals, plants, as well as humans, will not be able to enjoy that which was once there.

Conclusion

When we think about environmental ethics, we are working on a larger canvas than many of the dilemmas in the rest of this book. The environment predates the emergence of the human species and it is necessary if any form of life is going to continue on this planet. The environment transcends human time; it reaches far back into the past and is crucial for the future.

The focus of the chapter has been on the demands of the environmental future on humanity. The argument has stressed that it is important to recognize that the privileged place for humanity in this world brings with it certain responsibilities. We have a duty of care for animals, plants, and rocks. We do so not simply because our survival depends on such a disposition, but because we are simply renting space, with others, on this planet. Temporary occupants are not entitled to do "whatever they like." Responsible concern for the environment is a moral obligation on us all.

Notes

1 Taken from Martin Cohen, *101 Ethical Dilemmas* (London and New York: Routledge 2003) p. 119.
2 E. J. Mishan, *The Costs of Economic Growth* (London: Staples Press 1967) p. 8.
3 Ibid. p. 173.
4 Ibid. p. 127ff.
5 Ibid.
6 Jonathon Porritt, *Seeing Green* (Oxford: Blackwell Publishing 1984) p. 126.
7 Ibid. p. 126.
8 Garrett Hardin, "Lifeboat Ethics: The Case against Helping the Poor," *Psychology Today* September (1974) pp. 38–126.
9 Ibid. p. 40.
10 Ibid. p. 124.
11 David Landis Barnhill and Roger S. Gottlieb, *Deep Ecology and World Religions: New Essays on Sacred Ground* (New York: SUNY Press 2001) pp. 1–2.
12 See Robert Elliott, "Environmental Ethics" in Peter Singer (ed.) *A Companion to Ethics* (Oxford: Blackwell Publishing 1991) pp. 284–9.
13 Ibid. p. 287.
14 David Landis Barnhill and Roger S. Gottlieb, *Deep Ecology and World Religions: New Essays on Sacred Ground*, p. 6.
15 Tom Regan, *The Case for Animal Rights* (Berkeley, CA: University of California Press 1983).

16 Ibid. p. 285.

17 Ibid. pp. 324–5.

18 The section that follows is a modified version of my discussion of Peter Singer's speciesism, which is found in "Why should we suppose that our own death is any different from that of a pet cat or a squashed hedgehog? Questions people ask: is there really a life after death?" in *Expository Times* 107 (6) (1996) pp. 164–9.

19 Keith Ward, *The Battle for the Soul* (London: Hodder and Stoughton 1985) p. 152.

Part Three

Making a Decision

15

Becoming a morally serious person

As promised in chapter 1, my task in this book has been to be your guide on a journey around the world of ethics. In each chapter, the key names and main arguments have been introduced. Although complete "objectivity" is impossible, I have worked hard to be fair and accurate. However, in the last two chapters, it is necessary for your guide to become a conversation partner. In this chapter, I shall expose the hidden agenda behind this book; and in the next, I shall outline my position on the major questions that we have explored in this book.

My hidden agenda is simple: I want to encourage you to become a *morally serious person* (henceforth MSP). Instead of committing one to a set of axioms about what morality is, the idea is that MSP captures an underlying disposition to life – an attitude that believes moral questions are of fundamental importance. So you can be anything and an MSP, for example, a Catholic MSP, an evangelical MSP, a gay MSP, or a secular MSP. In this chapter I shall argue that becoming an MSP needs to be a primary goal for us all. Then in the rest of the chapter I shall sketch out the seven qualities or features of an MSP's life.

Why be an MSP?

What do you spend most of your time thinking about? It is very easy to limit one's horizon to the transient and immediate. What am I going to eat at lunchtime? Shall I go out tonight? I wonder if my friend knows that John is going out with Barbara? The routine pattern of work, eat, work, eat, telly, sleep, wake can become the entire world. Years can pass without this world being significantly disturbed.

Now what is wrong with a life so lived? The problem is metaphysical: the unreflective life does not fully appreciate the miracle of being human. Each person is a deep well of complexity: we have been given an intellect with a capacity to appreciate and locate the immediate. The irony of a deeply unreflective life is that it is an unappreciated life, for it depends on a certain degree of affluence which should provoke gratitude. However, the gratitude does not arrive because there is no reflection. If you are walking two miles a day for fresh water, which is the routine for many in Africa, then some form of reflection is forced on you. It is the unnoticed and unappreciated ease of the middle class life in the western world that makes it possible to create a world that is so small it stops at the limited interactions of oneself with the immediate environments.

One ironic value of emotional stress, illness, and death is that they force deeper reflection. The unreflective life handles such moments extremely badly. The individual who has enjoyed an unappreciated routine that has been so abruptly disturbed by, for example, unemployment or illness finds it difficult to gain an appropriate perspective. Coping with the changed circumstances can become very difficult.

The two main reasons, then, why the goal of becoming an MSP must be central is that it creates the disposition that *appreciates* the moment and prepares one to *cope* with the inevitable ambiguity, confusion, and sadness that encounters all lives at certain points and to different degrees of intensity. These two – appreciation and coping – are also the ultimate safeguards against selfishness. The selfish life is a life lived within very narrow parameters which doesn't reach beyond the horizons of the immediate. The MSP knows that the parameters of the moment need to reach out to the many around us.

MSPs are those who locate their preliminary concerns that are preoccupied with our relationships with family and friends (to use the terminology of the German theologian Paul Tillich)[1] in the wider context of our relationship to the national and international communities. The key is "care." Our care transcends the immediate and embraces to some degree everything else that is.

There are seven features that make up an MSP. These are:

1 responsible citizenship
2 intolerance towards discrimination
3 obligation to be empirically informed
4 disciplined reflection on the cultivation of virtue
5 consciousness of our sociological conditioning
6 an ordered interior life
7 commitment to moral conversation.

These seven features will now all be discussed in turn.

1. Responsible citizenship

An MSP recognizes a fundamental obligation to the community of which he or she is a part. When a child is born into a family, that child is also born into a million preexisting relationships. The child becomes part of a family which is part of a wider network. These include neighbors, clubs and societies, religious organizations, local and national government, and many much less formal connections between people. The security and success of that child's growth will, in many ways, depend on the strength of those networks. A good educational system, for example, depends on strong preexisting institutions. As that child grows into adulthood, so in turn, there is an obligation for the adult to now support the networks so that others can benefit from those networks.

Supporting these networks lies at the heart of responsible citizenship or what David Alton calls "active citizenship."[2] It involves supporting civic society. So, for example, one should get involved in political parties, become an officer of an organization (for example, Girl Guides or the Lions Club), and support one's local amateur dramatic association (either by attending or performing). These organizations are often very fragile: as anyone who is involved in these organizations knows. It is hard work making sure that they are financially viable and have sufficient participants. Yet if these organizations disappear then the networks are weakened and the potential for social decline increases dramatically.

This constructive participation in civic society runs parallel with a comparable obligation not to be destructive. Although one person behaving in an irresponsible way can have a minimal impact, the cumulative impact of a group (even if still a small minority) can be devastating. One person committing insurance fraud and claiming for their house to be repainted owing to a non-existent flood can be tolerated, but one hundred people doing the same leads to an increase in everyone's insurance premium and the potential breakdown of the system. One person taking legal action against a doctor in the quest for the windfall judgment can be tolerated, but one hundred people taking a class action can lead to doctors leaving the profession and increasing pressure on the health system, be it NHS or private. Destructive acts are not simply the illegal ones but include those that are not necessarily illegal (such as a legal action) but perhaps morally inadvisable.

The MSP is, then, both involved in civic society and avoids damaging civic society. It means that one should seek employment rather than "living off State benefits." State benefits are there as the safety net that keeps those unfortunate and unlucky alive; the exploitation of those benefits is wrong. MSPs are good parents – taking particular responsibility for those you have brought into the world is a fundamental moral obligation. The MSP participates in the democratic process – you vote, get informed, and perhaps even stand. The MSP gives a percentage of his or her income to others. Charitable giving is the indispensable evidence that one recognizes oneself as part of a wider world.

So the first feature of an MSP's life is this commitment to responsible citizenship. It is, in short, playing your part to sustain the social ecology that enabled you to thrive and survive.

2. Intolerance towards discrimination

There are certain axioms that an MSP simply accepts: for example, all humans are worthy of fundamental equality and respect. Generalizations about a gender or an ethnic minority are wrong. Prejudice is wrong. Prejudice by definition makes a pre-judgment. When a person asserts that "all black people are scroungers or criminals," then a pre-judgment has been made on non-rational facts.

It puzzles me deeply why so many can be so sanguine about racism and sexism. It is a certain lesson from history that racism and sexism are deeply destructive. James Cone (the African American theologian) attacks the blindness of white theologians, but his points stand against anyone who doesn't take the issue of race seriously. He writes:

> How do we account for such a long history of white theological blindness to racism and its brutal impact on the lives of African people? Is it because white theologians do not know about the tortured history of the Atlantic slave trade, which according to the British historian Basil Davidson, "cost Africa at least fifty million souls"? Have they forgotten about the unspeakable crimes of colonialism? Author Eduardo Galeano claims that 150 years of Spanish and Portuguese colonization in Central and South America reduced the indigenous population from 90 million to 3.3 million. During the 23-year reign of terror of King Leopold II of Belgium in the Congo (1885–1908), scholarly estimates suggest that approximately 10 million Congolese met unnatural deaths – "fully half of the territory's population." The tentacles of white supremacy have stretched around the globe. No people of color have been able to escape its cultural, political, and economic domination. Two hundred forty-four years of slavery and one hundred years of legal segregation, augmented by a reign of white terror that lynched more than five thousand blacks, defined the meaning of America as "white over black." White supremacy shaped the social, political, economic, cultural, and religious ethos in the churches, the academy, and the broader society.[3]

Given this history, it is amazing how many sons and daughters of white racists want to continue that tradition. It is so exhausting for black people to cope with that look (is it fear?) or action (e.g. the handbag is clutched a little closer). It is amazing how the black person in the smart executive suit has to fight the suspicion that it is only "positive discrimination." But most odd of all is the willingness of white people to continue to tolerate the racist joke, the crude generalizations, and the loaded observation, amongst their white "racist" friends. The continuing toleration of such ugly attitudes continues to exacerbate the suffering caused by racism.

As for sexism: there are still men who find it difficult to cope with the wife who earns more than they do. There are still couples where the wife lives in the kitchen serving the male who reads the newspaper and flicks through the TV channels. There are still numerous women who sit next to men doing the same work for a lower rate of pay. And most seriously, there are still women who live in fear for their lives because their drunken boyfriends or husbands might get angry. There are numerous other groups who are on the receiving end of discrimination. The adolescent, who discovers that he is not attracted to women, but to men, then also discovers a life of misunderstanding, suspicion, and unkindness.

The causes of racist or sexist attitudes lie deep in our psyche. The combination of education and a ruthless willingness to revisit one's talk and attitudes are essential components that can start to bring about a change. An MSP seeks diverse communities and company. This is the realm that can be both conceptually demanding (for example, the relationship of environment and biology in the social construction of genders) and intensely practical (for example, no husband is ever allowed to leave the kitchen until his wife can join him). The MSP knows how important all this is.

3. Obligation to be empirically informed

Many moral judgments depend on empirical ones. So, as we saw, Garrett Hardin wants to stop immigration because he believes that more people will lead to a decline in the standard of living of those already in the rich countries. His moral judgment assumes a certain judgment about the facts. In this case, his wrong facts are partly responsible for his misguided moral judgment.

An MSP works hard to make sure that he or she is informed. Finding a reliable source of news isn't easy. The source must concentrate on stories beyond Michael Jackson and gossip about the Royal family. It must convey the complexity of the world. However, it must be admitted that becoming empirically informed can be both time-consuming and perhaps, even more significantly make you very miserable.

It is necessary to think a little more about this difficulty because one reason often given by people who do not watch the news is that it makes them miserable.

185

It is one reason why the life of unreflective routine is so tempting. So let us look at this objection more carefully.

It is true that one of the great delights of going on holiday is that news suddenly becomes completely inaccessible. In a world where your horizon stops with those you meet, things you can see, or stories that others can tell you is a much less stressful world. It is as if you travel back in time to the middle ages, where there was nothing faster than a horse and few people in the course of a lifetime moved more than ten miles from the place of their birth. In this world, months could pass without hearing about disaster; instead the focus was local.

This world has disappeared forever. We all remember where we were when we heard of the death of J. F. Kennedy or the collapse of the World Trade Center towers. And we all heard within moments, perhaps hours, of it happening. CNN beams the action right into our homes moments after it has happened. There is clear evidence that the news junky is more stressed and unhappier than the person who opts instead for the soap opera.

Although it is tempting to evade the world of news, this temptation must be resisted. The secrets to being informed without being stressed are as follows. First, do remember that the vast majority of lives lived are very uneventful. Imagine a news broadcast that tried to represent the activities of everyone living in a particular country. It would run as follows: "Millions of people did their jobs today, came home, sat in front of a TV and went to bed. None of these people were murdered or mugged. They were not involved in a civil war or a tragic car accident. They did not have to cope with an earthquake. A very small number of people did have problems." But of course such a news report is not newsworthy. In other words, the news, by definition, informs the world about the extraordinary events and activities that have happened. It focuses on the spectacular. Even representative news would be extremely dull for 95 percent of the broadcasting time, with the disasters, thefts, and crises occupying the remaining 5 percent. It would not work. So disproportionate time is spent on the tragic and disturbing. It is important that we do not accept this disproportionately violent and tragic picture of our world: we must always remind ourselves this is the "spectacular news" not the "representative news." And linked with this, it is important that we do not "worry" disproportionately about the possible "outcomes" suggested in the news. The motivational thinker James Kilminster points out that 98 percent of our worries are in the end unjustified. He suggests the following helpful exercise: as an anxiety arises, write it on a slip of paper and insert it into your worry jar. One week later take out those slips of paper and marvel at the fact that the vast majority of those anxieties were unjustified. The point is simple: keep everything in perspective.

Second, pick a reliable news source and read, watch, or listen with care. Do not, however, be obliged to pick them all. Being informed does not require viewing the 24-hour news broadcasts that analyse to the point of tedium exactly what might happen to Michael Jackson.

Third, use the opportunities of travel to see the world from the vantage point of the other. Particular preoccupations of one country are not shared by other countries. And once this is seen, then it can reduce the significance of the particular preoccupation. The sense of significance changes when one lives abroad.

Fourth, locate the news story on a bigger canvas. One advantage of being religious is that the news story can become a context for prayer. One can commit the human tragedy to God. However, whether religious or not, the exercise of placing the immediate problem on a wider canvas is a good discipline. The study of history is helpful here. History locates your own time, normally to the advantage of your own time. It is worth remembering that the problems of today are not as great as the problems facing those during the First and Second World Wars.

Fifth, review and reflect on your judgments about time. One duty of the MSP is the periodical review of earlier social and political judgments that one has made. The great advantage of this is that it makes one realize the provisionality of one's own judgments and the unpredictability of history. Good newspaper columnists often use the New Year to reflect on their own judgments and predications. Anatole Kaletsky, writing in *The Times*, berates himself at the end of 2003 thus:

> For the first time in the 13 years that I have been chancing my arm with these annual forecasts, not even half my predictions have turned out to be right. This is a quite appalling performance, since a 50–50 outcome could presumably have been achieved by tossing a coin.[4]

This is a sign that at least in this respect Kaletsky is an MSP. He understands the importance of reflecting on his judgments and making a call as to the accuracy of them in hindsight. Given the intense feelings that a particular issue at a particular time can generate coupled with the discovery that often – in hindsight – we are not right, this exercise can mitigate the intensity with which we hold a position. Instead of our apocalyptic vision of the future, it becomes more thoughtful, measured, and balanced.

The exercise of being empirically informed is not just responsible for shaping our judgments of the moment, but feeds into the MSP's reflective practice of judgment, examination, and revision.

4. Disciplined reflection on the cultivation of virtue

The MSP will create space to reflect upon the life of virtue. Now this sounds very grandiose, however, it need not be in practice. A 20-minute commute in a car can serve the purpose: all it needs to be is a space where the mind can think about the appropriateness of one's decisions and behavior.

This is so important. Reflection is a necessary condition for satisfaction. There is a growing literature around happiness studies that draws attention to that old adage that "money does not make you happy." It is very odd how Europe and America have a majority of people who are comparatively rich, but not significantly happier. Ruut Veenhoven – the Dutch Professor of Happiness Studies – compared different sample groups of people in 68 countries. Amongst his findings, he showed that the British lifestyle generates as much happiness as the Guatemalan lifestyle: they both came in at 19th place.[5] The World Health Organization finds that the majority of clinically depressed people are in the wealthiest countries – United States, Canada, Australia, Japan, and the European Union.[6]

What is going on here? It is clear that at the very least there is a lack of a perspective. And this is the reason why creating space to reflect is so important. Perspective comes from reflection. It is as one reflects that one can transcend the ephemeral and start to appreciate what really matters.

Gregg Easterbrook in his *The Progress Paradox* identifies certain key characteristics of the wealthy that creates the sense of discontent. The main ones are complaint proficiency, complaint yearning, and the breakdown between needs and wants.

On complaint proficiency, Easterbrook explains:

> whether through natural selection, God's touch, or simply practice, human beings as a group are really good at complaining. We complain to our parents for bringing us into the world: complain to our teachers for educating us; complain to our bosses for employing us; complain to our shopkeepers who feed and clothe us; complain to our spouses who embrace us.[7]

Coupled with this capacity to endlessly complain, we are also gifted with the desire to be dissatisfied. This is Easterbrook's "complaint yearning." The great attraction of the complaining state is that one is freed from any obligation to care for others. He writes,

> If times are tough, or others are being unfair or unkind, or you've just had some unpleasant news, or you wanted something and didn't get it, or you loved someone and were not loved in turn, clearance is given to feel sorry for yourself. When you are sorry for yourself, you don't expect to help others or show kindness or to do important things. When you've got a grievance against the world, all the pressure is off.[8]

The third problem is the breakdown between needs and wants.[9] It is very easy to be glib at this point. It is not true, although often stated, that wicked advertising is responsible for creating needless wants. The pressures are much more subtle. The human hankering for a life-enhancing feature is understandable and often a good quality. It is because I want the holiday in Bermuda that I work a little harder to get that holiday. And, of course, although one could survive without that holiday (and certainly survive if it were in a less glamorous place), there is a sense in which one needs the opportunity to change scene, appreciate loved ones, and enjoy the break from the work routine. Some talk as if the distinction between needs and wants can be drawn strictly and clearly: this is not the case.

Nevertheless. The key word here is – as before in this chapter – perspective. It is not true to say that I need a plasma TV, four guest bedrooms, and a Porsche: it isn't even actually true, to take something a little less frivolous, that I cannot be whole without a life partner – singleness can be successful and fulfilling. We need to be able to stand back and see the big picture.

The cultivation of perspective is the reason why reflection is important. This is where we are able to stand back, offer a critique, force a judgment, and appreciate what is really going on. Historically, of course, this process was at the heart of the Christian practice of confession. This, in one form, involved "confessing" one's sins before a priest, in preparation for the taking of the Mass. Although confession can be abused (the priest has considerable power), the practice, when used properly, was a device for deep personal examination and disciplined cultivation of perspective.

Although the spiritual director continues to be important for many religious people, the secular equivalent of the confessor is the therapist. Although therapy can be invaluable, there is a problem with non-directive therapy. Therapy that simply affirms "where you are at" in an entirely non-judgmental way is not always what is needed. However, the idea of using another person to help you cultivate your virtue (be it a confessor, spiritual director, or therapist) is a good one. The MSP wants to be challenged out of the compliancy that we can all so easily lapse into. A good conversation partner can ensure that this happens. However, the conversation partner is always a supplement to the discipline of finding time oneself to reflect on the journey of virtue thus far.

5. Consciousness of our sociological conditioning

One of the great ironies of our age is that we spend our time celebrating the entitlement of a person to be an individual and shape him- or herself separate from the immediate social pressures, while at the same time knowing how much we are all shaped by the immediate environment. Humans are chameleons: we become part of the background of which we are a part. The MSP knows the significance of the immediate environment.

For all the differences that we imagine we have with the people in our social group, the shared assumptions are much greater. These shared assumptions express themselves in our language, expectations, descriptions, and aspiration. If all your friends like to hang out, smoke cannabis, and have anarchist sympathies, then it is likely that you will be similar. Alternatively, if your group is part of the aspiring aristocracy, who play polo, shoot, and privately educate their children, then it is likely that you will share many of the same aspirations and activities.

The fact is that changes in behavior and outlook are often "sociological." All forms of conversion, whether to the love of opera or to a religion, need to have a sociological component. One has to join a community and participate in certain shared activities. In the case of opera it will involve attending an opera, learning to appreciate the achievement, understanding the story, and perhaps subscribing to a magazine. The language will need to be learnt; certain words such as adagio (meaning slowly), allegro (meaning merry or cheerful and used to indicate a fast tempo), and aria (used to describe a song sung by one person) must all become part of your vocabulary. In the case of religion, it might involve attending a place of worship, learning to appreciate the liturgy, and interpreting your life differently. Conversion to anything (and this of course includes a secular worldview) starts with the moment one picks up a book or starts the conversation or attends a lecture or event. At that moment one is allowing oneself to be shaped by a certain community.

This is not frightening; it is just the way it is. It started when as children our parents introduced us to a certain language. A child in the school playground moves from community to community (from Pokemon to Digimon); in each case, he learns the names and skills of the characters. And as we grow older, we will find that we are members of many communities, some of which are relatively small (e.g. the gadget community), while others are larger (e.g. the soccer following community). Every time we learn to appreciate a new discourse, we are sociologically converted: a friend, perhaps, introduces us to this new world, we get enthralled, and slowly we start to belong. We find company in belonging: we find the sharedness with others a pleasure and delight.

For the MSP, this basic insight about human living has enormous ethical significance. Parents spot this intuitively: they worry about the influence the "bad crowd" might have on their children. And this is a legitimate worry. If a teenager joins the group that is shooting heroin, then it is likely that she might end up taking drugs with them. Perhaps she likes the talk, the rebellious, counter-cultural outlook; she sees that most users do not die and often manage to disguise their habit effectively; and before she knows where she is she is a drug addict who is slowly killing herself.

The basic rule for the MSP is to find others who are seeking to live life in a constructive and positive way. Join one of the millions of possible communities that celebrate life – from train spotting to rugby, and avoid those communities that are destroying life. The Internet has solved the problem of geography. For centuries, proximity was important. But now my eccentric interest in say 1950s train sets will be supported by an Internet chatroom and email list. This can be good and life enhancing.

But there are communities that are much less healthy. Pedophiles, suicide bombers, and white supremacists are all creating Internet communities that are deeply destructive of healthy living. An individual living in a big city who is thinking of becoming a pedophile finds it much harder without the support of a community; the community is the life-blood that keeps an evil tradition of behavior going. If one finds at a particular moment certain dark thoughts starting to develop, then, from the ethical point of view, the worse course of action to take is to do a "google" search. Finding someone else who shares your dark thoughts is the first step to a conversion to some evil act. The MSP, then, is committed to opposing such communities. He or she also wants to educate others about the dangers of these communities. We must be careful with the company we keep.

6. An ordered interior life

One temptation that pervades much contemporary ethical discourse is to draw a strong line between the imaginary life and real life. This is popular because most people intuit that while real actions make a real difference, imaginative actions don't make any difference to anyone.

It is true that the imagination is one of the greatest pleasures of being human. Although my body might be stuck in economy class on a jumbo jet, my mind enables me to become an airline pilot, a soccer star, a friend of Madonna's, or a tourist on a sun-soaked beach. It is the imagination that opens up other possibilities from the drudgery (or perhaps injustice) of the present. We can dream of a better world, as Martin Luther King Jr did, and, in so doing, create an option that didn't exist before.

However, most religious traditions insist that the moral life does require considerable discipline that extends to our imaginary life. They challenge the presumption that because our mental life doesn't directly involve action, then it doesn't matter. The constructive use of the imagination is good: Martin Luther King Jr's vision of an alternative world was a model use of imagination. The daydreams of a child or the fantasy modeling career of a bored shop assistant are clearly morally acceptable and can motivate and inspire a person to achieve more. However, while all of these mental activities are good, there are many others that are much less so.

Two words are used in the Christian tradition to describe inappropriate mental activity – covet and lust. Covet is part of the Ten Commandments, which reads: "You shall not covet your neighbour's house; you shall not covet your neighbour's wife, or male or female slave, or ox, or donkey, or anything that belongs to your neighbour" (Exodus 20:17). The idea here is that it is wrong to desperately desire the possessions of another. The reason for this is that the jealously can become corrosive. It eats away at your interior: it can preoccupy you and slowly become obsessive. It leads to discontentment with that which you have. Slowly the interior life of coveting you neighbor's possessions starts to affect your outlook and attitude to life and from there it starts to permeate your behavior. The other equally old and unfashionable word is lust. Lust is where you turn another person purely into an object of sexual desire. Pope John Paul II was ridiculed in the press for insisting that it is even wrong for a husband to lust after his wife.[10] However, what was not appreciated was that he was objecting to reducing love to sex. And even in marriage, it is wrong for the husband to turn the wife into a sex object. For the Christian tradition, an ordered interior life is one where the fantasies are constructive and ethical rather than destructive and unethical. The fantasies should not feed our darker side, which seeks to consume and possess.

Now between these two poles – the action only (i.e. the mental life doesn't matter) and the religious (the mental life needs to be carefully controlled), most of us would probably find ourselves in the middle. The single person's release of sexual energy through imaginative masturbation is probably both healthy and necessary. At the next level, there is the use of fantasy aids, such as pornography. This is a hot topic. There are some men who claim that pornography helps their behavior. It allows them to "lust" over a variety of women without seeking each one out, thereby assisting their monogamy. It is very widespread: over half of the rooms in a business hotel in the United States are viewing an "adult movie."[11] There are others who argue that pornography is not only degrading to women (turning them into sex objects – at this point some feminists coincide with the Pope!), but also feeds a culture of abuse and violence towards women. It is not necessary for us to resolve this disagreement. Instead let us concede that perhaps a fantasy life around mild pornography might be morally acceptable,[12] the problem remains that there is a vast array of resources now available that feed the imagination, which extends far beyond mild pornography. Adult men are surfing the web to find pictures of naked children: the sadomasochist is in search of forms of torture and degradation where pain is inflicted. Most macabre of all is the Internet chatroom where those who fantasize about eating another human being can meet up (construct a community) with those who fantasize about being eaten. Armin Meiwes, the so-called cannibal of Rotenburg, found Bernd Brandes in a chatroom and discovered their mutual sexual satisfaction could be realized in Meiwes consuming Brandes. On March 9, 2001, the deadly encounter took place.

At the points of paedophilia and cannibalism, we clearly have an interior life completely out of control. And the problem starts with the interior life: the obsession grew until it needed to be satisfied. However, at this point the "action only" advocate might complain that if the pedophile or cannibal managed to confine their sexual fantasy to their minds, then it would have been morally acceptable. It is at this point that the MSP invokes the important principle of healthy and respectful living (healthy in that it must be constructive – respectful in that other people should not be used for gratification). Even in our interior life, there are some thoughts we should not entertain, even if we don't act on them. Damage is caused to your own mind, even if you do not act on the fantasy.

While at this extreme, it might be clear that one should not entertain thoughts of cannibalism or paedophilia, the whole realm of fantasizing about your boss or secretary or your best friend's partner seems much less clear. However, it is worth appreciating the wisdom of the religious traditions at this point. They all teach that we should "resist" temptation (i.e. not entertain in the mind the possibility) and "avoid" temptation (i.e. not put yourself in a position where you might find it easy to succumb). The best way to remain happy and faithful to one's partner is to ensure that you do not entertain adulterous fantasies nor do you put yourself in a position where you might be tempted to realize the fantasy. In other words, if you are strongly attracted to a work colleague, then you should discipline your mental life and ensure that you do not engineer a business trip that involves a stopover in a hotel.

Constructive healthy relationships need to be built on integrity. The MSP knows that integrity is not simply action, but also internal. Recognizing that there are limits to where we will let our minds wonder is an important part of this integrity.

7. Commitment to moral conversation

An MSP knows that moral decision-making is complex. As we have seen chapter after chapter, there are good and valid arguments for opposing positions. Given this complexity the MSP welcomes pluralism (i.e. a range of contrasting cultural judgments about the nature of the good and how it can be realized) and therefore conversation or dialogue.

We need to commit to the conversation. The history of ethics repeatedly demonstrates the importance of fundamental disagreement between two value systems. The prophet Muhammad in the seventh century challenged the culture of infanticide for girls; the Reformers in seventeenth-century Europe challenged the culture of religious servitude that the Roman Catholic Church had inadvertently created; the secular Enlightenment challenged the culture of religious intolerance and patriarchy; and Martin Luther King Jr challenged the culture of racial segregation in the South.

Searching for a range of perspectives is an important quality of the MSP. We need diverse religious traditions, along with secular conversation partners. For this reason, the MSP appreciates the value of toleration. The MSP welcomes those who disagree with him or her into the community of discourse.

This trinity – *pluralism* (the fact of diversity) requiring *toleration* (allowing that which one fundamental disagrees with) leading to *conversation* (the sharing of different perspectives in the public square) – becomes a central feature of the MSP's outlook. Naturally, there are limits to this discourse. The pedophile, the racist, and the cannibal are not welcome to the conversation. But the MSP works hard to extend the conversation as widely as possible. The MSP is committed to these fundamental liberal values as the best way of arriving at moral insights.

Concluding reflections

It is important to note that these seven qualities of the MSP do not include any (well not many) direct prescriptions. It is not intended to be a list of dos and don'ts. It provides a framework for deliberation. The seven qualities commend certain attitudes, dispositions, and expectations. Although one should be informed, the MSP is not required to be a socialist or conservative. Most political options are available. Although one should be a responsible citizen, one could be wealthy or poor. One can be an MSP and an atheist, or gay person, or Tory, or socialist, or Catholic. The whole concept of the MSP is supposed to provide the moral boundaries within which a million different lives could be lived.

Yet we have seen in this chapter that there are clearly some prohibitions, many of which were historically contentious. For the MSP, living in the twenty-first century, racism and sexism are simply wrong. Fantasizing about children or eating another person is forbidden. This description of the MSP is building on the moral insights of our age: it should be interpreted as the minimum ethical expectations for participation in our society.

Now, as we can see, this boundary approach to ethics, coupled with a limited list of prohibitions, is an approach with its own ethical historical location. So one is clear, this chapter is advocating (and to an extent identifying) the code of moral expectation that is emerging in western life. It is post-Enlightenment (in its emphasis on feminism, equality, and the value of pluralism and tolerance), and religious (in its emphasis on care, respect, and the importance of the interior life).

The MSP should be the goal of all moral education in the State school system. Talk of schools as a "moral-free zone" is a manifest and dangerous nonsense. David Alton is right when he writes,

Education cannot be a value-free zone. There are many shared assumptions about what makes for a good and stable society. Why be embarrassed to teach children what these are? For each citizen to play their proper part, it is vital that they have the ability to discern the differences between right and wrong, good and bad, and recognize their own responsibility to act accordingly. That should be a top priority within our homes and schools.[13]

This is the boundary approach to ethics; it leaves open particular decisions about particular topics. This will be the subject of the next and final chapter of this book.

Notes

1 See Paul Tillich, *Systematic Theology*, vol. 1 (3 volumes) (Chicago, IL: University of Chicago Press 1973).

2 David Alton, *Citizen Virtues* (London: HarperCollins 1999) p. 151.

3 James Cone, *Risks of Faith*, pp. 131–2. For a good history of the slave trade see Hugh Thomas, *The Slave Trade: The History of the Atlantic Slave Trade 1440–1870* (London: Picador 1997).

4 Anatole Kaletsky, "How the Amazing Fed Upset My 2003 Predictions," *The Times* December 30, 2003, Business section, p. 23.

5 Taken from Gregg Easterbrook, "What money can't buy" in *The Sunday Times*, December 28, 2003.

6 Gregg Easterbrook, *The Progress Paradox: How Life Gets Better while People Feel Worse* (New York: Random House 2003) p. 181.

7 Ibid. p. 118.

8 Ibid. p. 120.

9 Ibid. pp. 136ff.

10 This was contained in two talks given by Pope John Paul II on October 1 and 8 1980.

11 For this statistic see the Timothy Egan, "Wall Street Meets Pornography," *New York Times* October 23, 2000. Egan writes, "Based on estimates provided by the hotel industry, at least half of all guests buy these adult movies, which means that pay-per-view sex from television hotel rooms may generate about $190 million a year in sales."

12 This is a good illustration of how the Christian ethic extends beyond this ethical minimum suggested for the potential Christian MSP. In Matthew 5:27–30, Jesus argues that the Christian ethic does not simply accept the letter of the law but goes beyond it. So it is not just adultery which is forbidden, but anyone who looks at a woman lustfully. It is clear that the ethic of Jesus does not permit mild pornography to aid a fantasy life.

13 David Alton, *Citizen Virtues*, p. 86.

16

Taking an ethical position

Unlike all the other chapters in the book, this chapter cannot stand alone. I shall assume that you have read the arguments outlined in the rest of the book. The purpose of this chapter is to offer my judgments on the major and serious issues that we have explored together. Standing back and simply presenting the arguments is very difficult; the issues are vitally important and I almost feel negligent in just presenting the options without serious comment and analysis. So in this the last chapter of the book, I shall revisit (without describing them all over again) the arguments in this book and explain exactly where I stand on these questions. Perhaps a word is needed about where "I am coming from." I am a middle-aged white male, born in England and now living in America, who is a Christian. I accept entirely that I have been shaped by my particular life story. And if my story had been different, then my judgments might be different. So what follows is the point at which I am now: I invite you to come from where you are at and enjoy engaging with my worldview.

The book started with the dangers involved in thinking about ethics. The worry at the start was that this book might undo all the good work of moral formation that you were given as a child. As I offer my own judgments on the issues we considered in this book, I shall start with the whole problem of the ultimate character of moral language that preoccupied us in Part One. In so doing, an additional argument about the dangers involved in ethical reflection will be raised. I shall show that the problem, then, with sustained ethical reflection is not simply the damage done to ethical formation, but that our increasing semi-detached disposition that many in our culture has to religion is making ethical discourse incoherent. Let me explain what I mean.

The nature of the ethical

Let me be clear: ethical discourse without a religious framework is ultimately unsustainable. This is not to say that all atheists are immoral. As we saw in the chapter on secular humanism, there is a strong ethical impulse embedded in that tradition, which attacks religion for its propensity to support, amongst other things, patriarchy, intolerance, and homophobia. Secular humanists are often very ethical: the problem is that they cannot make any logical sense of the discourse.

The reason for this is that the ethical must assume objective ethical values that transcend individuals, nations, and cultures. The word "wrong" is making a universal and transcendent claim. Universal in that it is a claim that applies to all people everywhere; transcendent in that this universality must imply a source for ethical that transcends the human race. So when secular humanists claim, rightly, that patriarchy is wrong, they do not mean "from my perspective and for my culture, patriarchy is something I do not like." It is the opposite. Cultures elsewhere in the world that are patriarchal are mistaken and ought (another moral term) to behave differently.

Secular humanists often have the right moral intuitions, but lack the framework in which these intuitions make any sense. The language requires an entity that transcends human communities and cultures. The fiction of the "ideal observer" is insufficient: the "ideal observer" needs to be real. The parallel with colors only works provided the value of good is truly objective, which then needs to be located in a broader narrative about the nature of the universe that gives rise to these objective values. So the primary reason why the study of ethics can be dangerous is that suddenly our moral intuitions about "right," "wrong," and "ought" are no longer justified. The temptation then is that other options might seem more rational. Perhaps one might cease to use moral language and live a life of rational egoism. At an extreme, one might decide that there is nothing wrong with murdering an innocent human being for vast sums of money, or at a more mundane level, being indifferent to a suffering world full of pain. A secular humanist is an MSP: however, it is possible that my secular humanist reader might decide that the lifestyle of an MSP makes no sense if we are simply complex bundles of atoms – products of a blind process of evolution – that face extinction when we die. Given this metaphysics, it is difficult for the secular humanist to provide an adequate answer to the question: why be an MSP?

At this point many secular humanists will want to invoke the argument described in chapter 6. If there is nothing else, then surely this adds to the significance of this life and human life in particular? This is a sentiment – an assertion, not an argument. If someone objects to this reasoning and asks, "why should I value human life, especially given there is nothing else?" then the secular human-ist has no adequate reply. It is fideism (a faith assertion not based on any rational argument). It is asking the agnostic to make a leap of faith (i.e. an act of fideism) to the life-affirming and altruistic view of the world. No reason can be given as to why you should leap, you are just invited to do so.

The next strategy the secular humanist might try is to point at the ethical systems of Kant or Bentham as secular systems of morality. Leaving aside the difficulties with the details of the systems, the problem of the "leap of faith" is required here as well. Why should I accept the utilitarian injunction that all people must be considered in my ethical decision-making? Why should I accept the Kantian version of the Golden Rule and accept that a moral law can be universalizable?

The secular humanist might be tempted to retort: why not make the leap into an ethical worldview?' The problem here is that the secular humanist narra-tive about the world makes the leap difficult. The scientific story of our origins and death, decoupled from any context of purpose and intention, supplemented with a view that different cultures invent different ethical systems makes the leap to a claim that a particular ethical system is true difficult.

The point of all this is that moral discourse needs a religious framework. Fortunately in most parts of the world this is no problem. Africa, Asia, Latin America, the Middle East, and North America are all intensely religious. The exception to this pattern is Europe.

In chapter 2 I briefly described the work of Grace Davie. She has suggested that there are two features of European religion that needs to be taken very seriously. The first is that Europeans are continuing to be religious, although in different ways. Church taxes continue to be collected in many European churches. And when national tragedy strikes (e.g. the death of Princess Diana), a whole set of religious rituals emerge. It is as if Europeans are happy for a small minority to be religious on their behalf. Grace Davie explains:

> For particular historical reasons (notably the historic connections between Church and State), significant numbers of Europeans are con-tent to let both churches and churchgoers enact a memory on their behalf (the essential meaning of vicarious), more than half aware that they might need to draw on the capital at crucial times in their individ-ual or their collective lives. The almost universal take up of religious ceremonies at the time of a death is the most obvious expression of this tendency; so, too, the prominence of the historic churches in particular at times of national crisis or, more positively, of national celebration. Think, for example, of the significance of European churches and church buildings after the sinking of the Baltic ferry *Estonia*, after the

death of Princess Diana or after the terrifying events of 11 September 2001.[1]

The second feature is that religion as an organization is stronger than many of the comparable organizations. Davie concedes that churches "no longer . . . supply a sacred canopy embracing every citizen within the nation in question." Instead she argues,

> They have become de facto, if not always de jure, influential voluntary organizations, capable of operating in a whole variety of ways – traditional as well as innovative. Placing the churches in the sphere of the voluntary sector or civil society is, in fact, the crucial point. In this sector of society the churches are key players; they are central to the structures of modern democracy and attract more members than almost all their organizational equivalents."[2]

It is true that compared with trade unions, women's guilds, or even attendance at soccer matches, churches are doing much better. What seems to have happened in Europe is that people have stopped gathering (or more strictly, they are happy to have others represent them at these organizations). People might go out and join an organization. They go to the pub or cinema, but not to an organization that involves participation and involvement. If this is the case, then Europe's problem is not unbelief but civic society. People, to use Grace Davie's expression, still believe but don't belong. And this lack of belonging is reflected in a lack of belonging to anything.

What is needed then is to recover a culture of belonging. In many ways, the community demands of religion can be helpful. The basic religious impulse sees the mystery beyond the immediate. It is, for example, that sense of awe cultivated by a newborn baby or the sunset. Doctrine can appear very silly, if this point is not grasped. Doctrine is the attempt to formulate a language about the underlying mystery that provides the context for all living. It is more properly seen as poetry than scientific description. Although it is attempting to describe an objective reality, it is not, and never intended to be, literal.

Regaining this sense of mystery, properly understanding religious discourse and participating in a faith community are the best ways to continue to use and appreciate moral categories. However, there are bound to be readers who cannot do this; secular humanists who find religion as odd as bingo and cannot look at the world in a religious way. To these people, I urge you to keep with your resolution that, despite the ultimate nothingness, you shall decide to affirm the moment. You have made a leap, which rationally is difficult to justify, but I rather you leap in this unjustified way, than cease to see the ethical priority in life.

It is clear then that I am committed to the objectivity of ethical assertions, grounded in the mystery of the transcendent. The basic principle that ethical injunctions can be worked out from the intentions of the creator in creation is sound. Natural law is correct at the macro level. H. Richard Niebuhr's stress on the responsible self provides a good way of reconciling the insights of the deontological and consequentialist accounts. We are seeking that action that is most "fitting" given the total context.

Business ethics

With the 1989 Eastern European Revolution, the radical Marxist left dissipated. It seemed clear then that the people decisively rejected a State-controlled command economy. Instead they wanted the basic liberal freedoms and the opportunity to trade goods and services, with the goal of improving life for themselves and their families. However, in recent years there has been a revival amongst the extreme left around the issue of globalization. The problem now according to the neo-Marxists is that global capital, under the control of multi-nationals and the World Bank, are working to protect the interests of the powerful elites in the world.

Marx has, in my view, done considerable damage to a proper understanding of the world and in particular economics. He had one good idea, which should be taken seriously. He saw that there is often an economic factor shaping the ideas, religion, law, and social organization of a society. However, the idea was overstated: economics is not the dominant or sole factor; it is simply one influence amongst many.

In Marx there is a social dualism. Management is set against workers; capitalists are opposed to labor; and business elites are working against the poor. Wicked capitalists, set on exploitation, are exploiting the labor of the poor, with the goal of making considerable profit, which isn't shared with those who did the work. This dualism oversimplifies the complexity of society; it feeds a conspiratorial worldview, which is rarely justified by the facts.

The truth is that capitalism, in the long run, only succeeds when it is ethical. This was the theme of the chapter on business ethics. The great opponent of Marx was the German sociologist Max Weber. It was Weber who said that ideas do change history. And one key idea behind the rise of capitalism was the religious disposition of Calvinism. It was this sense of "calling" that required a person to work hard and honestly – as if it were a duty to God. From its religious roots to today, the principle that capitalism depends on ethical integrity is still true. The best businesses succeed when they treat their employees well, create a good product, and advertise and sell with integrity. Successful capitalism depends on the rule of law and trust. It did at its origin and it continues to do so today.

The other problem with Marx is that he didn't understand economics. The presumption for many on the extreme left is that the economy is a cake: if I have a bigger slice then that leaves a smaller one for others. This is untrue. As we saw in the discussion on population in the environmental ethics chapter, more people can be good. More people create more demand for more goods and services that creates more opportunities for people to supply those goods and services, which leads to greater prosperity all round. And what is true in an economy is true globally. There is no reason why India, Pakistan, and China (to pick three potentially large economies) cannot have growing economies with richer citizens. Indeed there is a sense in which the wealth of the USA and Europe depends on the development of these markets. We need new markets in which we can sell our western expertise and knowledge. Globalization can lead to a reduction in inequalities, not an increase.

It is important, however, that those who are poorer and disadvantaged in terms of education and opportunity are included in the opportunities to create wealth. In that sense the programs of the center left political parties in Britain and America are important. But it is necessary that this inclusion of the marginalized needs to work within the framework of the market economy not against it.

Sadly some in business are not persuaded of the importance of business ethics. And this is the real threat to capitalism. It will not die from external attacks, but from misguided business leaders who decide the quick immediate buck is more important than building up sound businesses that can survive for generations to come. Business ethics, then, are vitally important. It isn't just good business, but it is the only adequate response to those who want to destroy capitalism.

Abortion

Let us start with two facts that most people would accept. The first is that the killing of people, however small, is wrong. Babies, for example, should not be killed and deserve legal protection. The second is that sex is a baby-making process. If one decides to have sex, especially without birth control, then there is a risk of creating a child. Although it is true, as many couples who are trying for a child well know, that sex doesn't always result in a baby, it still remains the case that those who are sexually active should recognize the risk of creating life.

Now is the unborn fetus a person? This is *the* question. Although the Roman Catholic Church today insists that human life starts at conception, the Church has not always held this view. In fact the older position – going back to Augustine (354–430 CE) and Aquinas (1225–74 CE) – is that the soul doesn't enter the embryo until later and quickening (the moment when a mother can feel movement in the womb) was considered significant. Indeed many Jewish, Muslim, and Christian thinkers (including Pope Gregory XIV in 1591) took the view that ensoulment occurs some 40 days after fertilization. It was not until 1896 that Pope Pius changed the Roman Catholic position and insisted that human life begins at conception.

Yet there is considerable wisdom in the older view. Given that two-thirds of fertilized ovum do not implant (they simply pass through the body), it is odd, theologically, to have a situation where the vast majority of human lives are never born. It means, for example, that heaven is predominantly populated with fertilized ovum, which makes one wonder why God bothered to create this earthly stage for the minority who are born. In addition, there is a scientific justification for moving the identification of human life beyond fertilized ovum. Richard Harries helpfully summarizes the argument when he writes:

> When it comes to the undifferentiated cells of the fertilized egg in its first fourteen days or so, before the formation of the primitive streak, which is the basis of the nervous system, such continuity of identify with the adult cannot be posited. For those cells also form the placenta and umbilical cord. Furthermore, and crucially, they can divide to form identical twins. Because there is no continuity of identity it would be more natural to refer to those undifferentiated cells as human life with the potential to become a person rather than a person.[3]

So instead of insisting that human life starts at conception (sperm meets egg), the gradualist view makes much more sense. This position believes that at some point between conception and viability (when the fetus can survive outside the womb) a human being is created.

However, one problem with the gradualist position is that we do not know precisely when the embryo becomes human. It is obviously important that we do not kill a person. Some distinction between human organism and a person is helpful. However, the characteristics of fundamental personhood, which is protected by the Fourteenth Amendment, must include babies. Given this, it must include anything which is viable (and close to viability) outside the womb. So the so-called "morning after pill" is acceptable: the small collection of cells that are forming are not a person and therefore to permit them to pass through the body (along with many other non-persons that do not implant) is morally acceptable. At the other extreme, to abort after 20 weeks is almost certainly killing a person; the entity is within weeks of viability.

Given what we know of the embryo early on (say, at six weeks), abortion is extremely serious. Ask almost any couple who have a miscarriage (often in the first trimester) and they will explain that they have lost a baby. We are at a very important moment in human development. Society clearly has an interest in protecting the lives of those who are most vulnerable.

The general principle is that abortion is extremely serious and ideally should not happen at all, and if it does, must only happen under very limited circumstances. The British legal approach to these questions is perhaps wiser than the US approach. The British approach retains a legal prohibition against abortion, save for various circumstances, which, in my view, should be much more restricted. Given that there is a social interest in protecting the growing embryo, to turn it into a privacy issue is difficult to justify.

What of Judith Jarvis Thomson's objection? The problem is that Thomson does not seem to appreciate the second fact on which most people would agree. One must approach the sexual activity with appropriate respect; it is possible that a child might be the result. Leaving the horrific tragedy of rape to one side (when there is no question that all options should be available), having sex with another person is not the same as being asleep, getting kidnapped, and finding that a famous violinist is now attached to you. Sex creates babies: it is wrong to embark on sexual activity unless one accepts the potential responsibility for the life that emerges at the end of the process.

Euthanasia

Given the advances in palliative care, the problem of dying in pain can be largely relieved. Providing medical practitioners with the freedom to manage pain effectively is important: the "ostensible" hastening of death owing to a large quantity of morphine is not in itself wrong, provided the intent is to relieve pain and not to kill. In addition medical practitioners are not obliged to treat every condition. If for example an elderly patient of 96 is suffering from Alzheimer's disease, then letting influenza take its natural course is an entirely appropriate decision.

A legal option of suicide would be very unwise. It moves decision-making from the practitioner to the courts. And it does raise the specter of unscrupulous relatives putting pressure on an elderly patient for the purposes of inheritance; in addition it might send a signal that the elderly are a burden and better off dead.

However, one fear that drives the euthanasia movement is that one will be left attached to a machine long after any meaningful mental and physical activity has dissipated. People worry that medical practitioners will want to keep them alive way beyond any healthy life. Therefore it is my view that the "living will" is good. Medical practitioners should take them seriously. It is right and proper that we are entitled to send a signal to our relatives and our doctor about the limits of appropriate treatment. The United States is good in this respect: it is commonplace for attorneys to provide carefully worded living wills that specify precisely when you would rather not be treated.

Advances in medical technology

This is probably one of the hardest areas in ethics, and continuing thought and ethical analysis are desperately needed. Around infertility treatments, many of the ethical issues are raised in the abortion debate. Given that I do not think that the small cluster of cells that form a fertilized ovum is a human person, IVF is an acceptable option for couples who are coping with the pain of infertility. Cloning, on the other hand, is much more problematic. It is not simply that as a science it is still in its infancy and therefore unlikely to work effectively, but that one is creating an option that is both unnecessary and disruptive of appropriate parent–child relationships. A parent is not supposed to bring up an identical twin. Generally when it comes to new medical technologies, it is important to be discriminating and tread very carefully. There are many undesirable options that perhaps we should not seek to create.

Sex

It is important in this realm to distinguish between the ideal and the pastoral. The ideal builds on the fact, as already noted earlier in this chapter, that men and women having sex produces babies. And babies need a secure reliable environment in which they grow. A child is a life-long commitment; hopefully, the child will outlive the parents. If one brings a child into the world, then there is an obligation to be there for that child. This applies not only to the mother, who literally brings the child into the world, but also the father, who supplies the sperm nine months beforehand. Marriage makes perfect sense: you need two adults who have committed to each other, as the setting for sex, which produces children. Then when children arrive, the framework that guarantees stability and presence is already established.

The pastoral however recognizes that in the complexity of living, this ideal cannot and will not work for everyone. In addition, in a world where it is possible, with birth control, to have sex without procreation, then the ideal is no longer necessarily the sole setting for sexual intimacy. Sometimes divorce is necessary; when a marriage reaches a point of irretrievable breakdown, then the husband and wife should separate. Sometimes a trial marriage or cohabitation makes sense: the actual institution of marriage is relatively modern; the commitment of two people in a framework of love and mutual support is much older. As the drift of the chapter suggested, if one is willing to permit birth control and have sexual activity unconnected to the procreative possibility, then same sex relations must be permissible. It is important that loving partners of gay men and women do have the legal safeguards in terms of inheritance.

Environmental ethics

Although many who worry about economic growth, pollution, animals, and the environment overstate their case, the underlying concern is one that we must take seriously. The way forward is "sustainable economic growth." This includes the quest for renewable energy sources, recycling, and making every effort to respect animals and the environment. For example, a tree and a dolphin should be treated with particular respect: trees are essential to the survival of life on this planet, while dolphins are extremely complex creatures which, along with other complex creatures, deserve considerable respect. It is right that we consider humans in a distinctive way and with greater rights than non-human life because this is what gives us our particular responsibility for the world in which we live.

War and violence

Although I admire the pacifism tradition, my view is that one is sometimes, sadly and reluctantly, required to take up arms against an aggressor. The Second World War is a clear example of a just war. The efforts to make peace without resorting to war went further than they should have: with Prime Minister Neville Chamberlain and the 1938 peace treaty with Hitler at Munich, it probably increased the number of Jewish lives that were lost. Hitler was not going to be stopped by passive resistance. It needed the war. Now the conduct of the war was not always appropriate; in that respect, it is very difficult to justify the indiscriminate bombing of Dresden or the nuclear bombs on Japan. However, the overall point is that sometimes it is necessary to fight to bring about a just peace.

Power and government

The problem with the classically liberal account of the State is that it is not true. We are not all individuals who mysteriously consent to sacrifice certain rights to live under certain rules in society. We are born into families which are part of a community that shares a certain culture. So when it comes to the account of the State the organic or communitarian view makes much more sense. Nations do form around cultures. However, it is not the case that we must try to protect a pure "culture." The discourse of the extreme right that is opposed to immigration and diversity is deeply misguided. More importantly, perhaps, it ignores certain economic realities: the world is changing and the cultures of nations need to change with it. The fact is, owing to the demands of the market (e.g. globalization), labor is much more mobile. Therefore diversity is increasingly characterizing every country in the world, especially those in Europe and North America.

This diversity means that the culture of many nations must change to accommodate this diversity. To think of the United Kingdom as Anglican or the United States as Protestant is impossible. These cultures are now pluralist. Naturally there is a preponderance of certain types in these countries: the United States, for example, is overwhelmingly theistic, even if there are many Roman Catholics, Jews, and Muslims adding to the millions of Protestant Christians. And the form of the State needs to recognize its changing culture and accommodate it. We have to get use to being bilingual or having in our town centers different places of worship for different religions.

However, Americans in particular must resist the notion that the only model for religious diversity is a secular State. Separation of Church and State in the American constitution has worked well; but it is not for everyone. Even in America, there are those who rightly complain about the way the First Amendment has been used to enshrine a secular outlook in the public square. With the vast majority of Americans being religious, it is absurd to suggest that "under God" should be taken out of the pledge of allegiance or that public schools cannot say "school prayers." To live together we must all make compromises. For atheists, they might have to listen to a prayer in school; for evangelical Christians, they might have to tolerate an Islamic "call to prayer" being broadcast from a mosque in their town. In addition, there is no way, for example, that Pakistan is going to opt for a secular constitution. Yet Pakistan, a predominantly Sunni Muslim country, has to handle its own diversity – significant numbers of Shiite Muslims live there, along with Christians, Hindus, and Sikhs.

Europeans are handling diversity slightly differently from the Americans. In the UK, for example, the Church of England continues to be privileged. The Queen is the head of the Church of England and bishops continue to sit in the House of Lords. Many Jews and Muslims prefer a state church rather than a vacant, secular center. To privilege one tradition is acceptable, provided that tradition feels obliged to represent all faith traditions and that there is fundamental legal recognition of all traditions. Now a model such as this is much more likely to be acceptable in Pakistan than the secular constitution of the United States.

The other theme of the chapter is the need for appropriate ethical behavior by those with power. A free press is vitally important: power must be always held accountable. Investigation and exposure of those that abuse power must be identified. However, the expectations should be reasonable. To require a bribe for a government awarded contract is clearly completely wrong; after an appropriate search to appoint someone who is politically sympathetic to a government position is not wrong. The latter is both inevitable and perhaps appropriate; the former is corruption.

Deciding

There are two reasons for this chapter. The first is that a reader is entitled to a straightforward description of the author's judgments in this area. The second is that it hopefully illustrates the process of decision-making. And I shall conclude this book with a short reflection on this task.

A good education should involve training in decision-making. Making decisions is difficult. When reading political pamphlets many people are easily persuaded to totally contrary positions. So it is worth just reminding ourselves of the process: the first stage is to make sure that one has correctly understood a position. Ideally one should be able to state and explain the arguments for a position in such a way that others find it persuasive. I hope as you read this concluding chapter, you feel that I have represented fairly the arguments that I disagree with. The second stage is to reflect on the hinge issues between positions. So, for example, on the abortion debate a key issue is the start of human life. Or, in the debate about war, one must decide on the permissibility of taking life under any circumstances. The third stage is to reflect on those hinge issues and form a view about them.

Forming a view is the hardest stage. Sometimes one finds a sense of "recognition." As one reads the arguments, say, for and against euthanasia, one finds oneself thinking "yes this is a very good statement of what I always thought." These moments of recognition are the bringing to consciousness of years of reflection, along with educational and parental influences. At other times it is a matter of "thinking it through." This is the process of weighing the various arguments. Is this position coherent? Is it compatible with other beliefs I hold? Is there good evidence for this or that claim? This latter stage can be a struggle; it takes time. However, it is good to do this. If one is going to think about the ethical realm at all, then it is important that it is done properly.

Notes

1 Grace Davie, *Europe: The Exceptional Case* (London: Darton Longman and Todd 2002) p. 18. When discussing this point with my good friend Stefan Weber from Germany he conceded this point entirely: 'I do not attend church but I pay the church tax because I know in time I will want to benefit from the club.'

2 Ibid.

3 Richard Harries, 'The Moral Status of the Early Embryo' in T. W. Bartel (ed.) *Comparative Theology: Essays for Keith Ward* (London: SPCK 2003) pp. 153–4.

Index